INSIGHT GUIDES

LONDON
smart guide

APA PUBLICATIONS

Part of the Langenscheidt Publishing Group

Contents

Areas

Below: the number 29 snakes its way into Trafalgar Square.

A–Z

Atlas

Below: The London Eye in
front of City Hall.

London

B y any calculation London rates as one of the greatest world cities; it is huge and diverse, stately and eccentric, with a long and fascinating history. It has been home to bankers and revolutionaries, tarts and bishops, artists and writers, royalty and waves of immigrants. Here are some of the best museums and galleries to be found anywhere, and a nightlife second to none.

London Facts and Figures

Population: **7.6 million**
Area: **610 sq miles (1,584 sq km)**
Open space: **30 percent**
Population density: **4,800 per sq km**
Languages spoken: **over 250**
Londoners born outside UK: **33 percent**
Visitors staying overnight: **26.1 million per year**
World Heritage Sites: **4**
Markets: **83**
Pubs: **3,800**
Black cabs: **21,000**
Nature reserves: **98**

A Commercial City

If Paris is a city of fashion and Vienna one of music, London is most definitely a city of commerce. The history and development of London is tied up with trade and empire, from the first Roman settlement on the river crossing, to the great Edwardian edifices of the early 20th century, to the latest additions to the City's skyline. For centuries making money has been, and in spite of recent turmoil is likely to continue to be, the central preoccupation of London's rulers and inhabitants.

Unlike Paris or San Francisco, London was never subjected to a wholesale rebuilding of its centre (even after the Great Fire of 1666, when a plan by Christopher Wren for a system of orderly boulevards was rejected) and the growth of the city has been haphazard, governed by commercial need and pressures rather than political or aesthetic considerations. On the whole this has added to, not detracted from, London's charm, though rampant consumerism and the city's inherent instinct for progression constantly butts up against the drive to maintain London's historic and quirky streets.

London's Villages

Perhaps unsurprisingly for a city as sprawling as this, London can feel like a collection of villages, or rather a conglomeration of districts and boroughs that have distinct identities and histories. These range from the posh and central (Kensington), to the deprived inner city (Tower Hamlets), to the more suburban such as Wimbledon and Dulwich. This is due in part to the vast spread of the city; as it moved out from its historic heart it gobbled up the towns and villages that lay in its hinterland. It is also expressed by the saying that 'no-one is as provincial as a Londoner'. Aside from the north-south (of the River Thames) divide that has caused rivalries for as long as the city has been in existence, each inhabitant is likely to be fiercely proud of their own immediate district, be that Chelsea, Brixton, Hackney or Hampstead. A further divide runs east–west, with the wealthier areas lying to the west, traditionally to keep upwind of the East End's polluting industries.

Below: a London cab driver.

Londoners

Centuries of incoming residents have made London's population highly diverse; today, the city is home to 40 percent of the UK's foreign-born residents and it is the most cosmopolitan city in the world. This multiculturalism is very much in evidence and London retains a reputation as one of the most tolerant places in the world in which to live. Between this, the pull exerted by London's economy and jobs market, and the city's vibrant culture and nightlife, the population is younger as a whole than the average across the UK (44 percent aged between 20 and 44 in 2007), and the general population is set to grow by another 15 percent by 2026.

Pros and Cons

Londoners are often the first to complain about the deficiencies of the city, particularly the overcrowded public transport system and high prices. Accommodation especially, both for living and visiting, is notoriously expensive. Nevertheless, Londoners are deeply proud of their city, its excitement, political importance and 'Blitz spirit', and many couldn't imagine living anywhere else, not least because the city retains an immense vibrancy and energy in its arts, fashion, ideas, nightlife and mix of peoples. Contradictory, chaotic and challenging it may be, but to most Londoners and many visitors, London is not only home, but the epicentre of the world.

Highlights

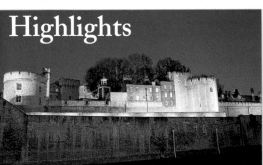

▲ **The Tower of London** The city's castle, palace and prison, redolent with history.

▶ **Palace of Westminster** Topped by the bell tower of Big Ben, this Gothic pile is home to the mother of Parliaments.

▶ **St Paul's Cathedral** Wren's great masterpiece, one of London's most iconic monuments.

▲ **Victoria & Albert Museum** London's museum of decorative arts is the largest in the world.

▲ **British Museum** Treasures from ancient Egypt and Greece on display at this superb museum.

▶ **National Gallery** Outstanding European painting collection, from the 13th to 20th centuries.

Westminster and St James's

The political heart of the city lies between parliament (the seat of government) and Buckingham Palace (the London residence of the Queen, the head of state). In between are government ministries, laid out along Whitehall and St James's Park. Across from the Palace of Westminster, as the Houses of Parliament are more properly called, is Westminster Abbey, final resting place of the 'great and good'. The area is not devoid of culture either; the grand National Gallery and Tate Britain are nearby.

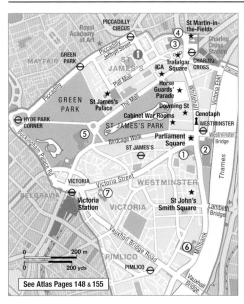

See Atlas Pages 148 & 155

Parliament Square has long been a favourite place for those with a grievance to let off steam and visitors will often see protests in action, but the longest-running is Brian Haw's anti-war encampment in the middle of the green (www.parliament-square.org.uk). He has been there since 2001 protesting for peace, despite repeated attempts by the government and police to shift him.

Around Parliament Square

The focal point for all this politicking and power is Parliament Square, flanked by **Westminster Abbey** ① and the **Palace of Westminster (Houses of Parliament)** ②. The clock tower is often erroneously called **Big Ben**, which is properly the name of the large bell that hangs inside.

The exterior of the 13th-century Gothic abbey has been greatly remodelled over the years and the inside is cluttered with the many tombs of monarchs, politicians, scientists, writers, artists and musicians. SEE ALSO CHURCHES, P.43; PALACES AND HOUSES, P.107

Whitehall and Trafalgar Square

The wide boulevard lined with imposing government buildings that runs north from

Parliament Square turns into **Whitehall** beyond the **Cenotaph** war memorial. Between the Treasury and Foreign Office (the first two buildings on the left) is King Charles Street, location of the **Cabinet War Rooms**.

The next road, gated and guarded, is **Downing Street**, home, at No. 10, to the Prime Minister and, at No. 11, to the Chancellor of the Exchequer. Beyond Downing Street, and also off to the left, is **Horse Guards' Parade**, site of the annual Trooping of the Colour.

At the top of Whitehall is **Trafalgar Square**, laid out on the site of of the old royal mews in 1820–45 by John Nash and Charles Barry. Its centrepiece is **Nelson's Column**, a 175ft (53.6m) homage to the admiral.

Left: Rodin's *Burghers of Calais* outside Parliament.

(named after a ball game popular in the 17th century). It is home to a number of gentlemen's clubs, of the classic leather armchair and afternoon snooze variety, including the Athenaeum, Reform and Royal Automobile clubs (all members only). At the western end of the road is **St James's Palace**, for centuries the seat of the royal court (though it is now considered to sit wherever the Queen is residing). Between Pall Mall and Piccadilly is **Jermyn Street**, a bastion of tradition with several exclusive shops, especially 'gentlemen's outfitters', and art galleries.

Pimlico and Victoria

To the west of Westminster is Pimlico, a generally wealthy residential area. It is enlivened by the superb collections of British art, including several Turners, at **Tate Britain** ⑥. To the north of the Tate, just off Victoria Street in guesthouse-dominated Victoria, where the city's main coach station is based, is the neo-Byzantine **Westminster Cathedral** ⑦, England's major centre of Catholic worship.
SEE ALSO CHURCHES, P.45; MUSEUMS AND GALLERIES P.82

Overlooking the square is the long facade of the **National Gallery** ③, while around the corner is the more discreet entrance to the great collection at the **National Portrait Gallery** ④. Just opposite is James Gibbs' lovely church, **St Martin-in-the-Fields**.
SEE ALSO CHURCHES, P.44; MONUMENTS P.78, 79; MUSEUMS AND GALLERIES, P.80, 81, 82

The Mall and the Parks

Leading off the southwest corner of Trafalgar Square is **The Mall**, the road that leads down to the Queen's London residence, **Buckingham Palace** ⑤. It is not the most architecturally distinguished palace in Europe but the royal cachet still draws the crowds, especially for the **Changing of the Guard**.
To the north and east of the palace are **Green Park**

and charming **St James's Park**. Lining The Mall, at the north end of St James's Park, is an elegant row of buildings that house the avante-garde **ICA** (Institute of Contemporary Arts).
SEE ALSO CHILDREN, P.38; MUSEUMS AND GALLERIES, P.80; PALACES AND HOUSES, P.106; PARKS AND GARDENS, P.112

St James's

Running parallel to The Mall is its companion, **Pall Mall**

Right: Trafalgar Square.

7

Soho and Covent Garden

These adjacent districts, separated by Charing Cross Road, are a magnet for younger, trendier visitors to the capital. Neither have 'sights' as such but both have a lively street-culture and nightlife, with a mix of shopping, restaurants, theatres and bars. Soho is the centre of London's thriving gay and lesbian scene, as well as its sex and film industries, while Covent Garden, previously London's fruit and vegetable market, has reincarnated itself as a shopping mecca and remains the heart of 'Theatreland'.

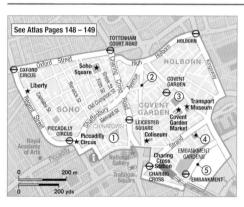

See Atlas Pages 148 – 149

Above: secondhand books on Charing Cross Road.

Soho

Bounded by Regent Street, Charing Cross Road, Oxford Street and the Embankment, Soho embodies the myths of both 1960s 'swinging London' and a more recent incarnation cashing in on so-called 'cool Britannia'. Although the maze of narrow streets may not quite live up to the promise of either of these, there is a definite buzz to the district, helped by being the focus of much of London's gay and lesbian scene and the location of many of London's youthful media companies.

Before the 17th century this was open fields and a hunting ground. These only began to be developed when what now is its heart, **Old**

Compton, **Gerrard**, **Frith** and **Greek streets**, were laid out in the 1670s.

These streets are lined with bars, restaurants and clubs and remain busy almost around the clock. Despite its position as the main nightlife centre in London, it's a considerably cleaned-up version of the old Soho, although there is still a red-light district tucked away in the quieter streets.
SEE ALSO GAY AND LESBIAN P.64–7

Leicester Square and Chinatown

To the south stood Leicester Fields, now **Leicester Square** ①. This tacky but famous piazza is surrounded by expensive multiplex cine-

mas (with the notable exception of the Prince Charles on Leicester Place) and crowded with street performers, touts and, at night, drunks; it is generally avoided by locals.

Gerrard Street, which lies between Leicester Square and Old Compton Street, is the main thoroughfare of London's **Chinatown**, packed with Asian shops. Chinese immigrants, mainly Cantonese from Hong Kong, started to settle the area during the 1950s, some moving in from Limehouse in the East End where there had long been a Chinese community. Once you are past the gateway on Gerrard Place there is a plethora of restaurants to try.
SEE ALSO FILM, P.59

8

Left: Soho buzzes through the day and night.

and the **Royal Opera** ③ on Bow Street. The concentration of theatre-goers ensures that the area is bustling all through the evenings.
SEE ALSO LITERATURE, P.77; MUSIC, P.99; SHOPPING, P.136; THEATRE, P.143

Around the Strand

Walking downhill towards the river from Covent Garden Piazza brings you to the **Strand**. At the western end is **Charing Cross Station**, in front of which is a 19th-century monument which replaced the last of the 12 crosses set up by Edward I in 1291 to commemorate the funeral procession of his wife from Lincoln to London. Also on the Strand is the **Savoy Hotel** ④ and to its side is the **Savoy Theatre**.

Heading down busy Villiers Street towards the Thames, turn left by Embankment tube for the pleasant **Victoria Embankment Gardens**. Opposite, on the bank of the river, is **Cleopatra's Needle** ⑤, an Egyptian obelisk.
SEE ALSO HOTELS, P.71; MONUMENTS, P.79; PARKS AND GARDENS P. 112

The name Soho derives from the hunting cry 'so-hoe', a legacy of its former role as a hunting ground.

Covent Garden

The other side of bookshop-lined **Charing Cross Road** is the Covent Garden district (named after a convent that once stood here). For about 300 years the piazza housed London's main veg and flower market. The area around the piazza was developed to a design by Inigo Jones in the 17th century, and the covered market buildings date back to 1830, based on Charles Fowler's designs (with considerable interference by the Duke of Bedford, the marketplace's owner).

By the 1960s it was becoming untenable to have such a volume of goods and traffic in the centre of town. In 1974, the market, now known as New Covent Garden, moved out to Nine Elms south of the river. A period of decline followed (not that it hadn't always had its more seedy side; the area to the north around **Seven Dials** ② was notorious in the 19th century for its criminal gangs) and it was only in the early 1980s that the central market was redeveloped as a shopping, eating and tourist hub.

Today, it is a popular shopping and entertainment district, with the piazza housing shops, a market and various entertainers. Quirkier, trendier spots can be found on the cobbled streets away from the piazza, particularly up Neal Street and along the narrow roads that stretch up to the Seven Dials and Soho.

Covent Garden is of course home to many of London's theatres, as well as its two resident opera companies, the **English National Opera**, based at the **Coliseum** on St Martin's Lane,

Below: the Chinatown gateway.

9

Oxford Street, Mayfair and Marylebone

Love it or loathe it, Oxford Street is the centre of London's shopping scene and a major draw for its temples to retail. It also divides the two wealthy areas of Mayfair and Marylebone. The former takes its name from a fair once held here, but today it is a rarefied bastion of the exclusive, its Georgian streets and squares packed with high-class shops, galleries and businesses. Marylebone is also smart but with a more relaxed, domesticated air, right down to the regular farmer's market held in its villagey heart.

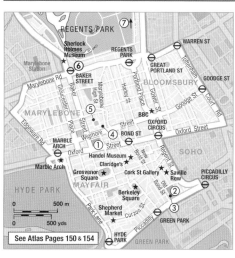

See Atlas Pages 150 & 154

Above: Mayfair's arcades are full of posh shops.

Oxford Street

Running between Mayfair and Marylebone is London's high street, the crowded shopping centre of Oxford Street, home to several top department and flagship stores, such as **Selfridges** ① and **Topshop**, amidst a fair bit of tat at either end of the mile-long thoroughfare. The relentless crowds mean locals really only come here for serious shopping, although plans to possibly pedestrianise the street may change this.
SEE ALSO FASHION, P.55; SHOPPING, P.137

Mayfair

Mayfair clings to its exclusivity, although many of the magnificent Georgian homes are now hotels, apartments, offices, shops and showrooms. **Bond Street** is Mayfair's version of a high street, where you will find London's most exclusive couturiers and designer boutiques, jewellery shops, antiques emporia and art galleries, as well as the headquarters of Sotheby's, the famous auctioneers founded in 1744.

Bond Street runs into **Piccadilly**, home to **The Ritz**

hotel and the southern boundary of Mayfair. Here, behind the imposing Renaissance-style facade of Burlington House, is the **Royal Academy of Arts** ②. The Academy stages big exhibitions all year and is especially famous for its Summer Exhibition. Next door, the **Burlington Arcade** ③ is home to prestigious shops, although archaic rules ban whistling and hurrying while passing through it.

Cork Street is the place for galleries, where many of Britain's top artists are represented. Just beyond is **Savile**

Left: Oxford Street is dedicated to the art of shopping.

of art assembled in the late 18th century.

Pretty **Marylebone High Street** is packed with small specialist food shops, pubs and boutiques. Georgian residential streets fill out the area, which is frequently cited as an example of 'urban village' dwelling in London.

Baker Street is best known as the place where Sir Arthur Conan Doyle set Sherlock Holmes up in residence. In a creaking Victorian terrace house, the **Sherlock Holmes Museum** carefully recreates the super-sleuth's home.

On busy Marylebone Road, the crowds alert you to the location of the phenomenally popular **Madame Tussaud's** ⑥ waxworks.

Heading north from here is the elegant **Regent's Park**, which spreads over 410 acres (166 hectares) framed by white Georgian terraces to the south and Regent's Canal to the north. **London Zoo** ⑦ is at the northeastern end of the park.

South of the park is Portland Place, home to the mass of **Broadcasting House**, headquarters of the BBC. The lovely **All Souls' Church**, with its circular design and slender spire, marks the beginning of **Regent Street**.
SEE ALSO ARCHITECTURE, P.31; CHILDREN, P.38, 41; MUSEUMS AND GALLERIES, P.84, 85; MUSIC, P.100; PARKS AND GARDENS, P.112

Many streets in this area take their names from 17th-century property speculators such as Sir Thomas Bond, Henry Jermyn and the Duke of Albemarle. Frequent bankruptcies interrupted progress and many buildings were left half finished for long periods, looking 'like the ruins of Troy', as one critic scornfully put it .

Row, traditional home of gentlemen's outfitters.

Curzon Street leads to **Shepherd Market**, a pedestrian enclave with a clutch of good pubs, places for alfresco dining and small galleries; its incongruity in the area makes it all the more charming.

Brook Street is home to **Claridge's Hotel**, one of London's premier hotels, and also the **Handel House Museum**, based where the composer lived for 35 years.

Park Lane runs from Hyde Park Corner to **Marble**

Arch, forming the western boundary of Mayfair. It is bounded on the other side by the 350 acres (142 hectares) of **Hyde Park**. The houses overlooking the park have largely been replaced by apartments and hotels, including the **Dorchester**.
SEE ALSO HOTELS, P.71, 72; MONUMENTS, P.79; MUSEUMS AND GALLERIES, P.84; PARKS AND GARDENS, P.113

Marylebone

North of Oxford Street is Wigmore Street, home to the Art Nouveau **Wigmore Hall** ④, one of London's most delightful concert halls. Nearby **Harley Street** has been the haunt of medical specialists since the 1840s.

In Manchester Square is Hertford House, home of the **Wallace Collection** ⑤, which houses a remarkable display

Right: step into the elegant Wigmore Hall.

Kensington
and Chelsea

Kensington and Chelsea contain many shades of upmarket. Serious South Kensington is the home of three legendary museums and the Royal Albert Hall, while the shopping quarter of Knightsbridge drips wealth. To the north lie the great stretches of Hyde Park and Kensington Gardens. Attractive Chelsea is more residential but also offers many opportunities to flex the credit card, its bohemian edge now mostly consigned to history, although a few offbeat reminders remain.

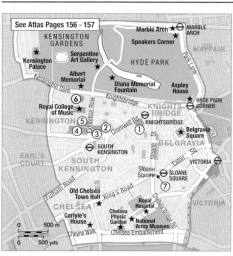

See Atlas Pages 156 – 157

Knightsbridge to South Kensington

From Hyde Park Corner, Knightsbridge heads west, lined with expensive shops, of which the most famous is **Harrods** ①. Further west stands the **Brompton Oratory** ②, a flamboyant Italian Baroque building. A short way on is the **Victoria and Albert Museum** ③, one of the three Victorian museums established in the wake of the Great Exhibition of 1851. On

Left: the Natural History Museum's Earth Galleries.

the other side of Exhibition Road is the neo-Gothic pile of the **Natural History Museum** ④, which encapsulates the Victorians' quest for knowledge. **The Science Museum** ⑤ in Exhibition Road traces the history of inventions from the first steam locomotive and is a favourite with children.

Behind the Science Museum is the **Royal College of Music** and nearby is the 1875 **Royal College of Organists**, with an elaborate, frescoed exterior; and the **Royal College of Art**, in a rather grim 1960s building.

These colleges surround the circular **Royal Albert Hall** ⑥, a huge, ornate building. Every summer the **Proms** are held here. Opposite is the **Albert Memorial**, designed by Sir George Gilbert Scott to commemorate Queen Victoria's Prince Consort.

SEE ALSO CHILDREN, P.40; CHURCHES, P.45; MONUMENTS, P.78; MUSEUMS AND GALLERIES, P.85, 86, 87; MUSIC, P.99; SHOPPING, P.137

Kensington Gardens

Kensington Gore runs alongside Hyde Park and Kensington Gardens, a single open space, but two distinct parks, divided by West Carriage

Left: the Royal Albert Hall.

and a great Saturday food market, run by Partridges food hall. On the left-hand side of the road stands the **Old Chelsea Town Hall**. SEE ALSO FOOD AND DRINK, P.61, THEATRE, P.144

Chelsea

On Royal Hospital Road, running parallel with King's Road, is the **Royal Hospital**, a magnificent building, inspired by the Hôtel des Invalides in Paris and built by Christopher Wren in 1692. This is home to Chelsea Pensioners, retired war veterans who are identifiable by their red uniform jackets. Beside the hospital is the **National Army Museum** and, close by, behind a high wall, the **Chelsea Physic Garden**, founded in 1676 for the study of medicinal plants.

At the foot of Royal Hospital Road, where it joins the Embankment at Albert Bridge, sits a statue of Scottish essayist Thomas Carlyle. Behind him a fine row of Queen Anne houses make up **Cheyne Walk**, one of London's most exclusive streets. Behind it is a network of small, pretty roads where you will find **Carlyle's House**, where he lived from 1834–81. The house is preserved exactly as it was: to the point of not having electricity. SEE ALSO PALACES AND HOUSES, P.108; PARKS AND GARDENS, P.113

The Chelsea Flower Show, one of the largest of its kind in the world, is a great social event held in the spacious gardens of the Royal Hospital in May. First held in 1862, the Royal Horticultural Society show has grown to encompass an impressive number of show gardens, hastily but immaculately built each year, plus an astonishing variety of plants and flowers.

SEE ALSO MUSEUMS AND GALLERIES, P.87; PARKS AND GARDENS, P.114

King's Road

From Knightsbridge, Sloane Street leads to **Sloane Square**, with a flower stall and a shady fountain of Venus. Here, Chelsea proper begins. On the east side of the square is the **Royal Court Theatre** ⑦, which dates from 1870. This is where John Osborne's mould-breaking *Look Back in Anger* was first staged in 1956, and it still has a reputation for good new material.

King's Road, leading west, rose to fame in the 'swinging '60s', and was the mecca for 1970s punk fashions. Today it's far from cutting edge, but pleasantly lined with fashion and homeware shops, cafés and restaurants. The Duke of York Square is home to the Saatchi Gallery

Drive. The lake in the middle of the park, known as the **Serpentine**, is in fact called the Long Water. Every Christmas Day, hardy swimmers dive in. Beside the lake, on the south bank, is a statue of J.M. Barrie's *Peter Pan*. The **Serpentine Art Gallery**, by the road bridge, stages adventurous contemporary exhibitions.

Kensington Gore eventually turns into **Kensington High Street**, a major shopping area and a pleasant alternative to the West End.

Right: Chelsea terraces.

13

Bloomsbury and Holborn

Bloomsbury is bounded to the north by Euston, St Pancras and King's Cross railway termini, but this is no typical station hinterland. It is London's intellectual area, home of the 1930s' Bloomsbury literati, and has a distinctly cultural and academic flavour, being the site of the British Museum and the University of London. Holborn is professional, 'legal London', encompassing the Inns of Court and the Central Criminal Court, although the streets still evoke the ghosts of Dickens and Johnson.

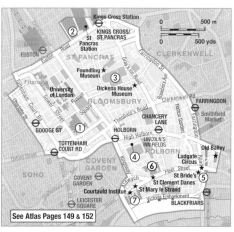

See Atlas Pages 149 & 152

Fitzrovia

North of Soho and west of **Tottenham Court Road** lies Fitzrovia, once a centre of radical and bohemian life. It's still a rather quirky district; its hip main thoroughfare, **Charlotte Street**, is packed with interesting and trendy restaurants, alongside the pubs known for being the haunts of bohemian writers in the 1920s and 30s.

Bloomsbury

The eastern side of Tottenham Court Road marks the start of Bloomsbury, London's literary heart. The

impressive neoclassical **British Museum** ① on Great Russell Street is the nation's greatest treasure house and London's most popular tourist attraction. It opened in 1759 and now owns more than 6½ million items.

The **British Library** ② is on Euston Road and houses 150 million books and periodicals. Opinion is split as to its external design, but the interior is light-filled and graceful.

Bloomsbury famously gave its name to a literary coterie that included Virginia Woolf, Vanessa Bell and Lytton Strachey, who lived here in the early part of the 20th century. Publishing houses and bookshops still flourish around the area's streets and squares.

The **University of London** comprises numerous buildings in the area around Gower Street, but is identified by the grey turret of Senate House, on the western side of Russell Square.

Coram's Fields ③ lies just beyond Great Ormond Street Hospital. Sea captain Thomas Coram started a hospital and school for abandoned children, and encouraged artists, such as Hogarth, to donate works to raise funds. The collection can now be seen at the **Foundling Museum**. The

Left: St Pancras Station.

Left: the Great Court.

of the domestic action in *Little Dorrit*, is only a step or two away from the bustle of **Hatton Garden**, the centre of London's diamond trade. The **Charles Dickens Museum** in Doughty Street, is where he lived from 1837–39.
SEE ALSO LITERATURE, P.76;
MUSEUMS AND GALLERIES, P.92, 93

Fleet Street and Aldwych

Temple Bar is marked by a menacing griffin on a plinth and is the boundary between Westminster and the City. It also marks the start of **Fleet Street**, home of Britain's national newspapers from 1702, when the first daily, the *Courant*, was published here, until the 1980s. **St Bride's** ⑤, the journalists' and printers' church, is on Fleet Street; and nearby, in Gough Square, is **Dr Johnson's House**.

On the site of the former Fleet Prison, just beyond Ludgate Circus, is the **Central Criminal Court** ⑥, universally known by the name of the street it stands on, **Old Bailey**.

On the Strand, by Waterloo Bridge, is **Somerset House** ⑦, which now accommodates the **Courtauld Galleries**, home to a collection of major 20th-century European art.
SEE ALSO CHURCHES, P.43;
MUSEUMS AND GALLERIES, P.92;
PALACES AND HOUSES P.109

Left: the national library.

area north of King's Cross is in the process of being transformed from their rough, industrial reputation of yore, part of the regeneration caused by the 2007 opening of the Eurostar terminal at King's Cross's sister station **St Pancras**, which has had its stunning glass roof restored and is now the city's most glamourous terminus.
SEE ALSO CHILDREN, P.39, 40;
MUSEUMS AND GALLERIES, P.91;
TRANSPORT, P.146

Holborn

Kingsway marks the western boundary of 'legal London'; Fleet Street borders it to the east, and in the Aldwych area, the Strand runs along the southern border; at its end are the **Royal Courts of Justice**, which deal with libels, divorces and all civil cases.

All around this area lie the **Inns of Court**, home of London's legal profession: Middle Temple and Inner Temple are on the Embankment, and Gray's Inn and Lincoln's Inn to the north of the High Court. Their name is taken from the crusading Knights Templar who built the Temple Church here in the 12th century.

Lincoln's Inn Fields were laid out by ambitious city planners in the 17th century. Here you'll find one of London's gems, **Sir John Soane's Museum** ④, a self-endowed monument to one of London's most important collectors, who died in 1837.

The ghost of Charles Dickens (1812–70) haunts the streets of Holborn. Bleeding Heart Yard, setting for much

Conservative though they may seem today, the Inns of Court used to be places of entertainment, some cultural, some rowdy. In 1601 the first performance of Shakespeare's *Twelfth Night* was given in the Inner Temple; other pastimes including dice, dancing, archery, football and wrestling, were all practised in the now-quiet quadrangles.

The City

For most of its 2,000-year history, the City *was* London. Standing roughly within the outline of the walls erected by the Romans, the City manages its own affairs, and maintains its own police force and archaic traditions. Throngs of suited business people, on a mission to make money, pack the district during the week while at the weekend the imposing streets are quiet. The City has been the site for many of London's most daring modern buildings, but the winding passages, evocative street names and churches tucked in between the towers are reminders of the area's lengthy history and a great contrast to the buzzy cut-and-thrust of one of the world's financial centres.

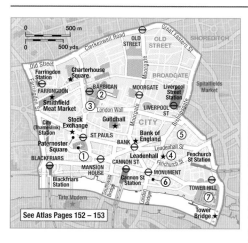

The Romans established the City in AD 45, but there are few remains. The Roman Wall was 2 miles (3km) long and had six magnificent gates but is now found only in fragments. There are remains on the approach to the Tower of London from Tower Hill station. The wall's course can be traced with the help of maps set up on the City's pavements.

St Paul's Cathedral

The City's rich past isn't readily accessible through its buildings. It has been devastated twice: in 1666 the Great Fire devoured four-fifths of the City, and in the Blitz of 1940–41 it was pounded by bombs night after night, leaving one-third in smoking ruins.

St Paul's Cathedral ①, Sir Christopher Wren's greatest work, stands at the western boundary of the City, and was miraculously unharmed by wartime bombs. As a result of the City's sky-high real estate values, the area around it – particularly the ancient market site known as

Paternoster Square – has been intensively developed.

There are several Wren churches between St Paul's and the river; and north of the Cathedral is the great block of **St Bartholomew's Hospital**, founded in 1122.

SEE ALSO CHURCHES, P.44

Clerkenwell to Cheapside

Smithfield meat market is a striking confection of iron and plaster, best visited early in the morning and the last of the great markets still on its original site. North of here is Clerkenwell, an area massively regenerated from the 1980s on, as its disused

warehouses were turned into modern flats and lofts. Today, Clerkenwell is vibrant and trendy, the district ripe with gastropubs, smart restaurants and web businesses.

To the northeast of Smithfield is the Georgian **Charterhouse Square**, with gas lamps and cobbles; and, to the left, St John's priory, founded by the crusading Knights of St John.

Just southeast of here is the modern **Barbican Centre** ②, the City's only residential complex, which also contains a renowned concert hall, theatre and galleries. Also by the ruins of London Wall is the **Museum of London** ③. It traces the city from its earliest beginnings, and holds more than a million objects, making it the world's largest urban history museum.

cream and maroon Victorian building, **Leadenhall**, once a wholesale poultry market, now a handsome commercial centre, popular with city workers at lunchtime.

Broadgate was overhauled at the same time as the adjacent **Liverpool Street station**. It's one of the most ambitious developments in the City, with 13 office-block buildings around three squares.

The distinctive **30 St Mary Axe** ⑤ building is a city icon, a 40-storey tapering glass tower designed by Lord Foster, known as 'The Gherkin'.

The best view of the whole area is from the top of the **Monument** ⑥, in Monument Yard, designed by Sir Christopher Wren to commemorate the Fire of London. Further east, there are several historical churches and reminders of the City's past, such as **Billingsgate Market**, lining the lanes around the riverfront.

East of the Monument, encircled by a now-dry moat, is the fairy-tale **Tower of London** ⑦, the City's oldest structure, begun by William the Conqueror in 1078.
SEE ALSO ARCHITECTURE, P.30, 31, 33; MONUMENTS, P.78; PALACES AND HOUSES, P.108

Craft guilds were enormously important in medieval London, and the 15th-century **Guildhall** is a good place to glimpse their past.

A flavour of the the City's trading past remains in the main shopping thoroughfare, **Cheapside**, behind St Paul's. On this old street stands the church of **St Mary-le-Bow**, home to the famous Bow bells, which define a true Londoner, or cockney: you have to be born within earshot.
SEE ALSO ARCHITECTURE, P.32; MUSEUMS AND GALLERIES, P.93; MUSIC, P.98; THEATRE, P.143

The City Centre

The triangular intersection known as **Bank** is dominated by the Bank of England. The **Stock Exchange**, just along Threadneedle Street, has changed enormously since 1986, when the 'Big Bang' led to radical changes in trading

practices. The real cut and thrust of trading takes place at the **London Metal Exchange** in Fenchurch Street and on the dealing floor in the **Royal Exchange** at Cornhill.

One of the first and most dramatic of the new buildings to go up in the City in the late 1980s was the **Lloyd's of London** ④ building in Lime Street, designed by Lord Richard Rogers. Beside this highly modern building is the

South Bank
and Bankside

The first bridge across the Thames was built by the Romans near London Bridge and in Shakespeare's day, the Bankside area was the place for putting on unlicensed plays. It retained its reputation as an area of vice and pleasure well into the 19th century, but successful, large-scale regeneration in recent years has made the most of the area's character while making the South Bank into London's cultural playground, with major attractions stretching all the way down the riverfront.

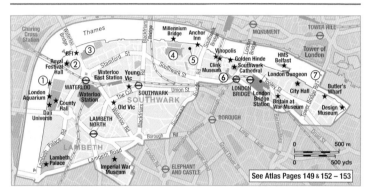

See Atlas Pages 149 & 152 – 153

South Bank

Lambeth Road leads away from the river to the **Imperial War Museum**, in an 1815 building that was once the Bethlehem hospital for the insane (known as Bedlam).

Back by the river, facing the Houses of Parliament, stands **County Hall**, the seat of the Greater London Council, which ran the city until it was abolished in 1986. It now incorporates two hotels, the **London Aquarium**, and the

> Once upon a time, Bankside was renowned for its brothels. The successive Bishops of Winchester made extra incomes from the fines they imposed on the prostitutes, who were known as 'Winchester Geese'.

Dalí Universe (featuring 500 of Salvador Dalí's works).

Towering over this is The **London Eye** ①, the world's largest observation wheel. At 450ft (135m), it is the fourth highest structure in London.

The **Southbank Centre** ② is Europe's largest arts complex. It's centrepiece, the **Royal Festival Hall**, is a concert venue that is dazzling and buzzy after a major refurbishment in 2007. On the upper level of the South Bank complex is the **Hayward Gallery**, a landmark of brutalist architecture with a cutting-edge programme of changing art exhibitions.

Next door is the revamped **BFI Southbank**, Britain's leading arthouse cinema complex, which holds more

than 2,400 screenings each year. It also runs the **BFI London IMAX Cinema**, on the roundabout at the south end of Waterloo Bridge. SEE ALSO ARCHITECTURE, P.32; CHILDREN, P.38, 39; FILM, P.58; MONUMENTS, P.79; MUSEUMS AND GALLERIES, P.94; MUSIC, P.99

Waterloo

On the east side of Waterloo Bridge is the modernist **National Theatre** ③. At night, one of its towers is lit up in beacon-like bright colour.

Waterloo Road leads down to the **Old Vic** theatre (1811) in The Cut. It was the first home of the National Theatre and is now a repertory theatre with Kevin Spacey as artistic director. Further along The Cut, the **Young Vic**, known

18

for its adventurous programme, is housed in a distinctively funky building.
SEE ALSO ARCHITECTURE, P.32; THEATRE, P.143, 145

Bankside

Beyond Blackfriars Bridge, the landmark **Tate Modern** ④ gallery occupies the former Bankside Power Station, identifiable by its tall brick chimney. The Turbine Hall houses massive sculptural works.

Giving pedestrian access to Tate Modern from St Paul's Cathedral over the river is the sleek **Millennium Bridge**, suspended by horizontal cables.

In the 16th century, **Shakespeare's Globe** ⑤ was built by the river. A replica of the building opened in 1996, staging summer performances in the round.

The 18th-century **Anchor Inn** by Southwark Bridge, is opposite the main entrance of **Vinopolis**, which offers a visual tour through the world's wine regions.

A single gable wall is all that remains of **Winchester Palace**, London residence of the Winchester bishops. The prison they founded in Clink Street is now the **Clink Prison Museum**. Nearby is a full-size replica of Sir Francis Drake's galleon, the **Golden Hinde**.

Southwark Cathedral, hemmed in by the railway, has

Left: the Tate Modern.

a lovely interior and is one of London's great historic churches. **Borough Market** ⑥, outside the Cathedral, is a renovated fruit and veg market dating from the 13th century that is now hugely popular.
SEE ALSO ARCHITECTURE, P.33; CHURCHES, P.42; FOOD AND DRINK, P.63; MUSEUMS AND GALLERIES, P.94; THEATRE, P.144

Around London Bridge

London Bridge, dating from 1967–72, is the latest of many on this site. In Tooley Street, the **London Dungeon** includes ghoulish exhibits of the Black Death and Jack the Ripper's exploits. Downstream is **HMS Belfast**, the last of the warships to have seen action in World War II. To its east, the oval-shaped glass building is **City Hall**, seat of the mayor and the Greater London Authority.

Tower Bridge ⑦, a masterpiece of Victorian Gothic (1894), has become a symbol of London. In the old warehouses to the east of Tower Bridge is **Butler's Wharf**, where there are several smart restaurants, near to the **Design Museum**.
SEE ALSO ARCHITECTURE, P.33; CHILDREN, P.38; MUSEUMS AND GALLERIES, P.94

Right: Tower Bridge.

North London

For centuries, North Londoners preferred to consign the seamier side of life to south of the river and today there is still a slight sense of superiority emanating from these parts. The gracious hilltop settings of Hampstead and Highgate do have some justification for this, however, having long been popular places to live and boasting a high count of famed former residents, as well as lots of greenery and attractive streets that retain a sense of the villages they once were. Closer to central London, Islington is a vibrant area popular for its range of cultural, eating and shopping opportunities, while Camden remains a distinctively alternative hub of the young and trendy.

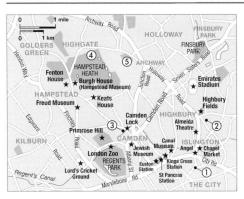

Above: Camden Lock.

Islington

Islington symbolises the new-style gentrification of London's Georgian and Victorian dwellings; a popular stereotype portrays it as the happy hunting ground of the liberal-minded middle-class. A fitting cultural icon here is the **Almeida Theatre** in Almeida Street, one of London's most innovative small theatres.

At the southern end of Islington, on Rosebery Avenue, leading down to Holborn, stands **Sadler's Wells** ①, a theatre built in 1683 and renovated as a stylish, cutting-edge space that is London's principal dance venue. The crossroads at the heart of Islington's shopping district, the **Angel**, is named

after a long-gone coaching inn. Close by, towards the shops and restaurants that line Upper Street, is the busy **Chapel Market**.

Nearby **Camden Passage** is a treasure trove of antique shops, ranging from simple stalls to grand shops.

Classic terraces can be found in squares such as Canonbury Square, where authors George Orwell and Evelyn Waugh once lived. The **Estorick Collection** ② is at Number 39a and features a fine collection of Italian Futurist and figurative art.

Just north of the intersection of Holloway Road and Upper Street lies **Highbury Fields**, a relaxed local green. This area is most associated

with football; Holloway Road leads to the enormous **Emirates Stadium**, home of Arsenal football club.

SEE ALSO DANCE, P.47; MUSEUMS AND GALLERIES, P.95; SPORTS, P.140; THEATRE, P.144

Camden

Resolutely alternative and grungy, Camden has quite a different atmosphere, and is frequented by a largely young and trendy crowd. **Camden Market** is the big draw for visitors. The main market (Camden High Street) has cheap clothes, while Camden Lock Market (off Chalk Farm Road) concentrates on crafts. The quality of goods has fallen as the crowds have risen. In 2008, a fire swept

Left: the view from Hampstead Heath.

doubles as **Hampstead Museum**, with a display on the landscape painter John Constable (1776–1837).

Sigmund Freud, fleeing the Nazis in 1938, moved to Maresfield Gardens with his daughter Anna. The **Freud Museum** preserves the house as they left it.

Kenwood House ④ was remodelled in 1764–79 by Robert Adam and overlooks Hampstead Heath. Its rooms showcase the **Iveagh Bequest**, a major collection with works by Rembrandt, Vermeer, Reynolds, Turner and Gainsborough.

SEE ALSO PALACES AND HOUSES, P.108, 109; PARKS AND GARDENS, P.114; PUBS AND BARS, P.120

Highgate

This pleasant hill-top suburb built round a pretty square, contains London's grandest **cemetery** ⑤, consecrated in 1839, where 300 famous people are buried. Besides its catacombs and impressive memorials, the main attraction is the stern bust of Karl Marx, who was buried here in 1883.

SEE ALSO PARKS AND GARDENS, P.114

Regent's Canal takes you through a secret side of London, and has some delightfully rural stretches. It is only about 4ft (1.2m) deep, and in most places wide enough for two narrowboats to pass. You can take a narrowboat trip from Camden (on the Jenny Wren, tel: 020-7485 4433) or Little Venice (Jason's Narrowboats, tel: 020-7286 3428).

Hampstead

Hampstead has long been a desirable address, historically popular with many artists and writers. Poet John Keats (1795–1821) wrote much of his work, including *Ode to a Nightingale*, during the two years he lived in Hampstead. **Keats House** contains memorabilia, including facsimiles of his letters.

The 3-sq-mile (8-sq-km) **Hampstead Heath** is the main 'green lung', leading down to Parliament Hill, which gives splendid views across London, as does the 110-acre (45-hectare) **Primrose Hill** overlooking Regent's Park to the south. History-laden pubs include the **Spaniards Inn** and the **Holly Bush**.

Tucked away among the quiet, countrified lanes is **Burgh House**, which has a fine music room, library and an award-winning garden. One of London's finest Queen Anne-style houses, it

through part of the market, claiming some of the local drinking landmarks too; they and affected Canal Market have since been rebuilt.

A nice way to view **Camden Lock** is along the **Regent's Canal**. Canalboats can be taken from here to London Zoo *(see box, above)*. This 8½-mile (14km) stretch of water running from Paddington in west London to Limehouse in Docklands was dug in the early 19th century.

SEE ALSO SHOPPING, P.139

Below: the tomb of Karl Marx.

East London

Long associated with poverty, over-crowding and grime, East London is now under the spotlight as the location of the 2012 Olympic Games, to be held in Stratford. The East End, synonymous with cockneys, also has a history of being the first stopping-point for immigrants and so being deeply multicultural. Proud of its heritage, the area retains a distinct character, where inner-city poverty, fashionable gentrification, genuine cultural diversity and both trendifying and impoverished artists bump up against each other. Over in Docklands, skyscrapers and glamourous riverside developments have been built on the site of the former docks, once so important to Britain's trade.

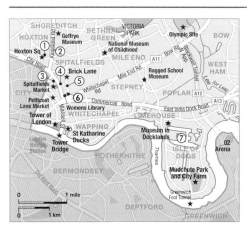

Above: White Cube gallery.

Hoxton and Shoreditch

In the 1990s, the depressed areas of Hoxton and Shoreditch, to the north and south of **Old Street**, became fashionable as young artists such as Damien Hirst and Tracey Emin moved in, creating studios in redundant warehouses. As they became successful, art dealers and web designers followed and urban desolation became urban chic.

Commercial galleries radiate from **Hoxton Square**, the location of the fashionable **White Cube** ① gallery. Despite a rash of trendy café-bars and rising property prices that has forced out the less successful artists, the area admittedly still looks inner-city bleak, and many of the more successful artists have now moved on. However, the Hoxton and Shoreditch area remains a major nightlife hotspot and a magnet for the trendy and artistic.

A few minutes' walk to the north-east, on Kingsland Road, the **Geffrye Museum** is the only British museum to deal with the interior decorating tastes of the urban middle classes from 1600 to the present day. Housed in a square of former almshouses built in 1714, it is a fascinating social chronicle.

SEE ALSO MUSEUMS AND GALLERIES, P.96; NIGHTLIFE, P.102

Bethnal Green

Once London's poorest area, Bethnal Green is now rapidly gentrifying. It is home to the **National Museum of Childhood**, a branch of the Victoria and Albert Museum. Displays range from classic children's toys to the development of nappies and the roots of adolescent rebellion.

Less than a mile away, the **Ragged School Museum** has a reconstructed kitchen and classroom to show how life was once lived by London's East Enders. The 'History of the East End' represents the changes the area has seen, from immigrants to abject poverty, to the Blitz and

It's worth taking a ride through Docklands on the Docklands Light Railway (from Bank to Greenwich) to see how property developers turned the place into an architect's adventure playground. Some find the variety intoxicating, others dislike the gigantic patchwork of glass, steel, concrete and high-priced apartment blocks lining the river.

recent regeneration. On Sundays, the **Columbia Road Market** ② specialises in flowers and plants.
SEE ALSO CHILDREN, P.40; SHOPPING, P.139

Spitalfields

Spitalfields contain several 18th-century streets of architectural interest, such as **Fournier Street**, where Huguenot silk weavers lived. **Dennis Severs' House** ③ in Folgate Street is laid out as if occupied by an 18th-century family and lit only by gaslight.

At the end of Fournier Street is **Christ Church** ④, considered the greatest of Nicholas Hawksmoor's churches. To the west lies **Spitalfields Market**, a former wholesale fruit and vegetable market, which now has antiques, crafts and organic food stalls. To the south, **Petticoat Lane Market** is still flourishing, packed on Sunday with over 1,000 stalls specialising in cheap clothes.

To the east of Fournier Street is **Brick Lane**, home to a large Bangladeshi community and famous for its cheap curry houses. It also has some of East London's best nightlife, much of which is held within the **Old Truman Brewery** ⑤, which is also home to quirky shops and a Sunday market.
SEE ALSO CHURCHES, P.44; MUSEUMS AND GALLERIES, P.95; SHOPPING, P.139

Right: stock up on flowers at the Columbia Road Market.

Left: the futuristic towers of Canary Wharf.

Whitechapel

On Old Castle Street, a Victorian bathhouse has been converted into **The Women's Library**, with a collection of suffragette memorabilia and banners. The **Whitechapel Art Gallery** ⑥ was founded by a local vicar and his wife in 1897. It mounts high-profile exhibitions in a spectacular space. To the south (just east of the Tower of London) is **St Katharine's Dock**. Built in 1828, it is a smart yacht marina, with a variety of restaurants and pubs.
SEE ALSO MUSEUMS AND GALLERIES, P.96

Docklands

London's obsolete docks were transformed in the 1990s with high-tech office buildings such as the **Canary Wharf** ⑦ complex, whose main tower is Britain's highest building, at 800ft (244m). Amidst the modernity, many former warehouses in the **India Quays** have been converted into bars and restaurants.

An incongruous attraction is the 34-acre (14-hectare) **Mudchute City Farm** on Pier Street. **The Museum in Docklands** on West India Quay recounts 2,000 years of history, and includes a model of Old London Bridge.
SEE ALSO ARCHITECTURE, P.31

South London

South London's residential locales offer parkland, galleries and café culture; places worth a visit include the very different areas of Brixton, Clapham, Blackheath and Dulwich, each with their own distinctive attractions. Back by the river, the naval and military heritage of Greenwich and Woolwich has been preserved and recorded with interactive exhibits at the museums. In contrast to the historical artefacts of this area, the former warehouses that stretch along the river are being rapidly turned into smart apartment complexes; a boat trip down the Thames reveals the extent of this redevelopment, although the streets away from the river remain poorer and more run-down.

Brixton

The diverse and multicultural community of people in Brixton is what gives this buzzy area its character and energy. Recording the history of black people in Britain are the **Black Cultural Archives** in Coldharbour Lane, a collection of artefacts and memorabilia. **Brixton Market** ① mixes Caribbean produce with traditional fruit, vegetables and fish, plus stalls of second-hand clothes and music. Nightlife is lively in Brixton, with many dance clubs such as **Mass**.
SEE ALSO FOOD AND DRINK, P.63; NIGHTLIFE, P.104; SHOPPING, P.139

Blackheath

Villagey Blackheath is most famed for its windy heath, where Henry V was welcomed home after beating the French at Agincourt in 1415. The **Paragon**, a crescent of colonnaded houses, overlooks the heath. **St Michael's Church** (1829) has a tapering spire known as 'the needle of Kent'.
SEE ALSO PARKS AND GARDENS, P.114

Clapham

Bustling Clapham is the preferred residence of many young professionals, something evident in the number of

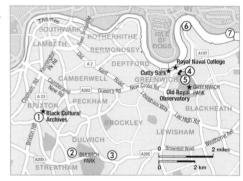

Above: in Brixton Market.

bars, cafés and restaurants that line the roads around attractive **Clapham Common**. There are few 'sights' as such, but the park, dining and nightlife options make it a popular place to live.

Dulwich

With leafy streets, elegant houses and a spacious park, Dulwich is a smart, picturesque enclave in southeast London. The grand building of the **Dulwich Picture Gallery** ② opened in 1814 as the country's first major public art gallery. It contains 300 important works, including by Rembrandt, Rubens and Murillo.

A mile to the east in Forest Hill, the **Horniman Museum** ③ combines rich collections of ethnography and natural history. It was founded in 1901 by a wealthy tea merchant, Frederick Horniman, and is set in 16 acres (6.5 hectares) of landscaped parkland, with great views over London.
SEE ALSO MUSEUMS AND GALLERIES, P.96

Greenwich

The **Cutty Sark** ship has been under wraps for a long time, after suffering a huge fire while

The heart of Greenwich lies just to the west of the maritime park, where a market spreads out from **Greenwich Church Street**, selling clothes, crafts, books and antiques. On the same street is **St Alfege's** church, built in 1712–18 by Hawksmoor. SEE ALSO CHURCHES, P.44; MUSEUMS AND GALLERIES, P.97

Woolwich

River trips continue downriver, sweeping back up the eastern side of the Isle of Dogs to **Blackwall Reach**, around the vast area reclaimed and cleared for **The O2** ⑥, formerly the Millennium Dome, an expensive exhibition arena and infamous damp squid, used for one year in 2000. Now a hugely successful concert, sporting and exhibition venue, with the superclub **Matter** in its bowels, the expectation is that it will also be used for some 2012 Olympics events.

Beyond here is the **Thames Barrier** ⑦, which protects 45 sq miles (117 sq km) of London from the very real danger of flooding.

Beyond is Woolwich, once the Royal Navy's dockyards and arsenal. The main attraction is **Firepower**, the Royal Arsenal's museum, which puts viewers in the midst of battle. SEE ALSO ARCHITECTURE, P.33; NIGHTLIFE, P.104

Eltham Palace is well worth a trip to see the splendid and luxurious Art Deco interior set in a medieval palace. The Great Hall is one of the few remaining intact relics of the palace, which was a royal residence between the 14th and 16th centuries. The palace can be reached by rail from London Bridge or Charing Cross. *See also Palaces and Houses, p.106.*

under renovation in 2007; it is due to reopen in 2010.

The **National Maritime Museum** ④ displays an unrivalled collection of maritime art and artefacts in galleries built around a spectacular space spanned by Europe's largest glazed roof. The **Queen's House**, now displaying the museum's art collections, was completed in 1637. It was England's first classical Renaissance building.

Greenwich Mean Time was established at the **Royal Observatory** in 1884, and the observatory has Britain's largest refracting telescope. A brass rule on the ground marks the meridian.

Flamsteed House, designed by Christopher Wren (himself a keen astronomer), has exhibits tracing the history of astronomy from its origins in ancient Sumeria and Egypt.

The elegant **Royal Naval College** ⑤ begun by Wren in 1696, was originally a royal palace, given over to the training of naval officers in 1873.

Right: the home of GMT.

West London

West London encompasses some of the most attractive and desirable real estate in London, particularly the Georgian stucco villas in hypergentrified Notting Hill, where Portobello Market remains a big draw. Further southwest, there's much to appeal to both residents and visitors; classic days out include trips to the glorious greenery of Kew Gardens, Barnes Wetland Centre, Richmond Park and Wimbledon Common, and visits to Hampton Court Palace or the many grand houses around Chiswick and Richmond. These areas started life as rural retreats and something of that atmosphere lingers in these parts, the closest London comes to the countryside.

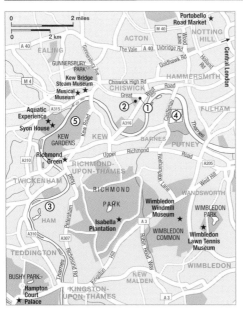

For day trips further west with a royalist bent, Windsor Castle and Hampton Court Palace are easily accessible by rail from Waterloo. Both are set in pretty riverside locations and are steeped in royal history. Windsor is an attractive town to wander about in, while Hampton Court boasts splendid, mature gardens and the famous maze. See also *Palaces and Houses, p.107.*

of London's most trend-conscious areas. Built on the site of a pig farm named for an English victory over Spain at Porto Bello in the Gulf of Mexico in 1739, **Portobello Road** hosts a famed and major antiques market. The road actually accommodates three markets: antiques, food and one mixing bric-a-brac with cutting-edge fashion.

On the August bank holiday each year **Ladbroke Grove** is the parade route for for the Notting Hill Carnival, a three-day Caribbean festival that has been held since 1966.

SEE ALSO ESSENTIALS, P.51; SHOPPING, P.139

Chiswick

This once rural area has two grand houses worth visiting. Off the Great West Road, **Hogarth's House** ① is the

Notting Hill

Notting Hill has long been known as a melting pot in which several races and extremes of just about every social class rub shoulders. Grand Georgian townhouses at the **Holland Park** end contrast with their run-down counterparts just to the north. With sky-high prices, it is one

Left: Portobello Road fashion.

modest residence of the father of political cartoons, William Hogarth (1697–1764) and displays his beautifully executed engravings, including *The Rake's Progress,* in an otherwise empty house. The romantic 18th-century villa and gardens of **Chiswick House** ② are rather grander.
SEE ALSO PALACES AND HOUSES, P.108

Wimbledon

This southwest suburb hosts the famed tennis tournament in June/July; its history is captured in the **Wimbledon Lawn Tennis Museum**, which has a rich collection, ranging from Victorian tableaux to Bjorn Borg's racket. Ground tours can be booked.

Wimbledon's village is a quintessential West London enclave of chic boutiques and family-friendly cafes, bordering the wilder **Wimbledon Common**, a partly wooded expanse with nature trails.

SEE ALSO PARKS AND GARDENS, P.115; SPORTS, P.141

Richmond

Richmond Park, at 2,345 acres (950 hectares) is the largest of the royal parks, and is grazed by herds of red and fallow deer who enjoy the bracken thickets and gather beneath the huge oaks. Rhododendrons and azaleas make the **Isabella Plantation** a particular high spot in May.

17th- and 18th-century buildings line **Richmond Green**, the handsome town centre. **Richmond Bridge** is the oldest on the river, and the waterfront is always lively.

Richmond Hill provides a grand view of the river. Below, along the towpath, is **Ham House** ③, a richly furnished 1610 Palladian building with stunning gardens. From here, you can take a foot ferry across the river to **Marble Hill House** and its lovely park in Twickenham.

Left: on Richmond Green.

SEE ALSO PALACES AND HOUSES, P.109; PARKS AND GARDENS, P.115

Barnes

Barnes, protected from the bustle of neighbouring Hammersmith by the natural boundary of the river, is a well-heeled village with several good pubs. Next to the pretty common is the **London Wetland Centre** ④, a habitat for rare wildlife. Birds, butterflies and water voles are among the creatures inhabiting the ponds, rushes and gardens.
SEE ALSO PARKS AND GARDENS P.115

Kew

Kew is synonymous with its **Royal Botanic Gardens** ⑤. The 295-acre (120-hectare) gardens, established in 1759, form a formidable repository and research centre. It is also very beautiful, with grand glasshouses, including the Palm House and Waterlily House, the Orangery, a mock Chinese pagoda, and the 17th-century **Kew Palace**, built for a Dutch merchant.
SEE ALSO PALACES AND HOUSES, P.107; PARKS AND GARDENS, P.115

Below: at the stunning Royal Botanic Gardens, Kew.

27

A–Z

In the following section London's attractions and services are organized by theme, under alphabetical headings. Items that link to another theme are cross-referenced. All sights that are plotted on the atlas section at the end of the book are given a page number and grid reference.

Architecture

L ondon's buildings reflect both the long history of the city and its readiness for innovation; no one style has ever been able to predominate. Over the years, fire and warfare have made their marks on the look of the city and today, futuristic designs for edifices made of steel and glass are transforming the look of London yet again. At the same time, older buildings are lovingly preserved or transformed, as in the case of the Tate Modern. With the upcoming 2012 Olympics on the agenda, further regeneration and building will ensure London's design landscape never stays static.

A History in Buildings

MEDIEVAL LONDON

The Norman Conquest brought Norman architecture to London in the 1070s. The **White Tower** and **St John's Chapel** in the Tower of London were built, the latter with the squat pillars and rounded arches that were this style's hallmarks. The only other surviving example of this is the Smithfield church, **St Bartholomew the Great** (1123).

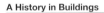

Below: Westminster Abbey was begun in Medieval times.

Gothic architecture was imported from France in the 13th century and remained in vogue until the mid-16th century. More delicate than Norman, it made outer walls thinner by supporting them with exterior buttresses. This allowed lancets and larger windows, which featured the Gothic pointed arch. Rib vaulting was a feature of Early English Gothic: its simple, unadorned geometric shapes can be seen at **Southwark Cathedral**. **Westminster Abbey** was begun in Gothic style in 1245.

Henry Yevele (1320–1400), the royal mason and London's first known architect, enhanced Westminster Abbey, as well as building the Jewel Tower and Westminster Hall, a huge space with a hammer beam roof.
SEE ALSO CHURCHES, P.42; PALACES AND HOUSES, P.108

TUDOR LONDON

A hallmark of the Tudor period, often called Elizabethan after Elizabeth I, is the use of half-timbering and red brick. **Staple Inn** in High Hol-

born is the city's sole survivor of this style. This era also saw the building of theatres, such as **Shakespeare's Globe**, now reconstructed close to its original Southwark site.
SEE ALSO THEATRE, P.144

CLASSICAL LONDON

Inigo Jones (1573–1652), Charles I's court architect, brought Italy's Classical Renaissance to Britain in the fine **Banqueting Hall** in Whitehall Palace, and **Queen Mary's House** in Greenwich, both still standing. Jones also designed the Palladian **Covent Garden** building, set around London's first square.

WREN'S LONDON

Sir Christopher Wren (1632–1723) designed 52 churches in the City (26 remain) as well as **St Paul's Cathedral**, after the Great Fire razed much of the city in 1666. The windows of these classical Baroque monuments bathe white and gold interiors with light. He also designed the Greenwich and Chelsea naval and military hospitals.
SEE ALSO CHURCHES, P.44

Left: Nash's sweeping terraces in Portland Place.

talist design also left a legacy of notable public buildings, the **Royal Festival Hall**, the **Barbican** complex and the **National Theatre** (see p.32).
SEE ALSO MUSIC, P.99; THEATRE, P.143

MODERN LONDON

The futuristic **Lloyd's of London** (see p.33) building was completed in 1986 and the following year building began on the mammoth Canary Wharf complex in Docklands. Today the tallest tower is Canary Wharf's **One Canada Square** at 800ft (244m), flanked by two 700ft (213m) blocks. It hasn't all been new builds either; in 2000, the **Tate Modern** (see p.33) opened in the transformed former Bankside Power Station.

Sir Norman Foster's bulbous glass **City Hall** (see p.33) near Tower Bridge opened in 2002, followed, in 2004, by the City's '**Gherkin**' (see p.33). Looking ahead, the **London Bridge Shard** is due for completion in 2012 and will boast a 1,016ft (310m) spire.
SEE ALSO MUSEUMS AND GALLERIES, P.94

Below: the Gherkin looms out.

With the **2012 Olympic Games** due to be held in Stratford, in London's east end, ambitious building plans are currently in the process of being realised. After the events, the extensive Olympic Park development will be given over to local housing, amenities and sports facilities, transforming this part of London.

GEORGIAN LONDON

John Nash (1752–1835), commissioned by the future George IV in 1811, designed some 50 elegant, formal villas in the Classical style, by what is now **Regent's Park**. He added theatrical terraces, with Doric and Corinthian colonnades. **Bedford Square's** houses are a good example of the simple elegance of typically Georgian style: uninterrupted brick terraced houses with long sash windows and elaborated porticoes.
SEE ALSO PARKS AND GARDENS, P.112

VICTORIAN LONDON

Sir Robert Smirke (1781–1867) was active as Italian influence waned and curiosity for all things Greek

became the vogue. Smirke built **Covent Garden Theatre** as a replica of the Temple of Minerva in Athens before going on to erect the monumental **British Museum**.

Meanwhile, Augustus Pugin (1812–52) lead the Gothic Revival after the old Palace of Westminster burned down in 1834. His design for the new **Houses of Parliament** took its inspiration from the **Henry VII Chapel** in Westminster Abbey. Gothic Revival was the cornerstone of Victorian architecture. George Gilbert Scott (1811–78) turned **St Pancras Station** into a temple of the arts and built the elaborate **Albert Memorial** in Hyde Park.
SEE ALSO MONUMENTS, P.78; MUSEUMS AND GALLERIES, P.91; PALACES AND HOUSES, P.107; TRANSPORT, P.146

POST-WAR LONDON

London was badly bombed in World War II and Britain was virtually bankrupted, which accounts for the depressingly utilitarian office and housing blocks built in this period. However, modernist and bru-

31

Modern Architectural Highlights

Oxo Tower (1929)

Barge House Street, South Bank; tube/rail: Waterloo; map p.152 B1

Beside the river on the South Bank, the distinctive Art Deco tower has pinprick windows outlining the words 'Oxo', a gimmick the makers of the beef extract of that name designed to get round a ban on advertising on the riverfront in the 1930s. The roof-level restaurant has stunning views.

Daily Express Building (1932)

121–128 Fleet Street, Holborn; tube: Chancery Lane; map p.152 B2

Built for the building's former occupants, the Daily Express, this sleek black Vitrolite and glass structure was designed by Sir Owen Williams in a highly Modernist style. The interior, however, is pure Art Deco, designed by Robert Atkinson. The lobby includes lots of silver and gilt. It is not open to the public, but the facade and entrance lobby can be seen from the street.

Southbank Centre (1951)

Belvedere Road, South Bank; tube/rail; Waterloo; map p.149 D2

Recently given a complete refurbishment, the Southbank Centre, with the Royal Festival Hall at its heart, is the only lasting monument of the Festival of Britain, a celebration marking the centenary of the Great Exhibition, and also intended as a 'tonic' to the nation after the ravages of World War II. It was built in a hurry, but is considered a triumph of post-war architecture and emblematic of optimism, with a Modernist, open design, in contrast to the brutalist designs of its neighbouring cultural institutions.
SEE ALSO MUSIC, P.99

Telecom Tower (1966)

60 Cleveland Street, Fitzrovia; tube: Goodge Street; map p.151 C3

This iconic tower dominates the local skyline. For thirty years it appeared on no maps, and was classed as officially 'secret', due to its telecommunications function. The revolving restaurant closed after a bomb attack in 1971.

Barbican (1969)

The City; tube: Barbican; map p.153 C3

This concrete complex profoundly divides opinion, some seeing it as a Modernist masterpiece, others as post-apocalyptic with its empty, windswept walkways. It is something of an anomaly, comprising around 6,500 flats, schools, amenities and the

The 21st century has seen the building of the graceful **Jubilee Bridges**, footbridges which run on either side of the Hungerford Bridge, from Embankment Station almost to the foot of the London Eye on the South Bank, offering wonderful views up and down river. The elegant stainless-steel scalpel-like **Millennium Bridge** allows easy pedestrian access to Tate Modern from St Paul's Cathedral across the river and was built using suspension cables.

The Open House London event is held annually in September and involves 700 buildings across the capital opening their doors for free, even those which, like the former Daily Express building *(see left)*, are not generally open to the public. For more information, see **www.londonopenhouse.org**

well-regarded Barbican Centre arts complex. It was built on an area flattened in the Blitz, in an attempt to create a microcosm community in the City.
SEE ALSO MUSIC, P.98; THEATRE, P.143

Trellick Tower (1972)

Golborne Road, Westbourne Park; tube: Westbourne Park

Erno Goldfinger's council estate was one of the last stands of experimental social housing and was modelled on Le Corbusier's *Unité d'Habitation* idea. High-rise architecture is most strongly associated with the welfare housing built in the 1950s and 60s and Trellick Tower was at one time touted as representative of the problems that went along with this. Today, the brutalist architecture has made it something of an icon of that period of design.

National Theatre (1976)

South Bank; tube/rail: Waterloo; map p.149 E2

Dramatically positioned at the side of Waterloo Bridge, the National Theatre literally glows at night, when the Lyttelton flytower is lit up with a changing series of bright-coloured lights, making it appear to shine in say, purple or red. This creative use of Denys Lasdun's concrete, Modernist structure keeps the design playful and fittingly theatrical.
SEE ALSO THEATRE, P.143

Left: Millenium Bridge links St Paul's to the Tate Modern.

Left: the Barbican's stark design divides opinion.

SEE ALSO MUSEUMS AND GALLERIES, P.94

City Hall (2002)
Queen's Walk, Bankside; tube/rail: London Bridge; map p.153 E1
Sir Norman Foster designed this tapering, spherical glass home for the Greater London Authority (GLA), which leans away from the river. This design conspires to make the building as environmentally friendly as possible, minimising the heat lost through the exterior, while various systems recycle the energy used within it, ensuring City Hall uses about a quarter of the energy of a typical office building.

Thames Barrier (1982)
Information Centre, 1 Unity Way, Woolwich; tube: North Greenwich
This massive barrier protects 45 sq miles (117 sq km) of London from the very real danger of flooding. The giant gates can rise to 15ft (4.6m) higher than the highest Thames tide, forming a wall of steel against the river's flow. This impressive construction is also the largest adjustable dam in the world.

Lloyd's of London (1986)
1 Lime Street, City; tube: Monument; map p.153 E2
Designed by Lord Richard Rogers, this postmodern structure was one of the first buildings to transform the City. It turned the traditional building inside-out, with all the usual internal workings, such as lifts, stairwells and ducts, on the outside. It is not open to visitors, but a walk around the outside is a modern City highlight.

The O2 (1999)
Millennium Way, North Greenwich; tube/boat: North Greenwich

Built on wasteland near the river in Greenwich, the former Millennium Dome was designed as an exhibition arena to be used for just one year, in 2000. It opened to great fanfare but was badly managed and caused a great deal of controversy. Today, it is finally in use again as a major concert arena. It is also due to be used as a sports venue for the 2012 Olympics.

Tate Modern (2000)
Bankside; tube: Southwark, London Bridge; map p.152 C1
The poster child for regeneration, this famed and successful gallery is housed in the former Bankside power station, a mammoth brick Modernist building. Architects Herzog and De Meuron transformed the massive spaces of the interior.

The Gherkin (2004)
30 St Mary Axe, City; tube/rail: Liverpool Street; map p.153 E2
Its distinctive tapering shape gave this skyline-dominating building its nickname. The shape is also beneficial environmentally, with a ventilated double skin reducing heating and cooling requirements and spiralling lightwells maximising natural light.

Wembley Stadium (2007)
Wembley; tube: Wembley Park, Wembley Central
The national stadium finally opened in March 2007. Crowned by a 1,033ft (315m) long arch, it seems to be worth the long wait and high cost for the acoustics and design engineered to avoid any view obstruction (the arch avoids the need for pillars).

SEE ALSO SPORT, P.141

Right: the O2.

Cafés

Café culture is part of the landscape in London, taking in everything from white-tablecloth tea houses to Italian caffs, French pâtisseries, greasy spoons, organic health-food spots, cultural centre cafés and communal wooden tables tucked inside delis. The emphasis may be on coffee and pastries or light meals, but London's café culture offers great opportunities to people-watch and absorb the local atmosphere. The various and varying-quality coffee house chains can seem ubiquitous, but the listings below suggest the alternative: some of the best individual cafés in London.

Soho and Covent Garden

Bar Italia
22 Frith Street; tel: 020-7437 4520; daily 24 hours; tube: Leicester Square; map p.148 B4
A Soho institution, reminiscent of the 1950s, it remains impervious to fashion and is a classic all-night hangout for coffees and bar food. It shows all-Italian football matches on a screen at the back.

Beatroot
92 Berwick Street; tel: 020-7437 8591; Mon–Fri 9am–9pm, Sat 11am–9pm; tube: Oxford Circus; map p.148 B4

Below: delectable cupcakes at the Hummingbird Bakery.

Choose between small, medium and large containers at this healthy veggie spot, which offers a daily selection of hot dishes, salads, tagines and quiches, amongst others.

The Breakfast Club
33 D'Arblay Street; tel: 020-7434 2571; Mon–Fri 8am–6pm, Sat 9.30am–5pm, Sun 10am–4pm; tube: Oxford Circus; map p.148 B4
Unusual and home-comfort breakfast foods are on offer here; there are also decent burritos, burgers and wraps for lunch. Free Wi-fi access.

Fernandez & Wells
73 Beak Street; tel: 020-7287 8124; Mon–Fri 7.30am–6pm, Sat–Sun 9am–6pm; tube: Piccadilly Circus; map p.148 A4
Great toasted sandwiches, custard tarts and cakes, washed down with Monmouth Coffee Company-supplied brews. You can also buy further creative sandwiches and selections of cheese and charcuterie at the sister shop on 43 Lexington Street and bring them over to eat here.

Maison Bertaux
28 Greek Street; tel: 020-7437 6007; Mon–Sat 8.30am–11pm,

For an old-fashioned and inexpensive British-food experience, London's greasy spoons are a fun place to stop off. These classic and cosy '**caffs**' tend to serve a variety of hot food, but the point is really the classic fry-up. Unfortunately, the dominance of the coffee-chains is driving many of the most atmospheric central spots out of business, although Soho and Covent Garden have quite a few remaining traditional, Italian-run caffs.

Sun 8.30am–7pm; tube: Leicester Square; map p.148 B4
This boho spot is a Soho icon these days and claims to be the oldest pâtisserie in London, dating from 1871. Likened to a corner of Paris, it is quirky and frothily decorated, with sugary baked goods on offer.

Neal's Yard Salad Bar
2 Neal's Yard; tel: 020-7836 3233; daily 8.30am–9pm; tube: Covent Garden; map p.148 C4
Tucked away in relaxed Neal's Yard, this charming vegetarian and vegan café is a bit of an institution, serving a range

Left: old Soho lingers on in Bar Italia.

(Bob Dylan played here and it was a centre of countercultural life in the 1960s), the 'Troub' is an atmospheric coffeehouse/folk club/café in Earl's Court. Favourites from the good menu include eggs benedict and fishcakes.

Bloomsbury and Holborn

Clerkenwell Kitchen
27–31 Clerkenwell Close; tel: 020-7101 9959; Mon–Fri 8am–5pm, Thur until 11pm; tube: Farringdon; map p.152 B4
In a sleekly designed space with an open kitchen, feast on tarts, soups and sandwiches, or larger hot meals, all featuring seasonal ingredients.

Hummus Bros
Victoria House, 37–63 Southampton Row; tel: 020-7404 7079; Mon–Fri 11am–9pm; tube: Holborn; map p.151 E3
At this healthy concept café, you order a delicious serving of pitta bread and hummous with your choice of topping –

of salads, sandwiches and hot dishes, washed down with delicious fruit juices.

Nordic Bakery
14a Golden Square; tel: 020-3230 1077; Mon–Fri 8am–8pm, Sat 9am–7pm, Sun 11am–6pm; tube: Piccadilly Circus; map p.148 A3
Immaculate Scandinavian style is the order of the day at this hip but cosy café, which offers fresh rye rolls with fillings like pickled herring or brie with lingonberry, enormous, sticky cinnamon buns and warming mugs of coffee.

Oxford Street, Mayfair and Marylebone

La Fromagerie
2–6 Moxon Street; tel: 020-7935 0341; Mon–Fri 8am–7.30pm, Sat 9am–7pm, Sun 10am–6pm; tube: Baker Street; map p.150 B3
Cheese is, unsurprisingly, the focal point of the café at the back of this popular deli, but charcuterie, fish plates, terrines and soups are also tasty, season-led options.

Scandinavian Kitchen
61 Great Titchfield Street; tel: 020-7580 7161; Mon–Fri 8am–7pm, Sat 10am–6pm; tube: Oxford Circus; map p.151 C2

At this relaxed and friendly Scandinavian specialist café, you can indulge in traditional fish, cheese or meatball open sandwiches on rye or a tasty platter. Alternatives range from hot dogs to salads.

Kensington and Chelsea

Hummingbird Bakery
47 Old Brompton Road; tel: 020-7584 0055; daily 10.30am–7pm; tube: South Kensington; map p.156 B2
This American-style sweet treats mecca boasts an amazing array of cupcakes, brownies and sweet pies, available to take away or eat in fittingly sugary-sweet surroundings.

Ladurée
Harrods, 87/135 Brompton Road; tel: 020-7893 8293; Mon–Sat 9am–9pm, Sun midday–6pm; tube: Knightsbridge; map p.154 A3
Extraordinary cakes and macaroons served in utterly opulent surroundings, with prices to match.

The Troubadour
263–267 Old Brompton Road; tel: 020-7370 1434; daily 9am–midnight; tube: West Brompton
Ripe with bohemian history

Most of the smart London hotels do **afternoon teas** for non-guests; they can be quite expensive but they are a delicious experience. You usually get a selection of cakes presented on old-fashioned cake stands, delicate little sandwiches, and hot buttered crumpets, along with tea. Many will have dress codes so check ahead of visiting; it's highly advisable to book well in advance at any rate. Some of the best and most atmospheric places include:

The Ritz, 150 Piccadilly, Mayfair; tel: 020-7300 2345.

Claridges, 55 Brook Street, Mayfair; tel: 020-7409 6307.

The Lanesborough, Hyde Park Corner, Kensington; tel: 020-7333 7254.

Left: alfresco space at Neal's Yard Salad Bar.

options; this Mediterranean deli-cum-bakery-cum-brasserie is a great choice for everything from breakfasts to meze and mint tea, to tasty burgers and sandwiches.

Konditor & Cook

10 Stoney Street; tel: 020-7407 5100; Mon–Fri 7.30am–6pm, Sat 8.30am–5pm; tube/rail: London Bridge; map p.153 D1

Now a mini-chain, this location is handy for Borough Market, although there is no indoor seating. It is famed for its hard-to-resist cakes and other baked goodies, but creative sandwiches and salads are also on offer alongside daily hot specials, all to take away.

Monmouth Coffee Company

2 Park Street; tel: 020-7940 9960; Mon–Sat 7.30am–6pm; tube/rail: London Bridge; map p.153 D1

In an atmospheric, open-fronted shop that chimes perfectly with neighbouring Borough Market's Dickensian architecture, excellent and strong coffee is the order of the day. You can also indulge in bread and jam or pastries at the communal wooden table.

The Table

83 Southwark Street, Bankside; tel: 020-7401 2760; Mon–Thur 8am–6pm, Fri 8am–11pm; tube: Southwark; map p.153 C3

Designed by the architects in whose offices it is situated – Allies and Morrison – this light, airy place does great breakfasts and has an extensive salad bar; there's a courtyard for warm weather.

North London

The Candid Café

3 Torrens Street, Islington; tel: 020-7837 4237; Mon–Sat noon–10pm, Sun noon–5pm; tube: Angel

---

the most popular ones are guacamole and chicken – and a side salad such as tabouleh.

Squat & Gobble

69 Charlotte Street; tel: 020-7580 5338; Mon–Fri 8am–5pm, Sat 9am–5pm; tube: Goodge Street; map p.151 D3

A fantastic spot for inexpensive and generous-sized sandwiches, jacket potatoes, soups and delicious salads, all with a variety of toppings.

The City

The Place Below

St Mary-le-Bow, Cheapside; tel: 020-7329 0789; Mon–Fri 7.30am–3pm; tube: St Paul's; map p.153 C2

> If you are looking for a coffee late in the evening and don't happen to be in Soho, or want to go to a noisy pub, the spacious foyers of the South Bank's cultural institutions are a great place to hang out. There are bars in the National Theatre *(see Theatre, p.143)* and the Royal Festival Hall *(see Music, p.99)* that serve until 11pm.

A godsend for hungry vegetarians is this uplifting café in the crypt of St Mary-le-Bow church, with seats in the churchyard in summer. There are fresh quiches and salads on offer, and there is always a hot dish of the day.

South Bank and Bankside

Benugo Bar & Kitchen

BFI Southbank, Belvedere Road; tel: 020-7401 9000; daily 11am–11pm, Sun until 10.30pm; tube/rail: Waterloo; map p.149 E2

This is the trendy bar and restaurant in the British Film Institute complex, in addition to the riverside café, perfect for sociable drinks as well lounging with the papers or enjoying the free Wifi. Food is traditional British and drinks include good wines, cocktails and coffees.

Del'aziz

5 Canvey Street; tel: 020-7633 0033; daily 7am–11pm; tube: Southwark; map p.152 C1

In the recently built piazza tucked behind the Tate Modern, you will find several eating

Mediterranean dishes, plus sandwiches, tea, coffee and cake at this tucked-away gem, with tables in the courtyard and scrubbed wood and comfy sofas inside.

Chaiwalla
4A–5A Perrins Court, Hampstead; tel: 020-7435 2151; daily 8.30am–8.30pm; tube: Hampstead

Try a chai, served in a clay pot, and a baked samosa at this smart Indian-style tea bar.

Pavilion Café
Highgate Woods, Muswell Hill Road, Highgate; daily summer 9am–9pm, winter 9am–4pm; tube: Highgate

Lots of outdoor tables and the Highgate Woods setting make this a good place to take children, who are well catered for.

S&M Café
4–6 Essex Road, Islington; tel: 020-7359 5361; Mon–Fri 7.30am–11pm, Sat 8.30am–11pm, Sun 8.30am–10.30pm; tube: Angel

This retro, cheerful place claims to provide 'the ultimate comfort food', with a huge list of sausages, mashes and gravies, as well as breakfast foods and pies.

East London

Brick Lane Beigel Bake
159 Brick Lane, Whitechapel; tel: 020-7729 0616; daily 24 hours; tube: Liverpool Street

Legendary beigels – try the salt beef, herring or smoked salmon – and the cheesecake's tasty too. Non-kosher.

Jones Dairy Café
23 Ezra Street, Bethnal Green; tel: 020-7739 5372; Fri–Sat 9am–3pm, Sun 8am–2pm; tube: Old Street, then bus: 55

This is a local institution, a small place with an attached shop selling a huge range of excellent cheeses. The café does all-day breakfasts and huge, creative salads.

South London

Dulwich Gallery Café
College Road, Dulwich; tel: 020-8299 8717; Tue–Fri 9am–5pm, Sat–Sun 10am–5pm; rail: North Dulwich

This gallery café has an attractive patio, and is a great place for afternoon tea.

Pavilion Tea House
Charlton Way, Greenwich Park, Greenwich; tel: 020-8858 9695; summer daily 9am–6pm, winter daily 9am–4pm; rail: Greenwich

The café in this attractive octagonal building has great views over the park and nearby Docklands. Hot and cold British dishes, breakfast and cakes are available.

West London

Kitchen & Pantry
14 Elgin Crescent, Notting Hill; tel: 020-7727 8888; Mon–Fri 7am–9pm; tube: Ladbroke Grove; map p.157 C4

Good value, buzzy and friendly café just off Portobello Road, perfect for coffee, brunch or a tasty wrap if you can find a free squishy leather sofa or chunky wood table.

Orange Pekoe
3 White Hart Lane, Barnes; tel: 020-8876 6070; Mon–Fri 7.30am–6pm, Sat–Sun 9am–6pm; rail: Barnes Bridge

In this elegantly-rustic but relaxed tearoom, you can try a huge number of tea blends. Also serves recommended scones, cakes and lunches.

London's French-style pâtisseries generally offer a good standard of coffee, cake and continental bites. The below locations are some of the handiest, but you will find these franchises dotted everywhere:

Paul: 29 Bedford Street, Covent Garden; tel: 020-7836 330; daily 8am–8pm; tube: Leicester Square; map p.149 C3

Patisserie Valerie: 162 Piccadilly, Mayfair; tel: 020 7491 1717; Mon–Fri 7.30am–7.30pm, Sat 8am–8pm, Sun 9am–7pm; tube: Green Park; map p.148 A3

Le Pain Quotidien: Upper Festival Walk, Belvedere Road, South Bank; tel: 020 7486 6154; Mon–Fri 7.30am–11pm, Sat 8am–11pm, Sun 9am–10pm; tube: Waterloo; map p.149 D2

Tom's Delicatessen
226 Westbourne Grove, Notting Hill; tel: 020-7221 8818; Mon–Fri 8am–7.30pm, Sat 8am–6.30pm, Sun 9am–6.30pm; tube: Notting Hill Gate; map p.157 E4

Breakfasts, salads, sandwiches and light meals in this quirky, popular spot.

William Curley
10 Paved Court, Richmond; tel: 020-8332 3002; Mon–Sat 9.30am–6.30pm, Sun 10.30am–6pm; tube/rail: Richmond

Tiny signature shop of the master chocolatier, which blends Japanese style with imaginative chocolate goodies and excellent coffee.

Below: tucking in at the S&M Café.

Children

Don't be put off by London's often grown-up seeming attractions: the city provides multiple options for keeping children entertained. From museums with interactive exhibits to city farms, river trips to West End treats, visiting with children could well unveil another side of London to adults too. If budget is a concern, remember that almost all attractions that charge an entry fee will offer discounts for youngsters, while many museums are free, as is most public transport. Meanwhile, the city's many parks offer countless diversions and space for youngsters to run around in.

Attractions

BBC Television Centre Tours
Wood Lane, White City; tel: 0370-901 1227; www.bbc.co.uk/tours; tours run regularly Mon–Sat, must be pre-booked; admission charge; tube: White City

See the news desk, weather studios and sets for TV shows. If you're lucky you may see some rehearsals in this look at what goes on behind the scenes. Note that the tours are not open to under-9's.

Changing of the Guard
Horse Guards Parade, Buckingham Palace, St James's; tel: 020-7766 7300; Mon–Sat 11am, Sun 10am; free; tube: Westminster; map p.148 C2

This half-hour ceremony is a colourful spectacle and children can have their photo taken with a mounted guard.

London Aquarium
County Hall, Westminster Bridge Road, South Bank; tel: 0871-663 1678; www.sealife.co.uk/london; Mon–Fri 10am–6pm, Sat–Sun 10am–7pm; admission charge; tube/rail: Waterloo; map p.149 D1

Lots of sealife in an atmospheric setting; sounds and lighting are used effectively.

London Dungeon
Tooley Street, Bankside; tel: 020-7403 7221; www.thedungeons.com; daily 10.30am–5pm, longer hours vary, see website; admission charge; tube/rail: London Bridge; map p.153 D1

Ghoulish exhibits of the gruesome parts of London's history, including exhibits of the Black Death, the Great Fire of 1666 and Jack the Ripper's exploits. Not for the very young or very nervous.

London Eye
Westminster Bridge Road, South Bank; tel: 0870-500 0600; www.londoneye.com; daily May–Sept 10am–9pm (July–Aug until 9.30pm), Oct–Apr 10am–8pm; admission charge; tube/rail: Waterloo; map p.149 D1

Pick out London's landmarks during a 30 minute ride in a capsule on the world's largest observation wheel.
SEE ALSO MONUMENTS, P.79

Madame Tussaud's
Marylebone Road, Marylebone; tel: 020-7935 6581; www.madame-tussauds.co.uk; Mon–Fri 9.30am–5.30pm, Sat–Sun and school/public holidays 9am–6pm; admission charge;

Below: crowds watch the Changing of the Guard.

Left: a captive audience at the Natural History Museum *(see p.40).*

nees, it's easy to find one that's a treat for children as well as adults. The Palladium Theatre is usually home to a family-friendly show. A much-loved choice is *The Lion King,* which has played at the Lyceum Theatre (21 Wellington Street; tel: 0870 243 9000; www.lyceum-theatre.co.uk) for several years.
SEE ALSO THEATRE, P.142

PANTO
Every Christmas season (Nov–Jan), the very British tradition of pantomime (children's stories such as *Aladdin* or *Jack and the Beanstalk,* incorporating song, slapstick and cross-dressing) comes to a number of family-friendly theatres.
Polka Theatre
240 The Broadway, Wimbledon; tel: 020-8543 4888; www.polkatheatre.com; admission charge; tube/rail: Wimbledon
This children's theatre stages productions well worth checking out year round, but is also famed for it's annual panto productions.

Museums
British Museum
Great Russell Street, Blooms-bury; tel: 020-7323 8299; www.britishmuseum.org; daily 10am–5.30pm (Thur–Fri until 8.30pm); free; tube: Russell Square, Tottenham Court Road; floorplan p.90; map p.151 E3
The Egyptian mummies tend to be the biggest draw for children, but there's lots on offer here and the British Museum strives to make it all as accessible as possible. The Hamlyn Family trails in different parts of the museum are designed to focus attention on the most interesting parts

tube: Baker Street; map p.150 B3
It's expensive, but the constant queues outside Madame Tussaud's demonstrates how popular it is. A key ingredient in its phenomenal success is that the models of celebrities are no longer roped off or protected by glass cases, so visitors can stroll right up to them. It also mounts temporary exhibits based on movies or television shows such as *Big Brother.* Otherwise, the mix is one of showbiz stars, sports celebrities, royalty and world leaders. Some are uncannily accurate, although quite a few of the models are not all that good. For a more gory take, there's the **Chamber of Horrors**, while you can view the historical **Spirit of London** tableaux from a sawn-off black taxi.
Tower of London
Tower Hill, The City; tel: 0870-950 4488; www.hrp.org.uk; Mar–Oct Tues–Sat 9am–5.30pm, Sun–Mon 10am–5.30pm, Nov–Feb Tue–Sat 9am–4.30pm, Sun–Mon 10am–4.30pm; admission charge; tube: Tower Hill; map p.153 E1
Take a tour with a uniformed

If your child has an accident, take them to any hospital with a casualty department (A&E). Your hotel will be able to tell you your nearest, or call NHS Direct (0845 4647). Great Ormond Street Hospital is child-specialist, but only treats referrals from other hospitals.

Beefeater to discover Traitor's Gate and the fascinating history of the Tower.
SEE ALSO PALACES AND HOUSES, P.108

Entertainment
CINEMA
BFI London IMAX Cinema
1 Charlie Chaplin Walk, South Bank; tel: 0870-787 2525; www.bfi.org.uk/imax; admission charge; tube/rail: Waterloo; map p.149 E2
The UK's largest cinema screen, with incredible acoustics. Films shown include specially-made 3D features and blockbusters.

MUSICALS
With the array of musicals staged in the West End, usually including bi-weekly mati-

Paddington Bear, 1980
Michael Bond's first Paddington Bear book appeared in 1958.
Gabrielle Designs began to make Paddington bear toys in
England in 1972.

In the basement, there is a more recreational area and it is a good place to bring younger children if they tire of the more serious exhibits. It contains **The Garden**, a play area for children aged 3–6, and **Things**, a hands-on 'how do things work?' gallery suitable for 7–11-year-olds.
SEE ALSO MUSEUMS AND GALLERIES, P.86

Parks and Animals

Battersea Children's Zoo
Battersea Park, Battersea; tel: 020-7924 5826; www.battersea parkzoo.co.uk; daily 10am–5pm; charge; free; rail: Battersea Park
This imaginative zoo has been designed to allow children to get up close with animals and handle the cuddlier ones.
SEE ALSO PARKS AND GARDENS, P.114

Coram's Fields
93 Guildford Street, Bloomsbury; tel: 020-7837 6138; www.coramsfields.org; daily 9am–7pm or dusk; free; tube: Russell Square; map p.151 E4
Heaven for kids: free sporting activities, sandpits, slides and swings, a paddling pool and a pets' corner, to name a few. No adults are allowed in unaccompanied by children.

Hackney City Farm
1A Goldsmith's Row, Hackney; tel: 020-7729 6381; www.hack neycityfarm.co.uk; free; Tue–Sun 10am–4.30pm; rail: Cambridge

to children of various ages, while the free Ford backpacks (available from the Paul Hamlyn Library) are full of different puzzles, games and other activities to do in the galleries.
SEE ALSO MUSEUMS AND GALLERIES, P.91

National Museum of Childhood
Cambridge Heath Road, Bethnal Green; tel: 020-8983 5200; www.vam.ac.uk/moc; Sat–Thur 10am–5.45pm; free; tube: Bethnal Green
Lots to enjoy for children and big kids alike. The vast collection of games, toys and other childhood paraphenalia includes a magnificent rocking horse to ride, detailed dolls' houses, model railways to activate and a dressing-up box to rifle. The sand-box is always popular too.

Natural History Museum
Cromwell Road, Kensington; tel: 020-7942 5000; www.nhm.ac.uk; daily 10am–5.50pm;

free; tube: South Kensington; map p.156 B2
This museum is perennially popular with children, thanks to the dinosaurs and other large creatures, including the blue whale and komodo dragons. The leafcutter ant colony in the Creepy Crawlies gallery is also a highlight.
SEE ALSO MUSEUMS AND GALLERIES, P.85

Science Museum
Exhibition Road, Kensington; tel: 0870-870 4868; www.sciencemuseum.org.uk; daily 10am–6pm; free; tube: South Kensington; map: p.156 B2
Most of the galleries here have hands-on exhibits to appeal particularly to children. **The Launch Pad** has fun interactive exhibits including two enormous sound receivers. A message spoken quietly into one is easily picked up by the other on the far side of the room.

The biggest difficulty when travelling with children in London is the sheer crush of fast-moving, impatient bodies on the underground at rush hour. Avoiding the tube between 8–9.30am and 5–6.30pm will make accompanying adults' experience far less stressful.

Left: penguins at London Zoo.

For all healthcare needs, the chain Boots has in-shop pharmacies with child-specialist products, plus stocks of baby gear. There are stores all over London; this branch's pharmacy stays open the latest. The branch at 490 Oxford Street also has long hours, including on Sundays (tel: 020-7491 8546; Mon–Fri 8am–10pm, Sat 9am–8pm, Sun 10am–7pm; tube: Marble Arch; map p.150 B2).

Heath, bus: 26, 48, 55

All kinds of domestic animals, plus pottery sessions and workshops. The on-site café, Frizzante@City Farm, is good for a child-friendly bite or an adult pick-me-up.

London Zoo

Regent's Park, Marylebone; tel: 020-7722 3333; www.zsl. org/london-zoo; Mar–Oct 10am–5.30pm, Nov–Feb 10am–4pm; admission charge; tube: Camden Town, bus: 274

Over 600 species, a Meet the Monkeys exhibit, the Gorilla Kingdom and the Clore Rainforest Lookout (displaying South American mammals, birds and reptiles) are just some of the attractions here. The children's enclosure allows visitors to handle animals such as llamas and rabbits. Check the website for feeding times.

SEE ALSO PARKS AND GARDENS, P.112

Shopping

ESSENTIALS

Boots

114 Queensway, Bayswater; tel: 020-7229 1183; www.boots. com; store: Mon–Sat 9am–8pm, Sun noon–6pm, pharmacy: Mon–Sat 9am–midnight, Sun noon–6pm; tube: Bayswater; map p.157 E4

TOYS

Hamleys

188–196 Regent Street, Mayfair; tel: 0870-333 2455; www.hamleys.com; Mon–Fri 10am–8pm, Sat 9am–8pm, Sun noon–6pm; tube: Piccadilly Circus; map p.151 C1

The enormous selection and manic atmosphere is overwhelming, yes, but Hamleys is a great inducement to good behavior if all else fails.

Traditional Toys

53 Godfrey Street, Chelsea; tel: 020-7352 1718; www.traditionaltoy.com; Mon–Sat 10am–6pm; tube: Sloane Square; map p.156 C1

This charming toyshop stocks an enormous collection of toys with a distinctively 'English' character, including high-quality wooden toys, dolls, dolls' houses, fancy-dress costumes, teddy bears, games and educational toys.

Transport

Under-11s travel free at any time on London's public transport, including buses, tubes, DLR and trams, provided they are accompanied by a ticket-holding adult. Up to four children can travel free per adult.

11–15 year-olds can travel free on buses at any time and are eligible for child fares on tubes and trains, but they will need to be in possession of an Oyster photocard, which needs to be ordered at least three weeks in advance of travel and then collected from a Travel Information Centre. Under-16s will not need a photocard for day travelcards or cash-bought tube travel, only for cheaper Oyster pay-as-you-go fares or weekly travelcards. For more details, see **www.tfl.gov.uk**.

For a more relaxed way of viewing the city, open top buses offer a chance to get a proper sense of London's topography while keeping children diverted. See **Original Tour** (tel: 020-8877 1722; www.theoriginaltour.com) or the **Big Bus Company** (tel: 020-7233 9533; www.bigbus.co.uk).

SEE ALSO TRANSPORT, P.147

Right: the London IMAX.

Churches

London has a wealth of historic churches. In terms of architecture, certain names stand out, not least Sir Christopher Wren and his successors Nicholas Hawksmoor and James Gibbs. Between them, they are responsible for many of the loveliest and most enduring churches and cathedrals. Unless specified, the churches listed below belong to the Church of England or Anglican tradition. In addition to the many historical Christian places of worship, London's diversity is visible in the striking examples of mosques, synagogues and temples that cater to the city's vibrant multicultural population.

Medieval Churches

Despite fire, bombing and general time erosion, these churches and cathedrals retain at least some of their original structure.

St Bartholomew the Great
West Smithfield, The City; tel: 020-7606 5171; Mon–Fri 8.30am–5pm (mid-Nov–mid-Feb until 4pm), Sat 10.30am–4pm, Sun 8.30am–8pm; admission charge; tube: Barbican; map p.152 B3
This medieval church, begun

Below: memorial to Shakespeare at Southwark Cathedral.

in 1123, is one of the oldest in the city, and one of the most beautiful. The interior has been used as a setting for several films: *Four Weddings and a Funeral*, *Shakespeare in Love* and *The End of the Affair*. It also has a strong musical tradition.

Chelsea Old Church
64 Cheyne Walk, Chelsea; tel: 020-7795 1019; Tue–Thur 2–4pm; free; tube: Sloane Square
The church was painstakingly rebuilt after being destroyed by a landmine in 1941, but retains several fine Tudor monuments. The site was formerly occupied by a 12th-century Norman church. Henry VIII, who had a house on the river where Cheyne Walk now is, supposedly secretly married his third wife, Jane Seymour, here, several days before the official ceremony.

Southwark Cathedral
London Bridge, Bankside; tel: 020-7367 6700; daily 8am–6pm; free; tube/rail: London Bridge; map p.153 D1
Hemmed in by the railway, this is one of London's great historic churches. In the 12th

In 1533, King Henry VIII broke away from the Roman Catholic Church when the Pope refused to grant him a divorce in order to marry Anne Boleyn; the **Act of Supremacy** the following year declared the monarch as the head of the Church of England. This was the beginning of the English Reformation and forced a national conversion to Protestantism. Other than during Mary I's five-year reign, when the country was briefly returned to Catholicism, the Church of England, or Anglicism, has been the UK's official religion ever since.

century it was a priory church, and it has a Norman north door, early Gothic work and a number of medieval ornaments.

A memorial to Shakespeare in the south aisle, paid for by public subscription in 1912, shows the bard reclining in front of a frieze of 16th-century Bankside. Above it is a modern (1954) stained-glass window depicting characters from his plays. Shakespeare was a parishioner for several

Left: St Pauls' interior.

the area around St Paul's designed by Wren, was so-named because it stood near a royal store house, the Great Wardrobe, where King Edward III kept his state robes and other effects. The square-towered exterior is plain, but the inside is embellished with attractive carved woodwork.

St Bride's

Fleet Street, The City; tel: 020-7427 0133; Mon–Fri 8am–6pm, Sat 11am–3pm, Sun 10am–1pm, 5–7.30pm; free; tube: Temple; map p.152 B2

Known as 'the journalists' and printers' church', St Bride's was one of 87 churches destroyed by the Great Fire; it re-opened in 1675. The elegant spire makes it Wren's tallest church and it is said to have inspired the first tiered wedding-cake.

There is a small museum of Fleet Street in the crypt, where a collection of Roman mosaics from a villa on this site, Saxon church walls, William Caxton's Ovid and a large number of coffins are stored; much was revealed when the building was badly bomb-damaged in World War II. Diarist Samuel Pepys was baptised here.

Below: St Bride's.

---

years. John Harvard, who gave his name to the American university, was baptised here, and is commemorated in the Harvard Chapel.

Westminster Abbey

Parliament Square, Westminster; tel: 020-7654 4832; Mon–Tue, Thur–Sat 9.30am–4.30pm, Wed 9.30am–7pm; guided tours from 10am; admission charge; tube: Westminster; map p.155 D3

The most historic religious building in Britain, this is also an outstanding piece of Gothic architecture, which is probably more striking from the detail on the inside than from its outward aspects. Much of the abbey was built in the 13th century by Henry III. In the 16th century, Henry VII added the remarkable chapel in the late Gothic Perpendicular style. During the 18th century, Nicholas Hawksmoor designed the distinctive towers at the main west entrance.

The Abbey has always had a special place in national life because of its royal connections. The Coronation Chair has been used for every coronation in the Abbey since 1308. So many eminent figures are honoured here that large areas of the interior have the cluttered appearance of an over-crowded sculpture museum.

Poets' Corner is the burial place of Chaucer, Shakespeare, Milton, Tennyson and Keats, among others, while in the Tomb of the Unknown Warrior there is a body brought back from France at the end of World War I, along with the soil for the grave.

Wren's Churches

In the wake of the Great Fire of London in 1666, Sir Christopher Wren (1632–1723) was appointed one of the architectural commissioners overseeing the reconstruction of the city. His plans for a complete redrawing of the city streets were rejected, but his masterpiece, St Paul's Cathedral, and 51 churches were built to his designs; 26 remain today.

St Andrew-by-the-Wardrobe

Queen Victoria Street, The City; tel: 020-7329 3632; Mon–Fri 10am–4pm; free; tube: Mansion House; map p.152 C2

This church, one of several in

C

Above: Westminster Cathedral's distinctive exterior.

After the roof of Christ Church Spitalfields was rebuilt in 1966, the building was put to good use. The crypt of the then-derelict church was used as a shelter for homeless men.

18th-century organ, as much of the original is intact.

St Alfege's Church
Greenwich Church Street, Greenwich; tel: 020-8691 8337; Sat 11.30am–4pm, Sun noon–4pm, other times by appointment; free; rail/DLR: Greenwich

There has been a church on this site since 1012 following the martyrdom of St Alfege, Archbishop of Canterbury, who was murdered here. St Alfege's was built in 1712–18 by Hawksmoor to replace an earlier church in which Henry VIII had been baptised. It was restored in 1952 after being badly bombed in World War II. General James Wolfe, victor of the Battle of Quebec, is buried here (1759), as is Thomas Tallis (1585), known as 'the father of English church music'. There are often (free) concerts and recitals on Thursdays at 1.10pm.

St George's
Bloomsbury Way, Holborn; tel: 020-7242 1979 ; daily 1–4pm; free; tube: Holborn, Russell Square; map p.151 E2
Hawksmoor's church was modelled on the tomb of King Mausolus and is topped by a statue of George I in a toga. It recently underwent a £9 million renovation.

St Martin-in-the-Fields
Trafalgar Square, Westminster; tel: 020-7766 1100; daily 8am–6pm; free; tube: Charing Cross; map p.148 C3
The oldest building in Trafalgar Square, built in 1724 by Gibbs, when this venue really

St James's Piccadilly
197 Piccadilly, Mayfair; tel: 020-7734 4511; daily 8am–6.30pm; free; tube: Green Park; map p.148 A3
This graceful red-brick church was consecrated in 1684. The carved marble font and wooden reredos are the work of Grinling Gibbons. The churchyard is home to busy market stalls and there is a full evening events programme, including regular classical concerts.

St Paul's Cathedral
Ludgate Hill, The City; tel: 020-7246 8357; Mon–Sat 8.30am–4pm, tours at 10.45am, 11.15am, 1.30pm, 2pm; admission charge; tube: St Paul's; map p.152 C2
The first purpose-built Protestant cathedral is Wren's greatest work. Begun in 1675, it was not completed until 1710. A tablet above Wren's plain marble tomb reads: *Lector, si monumentum requiris, circumspice* (Reader, if you wish to see his memorial, look around you).

Just below the 24 windows in the magnificent dome is the Whispering Gallery, more than 30m of perfect acoustics. A whisper can be heard across the gallery, 10ft (33m) away. A chapel behind the High Altar, damaged in 1940s bombing

raids, was restored as the American Chapel, with a book of remembrance paying tribute to the 28,000 American citizens based in the UK who died during World War II.

Hawksmoor and Gibbs

Nicholas Hawksmoor (1661–1736) was Wren's protégé and worked on many of his projects. However, both he and James Gibbs (1682–1754) ultimately left their marks on London architecturally due to the 1711 decree that 50 new churches should be built (only 12 actually were) to accommodate the expansion of London.

Christ Church Spitalfields
Fournier Street, Spitalfields; tel: 020-7377 6793; Tue 11am–4pm, Sun 1–4pm, also Mon, Wed–Fri 11am–4pm if not in use for events, call to check; free; tube/rail: Liverpool Street, Aldgate East; map p.153 E3
Christ Church, with its elegant, slender spire, is the size of a small cathedral. Completed in 1729, it is considered the greatest of Hawksmoor's churches. Badly renovated and changed in the 1860s, then neglected for many years in the first half of the 20th century, it has now been restored to its original, sumptuous appearance. There are also plans to restore the mighty

Right: the London Central Mosque in St John's Wood.

44

Above: Brompton Oratory.

was in fields outside the city. Nell Gwynne, mistress of Charles II, is one of several famous people buried in this parish church of the royal family, so fashionable in the 18th century that pews were rented out on an annual basis.

Lunchtime and evening candlelit concerts are held here regularly. The church underwent a programme of renovation in 2006–7.

Catholic Churches

After centuries of oppression, the Catholic Relief Act of 1829 removed the legal restrictions on those who practised Catholicism; consequently, the grandest of their churches date from the 19th century.

Brompton Oratory
Brompton Road, Kensington; tel: 020-7808 0900; daily 6.30am–8pm; free; tube: South Kensing-

ton, Knightsbridge; map p.156 B2
A flamboyant Italian Baroque building designed by Herbert Gribble, whose career took a sudden step forward as a result. It was opened in 1884 and has a nave wider than St Paul's Cathedral. It also contains much older elements: the figures of the 12 apostles in the nave were carved for Siena cathedral in 1680 and the altar and reredos in the Lady Chapel date from the 17th century. The church used to host the city's main Roman Catholic congregation, but this role has been supplanted by Westminster Cathedral.

Westminster Cathedral
Victoria Street, Westminster; tel: 020-7798 9055; Mon–Fri 7am–6pm, Sat 8am–6.30pm, Sun 8am–7pm; free; tube: Victoria, bus 11, 24; map p.155 C2
The most important Catholic church in London. Its bold red-and-white brickwork makes it look like a gigantic layer cake. Built at the end of the 19th century in an outlandish Italian-Byzantine style not seen elsewhere in London, it has a 330ft (100m) striped tower incorporating a lift for public use (admission charge). The views from the gallery at the top are superb. The interior is sumptuous and impressive; many of the chapel walls are enriched with coloured marble cladding.

London's diversity of cultures is reflected in the variety of mosques, temples and synagogues that can be seen around the capital. Bear in mind that specific etiquette may apply when visiting these sites and will generally be signposted at the entry, but in all cases, it is advisable for both men and women to dress modestly when visiting.

Buddhapadipa Temple (14 Calonne Road, Wimbledon; tel: 020-8946 1357; www.buddha padipa.org; Temple: Sat–Sun 9am–6pm, grounds: daily 9am–6pm; free; tube/rail: Wimbledon, then bus: 93)
The only Thai Buddhist temple in Europe, situated in lovely, peaceful gardens and running Buddhist courses and retreats.

London Central Mosque (146 Park Road, St John's Wood; tel: 020-7724 3363; daily dawn–dusk; free; tube: Baker Street; map p.150 A4)
The gleaming golden dome and slender minaret of the mosque are now familiar sights. Completed in 1978, it adjoins the Islamic Cultural Centre. Guided tours of the centre are available; book on tel: 020-7725 2212.

New West End Synagogue (St Petersburgh Place, Bayswater); tel: 020-7229 2631; Mon–Thur 10am–1pm; free; tube: Bayswater; map p.157 E3)
One of the most historic synagogues in London, dating from 1879; stained glass windows illustrate different aspects of Jewish tradition.

BAPS Shri Swaminarayan Mandir (105–119 Brentfield Road, Neasdon; tel: 020-8965 2651; daily 9am–6pm, Shrines 9–11am and 4–6.30pm; free; tube: Neasden)
This Hindu temple is astonishing to look at: a confection of frothy white Italian marble and Bulgarian limestone, shipped to India for traditional skilled craftsmen to work on.

Dance

While it's not quite as high profile as other aspects of London's arts culture, the capital's dance scene is thriving. Challenging, innovative contemporary works are performed alongside classical dance in spectacular spaces. The Royal Ballet, founded in 1931, continues to be prestigious and popular, its legacy created by choreographers like Frederick Ashton and ballerinas such as Margot Fonteyn and more recently, Darcey Bussell. Today, the availability of dance training in virtually every style ensures that there is a wealth of talent out there; these listings suggest some venues where you can go to see it.

Classical Dance Venues

Coliseum
St Martin's Lane, Covent Garden; tel: 0870-145 0200; www.eno.org; tube: Charing Cross; map p.148 C3
The home of the English National Opera, the London Coliseum also hosts ballet performances by the Royal Ballet and the English National Ballet, as well as visiting companies; it is particularly popular with visiting Russian Ballet companies.

Royal Albert Hall
Kensington Gore, Kensington; tel: 0845-401 5045; www.royal alberthall.com; tube: South Kensington; map p.156 B3
Ballet is often featured on the extensive programme here; the English National Ballet regularly performs a summer season in the round. Ballroom dancing, salsa and flamenco, among other dance forms, have also been staged.

Royal Opera House
Bow Street, Covent Garden; tel: 020-7304 4000; www.roh.org.uk; tube: Covent Garden; map p.149 C4
Home to the Royal Ballet and the Royal Opera, the building was extensively refurbished for the millennium. The stage and the auditorium are splendid, as are many of the performances, but tickets are expensive and hard to get, particularly when artists such as Carlos Acosta and Sylvie Guillem are dancing.

Backstage tours are available on many week days; leave time for a drink on the roof terrace with views over Covent Garden.

Contemporary Dance Venues

Barbican Arts Centre
Silk Street, The City; tel: 020-7638 8891; www.barbican.org.uk; tube: Moorgate, Barbican; map p.153 C3
Although the Barbican Centre is sometimes more associated with classical music and theatre than with dance, the latter forms a substantial part of its programme, and features innovative companies, both home-grown and international.

Jackson's Lane
Jacksons Lane Community Centre, 269a Archway Road, Highgate; tel: 020-8341 4421; www.jacksonslane.org.uk;

Above: the prestigious Royal Opera House.

tube: Highgate
North London's leading and busiest arts centre features a wide variety of artistic performances, including dance, throughout the year. The five-week dance season, Zone 3, is highly regarded and relatively inexpensive to attend.

Peacock Theatre
Portugal Street, Covent Garden; tel: 0844-412 4300; tube: Holborn; map p.149 D4
This is the West End venue of Sadlers Wells *(see right)*, where performances of a similarly high standard can be seen.

Left: male swans in Matthew Bourne's *Swan Lake*.

Those interested in doing some dancing themselves should hot-foot down to one of these studios, where regular classes are held. There are daily membership fees in addition to a charge for taking the class, however, these are not high.
Pineapple Dance Studio, 7 Langley Street, Covent Garden; tel: 020-7836 4004; www.pineapple.uk.com.
Danceworks, 16 Balderton Street, Mayfair; tel: 020-7629 6183; www.danceworks.net.

The Place
Duke's Road, Bloomsbury; tel: 020-7121 1000; www.thep lace.org.uk; tube/rail: Euston; map p.151 D4
London Contemporary Dance School, Richard Alston Dance Company and the Robin Howard Dance Theatre all perform here. A great place to see modern dance, and at ticket prices much lower than in most other venues.
Sadlers Wells Theatre
Rosebery Avenue, Islington; tel: 0844-412 4300; www.sadlerswells.com; tube: Angel
Extensive renovation has

made this a flexible, state-of-the-art performance space, offering an exciting and innovative programme of dance. It is London's leading venue for contemporary and classical dance, where you can rely on seeing excellent performances from renowned companies. Matthew Bourne's popular ballets are frequently performed here.
South Bank Centre
Belvedere Road, South Bank; tel: 0871-663 2500; www.south bankcentre.co.uk; tube/rail: Waterloo; map p.149 D2
A diverse range of dance performances are staged in newly renovated spaces at the South Bank Centre. Featuring many experimental productions as well as international dance, this is an accessible place to view innovative performances.

Dance School Spaces
Chisenhale Dance Space
64-84 Chisenhale Road, Bow; tel: 020-8981 6617; www.chisenhaledancespace.co.uk; tube: Mile End
It's somewhat off the beaten track in Bow, but this is an interesting venue for contem-

porary dance which holds offbeat events and hosts community-focussed workshops. Student performances can be seen in the summer.
Laban Centre
Creekside, Deptford; tel: 020-8691 8600; www.laban.org; DLR: Cutty Sark
The Laban Centre building has garnered a lot of attention for its striking, prize-winning design but what goes on inside is often just as exciting. Contemporary dance is performed by the resident company, Transitions, as well as visiting troupes and community groups. The school's emerging dance artists choreograph and perform their own work regularly.
Siobhan Davies Studios
85 St George's Road, Southwark; tel: 020-7091 9650; www.siobhandavies.com; tube: Elephant and Castle
The RIBA award-winning conversion of a disused Victorian building into an innovative space holds frequent events, workshops and occasionally open rehearsals. Every month, The Open Space showcases new work from dance artists, both established and emerging, in an informal setting.

Below: the striking Laban Centre.

Environment

Until the Clean Air Act of 1956, London suffered from extreme smog: when smoke particles from factories, power stations and domestic fires mixed with fog, giving it a murky yellowish colour. While use of electricity and gas as fuel sources has long alleviated this problem, awareness of other environmental concerns has greatly increased in recent times. With increasing attention from the government and Greater London Authority, there is currently a firm focus on pressing green isssues and measures are being taken to reduce London's massive and size-disproportionate output of waste and pollutants.

A Crowded City

Like all major cities, London suffers from overcrowding. Although there is a constant exodus of young families to the suburbs, there is a larger influx of people coming into the city from all over the country and the rest of the world. Many come looking for work or for a better life and in the case of many young people, simply looking for fun.

All this makes the city a hugely vital and interesting place but also a crowded one: 7.6 million residents, officially, generating a high volume of waste, transport emissions, and consuming large amounts of electricity and other fuels.

Transport Problems

London's transport system is still very congested, as anybody travelling on the underground during rush hour is painfully aware. Improvements tend to be slow in coming and the age of many of the tube lines show in the regular glitches. The aim of the Greater London Authority (GLA) has been to tempt people out of their vehicles, with reasonable success. However, the constantly spiralling costs of travelling by public transport and lack of comfort continue to put a lot of people off.

Above ground, London suffers from pockets of bad traffic, but the introduction of the £8 congestion charge in 2003, levied on all cars brought into central London and now parts of west London on weekdays between 7am and 6pm, has helped alleviate the more widespread problem. Traffic entering the central zone is estimated to be down by 21 percent in the original zone and by 14 percent in the western extension zone.

Positively, the number of people choosing to cycle around the city increased by 107 percent between 2000 and 2009. Investment in cycling infrastructure such as bike lanes and parking spaces has had the effect desired by the GLA. Currently, about 550,000 journeys in London each day are made by bicycle; the planned introduction of a Paris-style bike hire scheme in 2010 is expected to further increase this number.

In December 1952 an anti-cyclone settled over London, causing a thick fog to form. What became known as the **Great London Smog** lasted for five days, causing a seven-fold increase in sulphur dioxide levels, and leading to around 4,000 deaths. It was this that led to the 1956 Clean Air Act, which introduced zones in which smokeless fuels had to be used.

Below: crowds face rush hour on the day of a train strike.

Left: a summer haze over the towers of London.

ban in all enclosed public spaces, driving smokers increasingly onto the streets. Cigarette butts and other smoking parephenalia are said to account for around 40 percent of London's litter, in spite of the threat of £50 fines for those caught in the act. The added problem with cigarette ends is their ability to fall into grates and get into the water system, spreading toxins to wildlife.

A Green City

Despite all the hazards associated with a major city, London benefits from several green lungs, in the form of the city's many parks. The natural world is also preserved in the city farms which thrive in places from Mudchute to Hackney, dedicated botanical areas such as Kew Gardens and the Barnes Wetland Centre, not to mention the Camley Street Natural Park, a wildlife reserve just north of the very central King's Cross station. SEE ALSO PARKS AND GARDENS, P.112

Cleaning Up the River

The Thames is actually the cleanest metropolitan river in Europe, but untreated sewage and rainwater is still a problem. To cope with the increased population and climate changes, a tunnel is to be built to address the estimated 52 million cubic metres of waste that go into the river every year. The tunnel, which will cost an estimated £2 billion and stretch for 20 miles (32km), is

Below: look out for the 'C' – it means you're in a Congestion Charge zone.

designed to catch sewage and rainwater discharged along the river and carry it to a treatment plant in east London. There's a way to go yet, however; the projected completion date is 2020.

Litter in London

London suffers from the same problems with litter as most other cities. While most people are quite conscientious, many areas suffer from a lack of rubbish bins, particularly at rail and tube stations. The situation is exasperated in central London by the vast amount of food packaging generated by consumption of sandwiches, coffees and the like, and currently, by the growth of free daily newspapers, which many people read and discard freely.

It's not all bad news, however. Increased focus on the importance of recycling has led to a rise in the number of recycling bins near stations and popular lunch spots, especially for paper, glass and aluminium.

In July 2007, England became subject to a smoking

One way in which visitors to London can consider their environmental impact is in how they arrive. Air travel produces a huge amount of carbon dioxide, so, if possible, take the train to your destination *(see Transport, p.146)*. However, many travellers, especially those from the US, will find it impossible to do this and will arrive by air. Consider 'offsetting' the CO_2 through an organisation like Climate Care (www.climatecare.org). Their on-line calculator will tell you your carbon emissions for your trip and how much you should donate to the scheme.

Essentials

Finding your way around an unknown city of this size can be quite daunting, but London is so international and geared towards visitors that it is usually easy to find information. Most hotel reception staff are a mine of information and will generally help with communication problems and bookings. English people are not renowned for their grasp of other languages, but they are also undeserving of their standoffish reputation (except when on the tube) and are generally happy to help when asked. This section gives you the basic useful facts, but for specific practical information, see *Transport, p.146–7*.

Embassies

Australia: tel: 020-7379 4334
Canada: tel: 020-7258 6600
France: tel: 020-7073 1000
Ireland: tel: 020-7235 2171
New Zealand: tel: 020-7930 8422
US: tel: 020-7499 9000

Emergencies

For police, ambulance and fire brigade, dial 999.

Entry Requirements

To enter Britain you need a valid passport (or any form of official identification if you are an EU citizen). Visas are not needed if you are from the US, a Commonwealth citizen or an EU national (or come from most other European or South American countries).

Health and Medical Care

If you are an EU national, you are entitled to free medical care for illnesses arising while in the UK. You should obtain a European Health Insurance Card (EHIC), available free in your own country. Many other countries also have reciprocal arrangements for free treatment. Other visitors should ensure they have health insur-

The climate in London is generally mild year-round. Snow is rare and January temperatures average 6°C (43°F). In the summer months, they average 18°C (64°F) but can soar, causing the city to become very stuffy. Rainfall is unpredictable and it's wise, even in summer, to keep an umbrella handy.

ance. However, emergency treatment is always free and usually very good.

EMERGENCY DENTAL CARE
Guy's Hospital
St Thomas Street; tel: 020-7188 7188; Mon–Fri 9am–5pm (queuing begins at 8am); tube/rail: London Bridge

HOSPITALS
All of these have 24-hour Accident and Emergency service.
Charing Cross Hospital
Fulham Palace Road; tel: 020-8846 1234; tube: Hammersmith
St Mary's Hospital
Praed Street; tel: 020-7886 6666; tube/rail: Paddington
St Thomas's Hospital
Lambeth Palace Road; tel: 020-7188 7188; tube/rail: Waterloo

PHARMACIES
Boots is a large chain of pharmacies with branches throughout London that will make up prescriptions. For details of late-opening branches, *see Children, p.41*.

Internet

If you have brought a laptop, you may be able to plug it in or access wireless services in your hotel room. Cafés around town offer Wi-fi too. Alternatively, internet cafés are found all over town, see **www.easyinternetcafe.com**.

Money

The pound sterling (divided into 100 pence) is the currency, but many large stores will accept euros.

ATMs are everywhere: you can withdraw cash with a credit or debit card as long as you have a PIN (Personal Identification Number). Your bank may charge you a withdrawal fee; check in advance.

International credit cards are accepted almost universally; look for signs if in doubt.

Most banks open Mon–Fri 9.30am–5pm and some on

Left: it is always wise to carry an umbrella.

Bank (Public) Holidays
New Year's Day (1 Jan); Good Friday (moveable); Easter Monday (moveable); May Day (Mon of 1st weekend in May); Spring Bank Holiday (Mon of last weekend in May); Summer Bank Holiday (Mon of last weekend in Aug); Christmas Day (25 Dec); Boxing Day (26 Dec)

Telephones
Dial **100** for the operator and **118 118** for directory enquiries. Public phones are much cheaper to use than those in hotel rooms, with a minimum charge of 40p; most will also accept phone cards, which are available from post offices and newsagents. Credit card phones can be found at major transport terminals and on busy streets.

To call an international number, dial 00 followed by the international country code, and then the number. Country codes: Australia (61); France (33); Germany (49); Ireland (353); New Zealand (64); South Africa (27); Spain (34); US/Canada (1).

Toilets
During the day, department stores and museums are a good bet for free toilets, or pay a small fee (20–30p) to use those at rail stations. Facilities in pubs, cafés and restaurants are generally only for customers.

Tourist Information
Britain & London Visitor Centre
1 Lower Regent Street; tel: 020-7808 3800; www.visit london.com; Mon–Fri 9am–6.30pm (Mon from 9.30am), Sat–Sun 10am–4pm; tube: Piccadilly Circus; map p.148 B3
The official tourist office.

Saturday morning in shopping areas. Major banks offer similar exchange rates. Banks charge no commission on sterling travellers' cheques.

Thomas Cook travel agents operate bureaux de change at comparable rates. Alternatively, **Chequepoint** are a reputable chain of bureaux de change and can be found at 550 Oxford Street (tel: 020-7724 6127; www.cheque point.com; tube: Marble Arch) and elsewhere around town. There is a charge for buying or selling cash, or cashing travellers' cheques, unless you do so at a post office (see below).

Postal Services
Post offices are open Mon–Fri 9am–5pm, Sat 9am–noon. Stamps are available from post offices, as well as many newsagents.
Trafalgar Square Post Office
24–28 William IV Street; tel: 0845-722 3344; www.postof fice.co.uk; Mon–Fri 8.30am–6.30pm, Sat 9am–5.30pm; tube: Charing Cross; map p.149 C3
The most central and latest-opening branch.

Public Holidays and Events
On bank holidays (see box, above), transport and shops mostly keep to Sunday hours, except on Christmas and Boxing Days, when virtually everything shuts down.

Major public events to enjoy for free include the **London Marathon**, held in the spring, which attracts 40,000 participants and a further half a million who line the route between Blackheath and St James's Park. Europe's largest street festival, the **Notting Hill Carnival**, takes place over the Summer Bank Holiday, with parades, music and dancing.

Below: the iconic red postbox.

Fashion

The most 'street-style' of the major fashion capitals, London fashion is characterised by a quirky mix of the creative and the traditional. The most successful of the British designers have worked in this vein, but there is room for virtually every style somewhere in London. The range of fashion stores on offer reflects this; every budget and taste is catered for by a huge range of designer boutiques, inexpensive high-street chains and everything in between. Meanwhile, those looking for one-offs can peruse the city's vintage shops. For department stores and markets, see *Shopping, p.136*.

The Fashion Scene

Fashion in London is energetic. Young designers constantly reinvent Britain's style history into edgy, creative fashion that is influential worldwide, not least in the high-street stores which interpret the big looks in double-quick time. Less formal than in other major style cities like Paris, New York and Milan, trend-setting looks are not confined to the catwalk or the very wealthy, but created and translated in different ways by the fashion-conscious people who live and work here, and equally, designers look to the streets for their inspiration.

Much of London's creativity is due to the encouragement given to young designers. London is internationally reputed for its fresh design talent, often alumni of Central St Martins, as well as its rich heritage of quintessentially British houses such as Burberry and Daks, not to mention the traditional gentlemen's tailors, who are updating their styles without losing their techniques. This influ-

ence, combined with the fast-fashion of the high-street and markets, and finds from the many vintage treasure-trove stores, is representative of a city that has always prided itself on being in fashion.

The Fashion Trail

The sheer diversity of London's districts means that trends can vary wildly in the different shopping areas. Glamourous, high-class fashion is prevalent in the designer stores of **Mayfair** and **Knightsbridge** while **Notting Hill** is home to shops promoting a luxe, bohemian style. **Covent Garden** offers some of the best streetwear, denim and youth fashion shops in town. **Shoreditch** is all edgy boutiques and pop-up shops, while **Spitalfields** is good for vintage shops and new designers, in contrast to **Oxford Street**, the busiest and most famous high street in London, with a presence by all of the major mainstream high-street chains and many of the best department stores. **Regent's Street** boasts several of the more

upmarket chains as well as a handful of designer outlets.

The **Westfield London** Shopping Centre in Shepherd's Bush opened in 2008 and offers a vast range of fashion shops, from all the big high-street names to streetwear labels, more unusual international brands and, in the Village, a collection of designer names.

While all the major international brands, both high-end and high-street, have a presence in London, the listings below focus on some of the best British brands and shops. Many of the shops listed will have a few, and sometimes multiple, branches around London; the details given refer to the flagship stores.

Size Conversions
Women:
10 (US 8, Europe 38)
12 (US 10, Europe 40)
14 (US 12, Europe 42) etc.
Men:
(suits) 36 (US 36, Europe 46)
38 (US 38, Europe 48) etc.
(shirts) 14 (US 14, Europe 36)
15 (US 15, Europe 38) etc.

Left: models strut their stuff at London Fashion Week.

through the latest and best in designer fashion.

Koh Samui
65–67 Monmouth Street, Covent Garden; tel: 020-7240 4280; www.kohsamui.co.uk; Mon–Sat 10.30am–6.30pm (Thur until 7pm), Sun noon–5.30pm; tube: Covent Garden; map p.148 C4
This boutique mixes vintage fashions with major labels and is still very popular. Lines include those by Chloe, Balenciaga and Marchesa. Independent labels are also given space, as are designer shoes (colour co-ordinated with the clothes) and menswear.

Boutiques

Browns
23–27 South Molton Street, Mayfair; tel: 020-7514 0000; www.brownsfashion.com; Mon–Wed 10am–6.30pm, Thur 10am–7pm, Fri–Sat 10.30am–7pm; tube: Bond Street; map p.150 B2
Numerous leading designers are stocked in Browns' five interconnecting shops on South Molton Street, as well as the directional Browns Focus and the discount shop, Browns Labels for Less. Over 100 labels are represented, from perrenial favourites such as Marc Jacobs and Sophia Kokosalaki, to newer hot names like Alexander Wang, Preen and Derek Lam.

The Cross
141 Portland Road, Notting Hill; tel: 020-7727 6760; www.the crossshop.co.uk; Mon–Sat 11am–5.30pm; tube: Holland Park; map p.157 C2
One of London's original fashionista boutiques and still one of the most popular. Boasting an eclectic mix of designers, including Clements Ribeiro, Gharani Strok and Betty Jackson, The Cross also stocks American lines such as Dosa and Juicy Couture and a fantastic line of own-brand cashmere.

Dover Street Market
17–18 Dover Street, Mayfair; tel: 020-7518 0680; www.dover streetmarket.com; Mon–Wed 11am–6pm, Thur–Sat 11am–7pm; tube: Green Park; map p.148 A3
At the vanguard of cutting-edge shopping is this conceptual fashion bazaar, inspired by London's covered markets and the creation of Comme des Garçons designer, Rei Kawakubo. Six floors of both cutting-edge and established labels, such as Azzedine Alaia and Lanvin, set in creative, deconstructed spaces and punctuated by fittingly avant-garde art.

Harvey Nichols
109–125 Knightsbridge; tel: 020-7235 5000; www.harveyni chols.com; Mon–Sat 10am–9pm, Sun 11.30am–6pm; tube: Knightsbridge; map p.154 A3
Less of a boutique than a department store, but elegant and urban Harvey 'Nicks' is the preferred destination for those who want to browse

Designer Fashion

Alexander McQueen
4–5 Old Bond Street, Mayfair; tel: 020-7355 0088; www.alexandermcqueen.com; Mon–Sat 10am–6pm (Thur until 7pm); tube: Bond Street; map p.148 A3
The former *enfant terrible* of British fashion has toned down his outrageousness a bit from days gone by, but he still produces immaculately tailored clothes.

Aquascutum
100 Regent Street, Mayfair; tel:

Below: high fashion at the Dover Street Market.

Right: modern British cool on offer at Luella.

020-7675 8200; www.aquascutum.com; Mon–Sat 10am–6.30pm (Thur until 7pm), Sun noon–5pm; tube: Piccadilly Circus; map p.148 A3
This luxury label, known for its smart raincoats ('Aquascutum' comes from the Latin for water and shield) has been serving London since 1851 and holds a number of royal warrants. This flagship store reflects the label's combination of English traditionalism with sleek contemporary touches.

Burberry
21–23 New Bond Street, Mayfair; tel: 020-3367 3000; www.burberry.com; Mon–Sat 10am–7pm, Sun noon–6pm; tube: Bond Street; map p.150 C1
While many visitors still head here for the classic items (raincoats, scarves etc.), style-conscious regulars are more interested in the Burberry Prorsum collection, designer Christopher Bailey's stylish range with a fresh take on classic British sensibilities.

Luella
25 Brook Street, Mayfair; tel: 020-7518 1830; www.luella.com; Mon–Sat 10am–6pm (Thur until 7pm); tube: Bond Street; map p.150 C2
Luella Bartley's label is one of the most synonymous with trendy young Londoners such as Alexa Chung and filters very English, feminine clothes such as floral dresses through a rock 'n' roll aesthetic.

Matthew Williamson
28 Bruton Street, Mayfair; tel: 020-7629 6200; www.matthewwilliamson.com; Mon–Sat 10am–6pm; tube: Green Park; map p.150 C1
One of Britain's most successful designers, specialising in brightly-coloured and patterned clothes, often intricately embellished and with an Asian-inspired or bohemian aspect. This bright flagship store reflects the pieces.

Stella McCartney
30 Bruton Street, Mayfair; tel: 020-7518 3100; www.stellamccartney.com; Mon–Sat 10am–6pm (Thur until 7pm); tube: Green Park; map p.150 C1
One of the most visible designers of 'London' style is based in this converted Georgian townhouse. The style is femininity with an edge; pretty tops, skinny trousers and 'vegetarian' shoes displayed in airy rooms, with a boudoir space upstairs for the lingerie.

Temperley
2–10 Colville Mews, Lonsdale Road, Notting Hill; tel: 020-7229 7957; Mon–Fri 10am–6pm (Thur until 7pm), Sat 11am–6pm; tube: Notting Hill Gate; map p.157 D4
Alice Temperley has been one of the greatest success stories of the last few years, creating feminine, romantic pieces with intricate embellishment and attention to detail. Her signature pieces remain the dresses, but there is also an expanding range of daywear.

Vivienne Westwood World's End
430 King's Road, Chelsea; tel: 020-7352 6551; Mon–Sat 10am–6pm; tube: Fulham

Below: crowds outside Topshop, the high street superstar.

Broadway, bus: 11, 22

This quirky and iconic shop, situated near the bend in the King's Road, is easily identifiable by the large clock that tells the time backwards on its shop front. This shop stocks the diffusion line, Anglomania, a highly wearable range that still fits the Westwood mould of distinctive tailoring. The World's End and Men lines are also available here.

High Street Fashion

French Connection

396 Oxford Street, Marylebone; tel: 020-7629 7766; www.frenchconnection.com; Mon–Fri 10am–8pm, Thur until 9pm, Sat 10am–7pm, Sun noon–6pm; tube: Bond Street; map p.150 B2

Having ditched the risqué FCUK advertising campaign and slogan tees; the onus is now all on the catwalk-conscious clothes. On-trend little dresses, floaty tops and chic tailored separates and knitwear make this a great stop-off for both work and weekend wear. This store also sells menswear and beauty products.

Oasis

13 James Street, Covent Garden; tel: 020-7240 7445; www.oasis-stores.com; Mon–Sat 10am–7pm (Thur until 8pm), Sun noon–6pm; tube: Covent Garden; map p.149 C4

The fashion at this chain comprises ladylike styles and retro-influenced separates alongside up-to-the-minute styles and colours. This store sells the New Vintage range as well as a great selection of shoes and accessories.

Reiss

116 Long Acre, Covent Garden; tel: 020-7240 7495; www.reiss.co.uk; Mon–Fri 10.30am–7.30pm (Thur until 8pm), Sat 10.30am–7pm, Sun noon–6pm; tube: Leicester

Square; map p.149 C4

This rapidly expanding brand positions itself between the high-street mutiples and designer fashion. The prices reflect this, but so do the clothes, which are contemporary and understated, with a distinct look and quality detailing. Grown-up, sexy tailoring is a particularly strong point.

Topshop

36–38 Great Castle Street, Oxford Circus, Marylebone; tel: 0844-848 7487; www.topshop.com; Mon–Sat 9am–9pm, Thur until 9pm, Sun 11.30am–6pm; tube: Oxford Circus; map p.151 C2

This flagship branch of this unstoppable high-street juggernaught is now established as a London institution and the largest fashion store in the world. Topshop has become a byword for affordable, bang-up-to-date trends and this branch features ranges by guest designers, including the Kate Moss range, as well as recent graduates. There's also a fantastic shoe department, a vintage boutique and several smaller labels downstairs.

Whistles

12 St Christophers Place, Marylebone; tel: 020-7487 4484; www.whistles.co.uk; Mon–Fri 10am–7pm, Sat 9am–6pm, Sun noon–5pm; tube: Bond Street; map p.150 B2

Having been taken over by Jane Shepherdson, the force behind Topshop's renaissance, Whistles is now undergoing a resurgence of its own and is turning out line after line of wearable clothes for stylish urban girls, from silk blouses to leather jackets. It's good value for trend-referencing but distinctive designs.

Lingerie

Agent Provocateur

6 Broadwick Street, Soho; tel: 020-7439 0229; www.agent

provocateur.com; Mon–Sat 11am–7pm, Thur until 8pm, Sun noon–5pm; tube: Tottenham Court Road; map p.148 B4

The original high-end raunch purveyors are still exhibiting saucy but classy lingerie at their first store. The range includes decadently sexy bras, basques and suspenders in silk, satin and lace.

Myla

The Village, Westfield Shopping Centre, Ariel Way, Shepherd's Bush; tel: 020-8749 9756; www.myla.com; Mon–Fri 10am–9pm, Sat 9am–9pm, Sun noon–6pm; tube: Shepherd's Bush Market, Wood Lane

Gorgeous, romantic lingerie is available at this girlie boutique devoted to sensuality, amidst swimwear, nightwear and upmarket toys.

Coco de Mer

23 Monmouth Street, Covent

Below: hosiery to kick your heels up in.

55

Garden; tel: 020-7836 8882; www.coco-de-mer.com; Mon–Sat 11am–7pm (Thur until 8pm), Sun noon–6pm; tube: Covent Garden; map p.148 C4

Risqué erotica emporium, selling beautiful underwear that perfectly combines the saucy with the classy, alongside the naughtier goodies.

Menswear

Aware Underwear
25 Old Compton Street, Soho; tel: 020-7287 3789; www.awarelondon.com; Mon–Sat 11am–8pm, Sun noon–7pm; tube: Leicester Square; map p.148 B4

Catering to the trendy, well-groomed Soho crowd, this men's underwear store is packed with boxers and briefs from designers such as Calvin Klein, Hom and Dolce & Gabbana. There's a good swimwear range too.

Gieves & Hawkes
1 Savile Row, Mayfair; tel: 020-7434 2001; www.gievesand hawkes.com; Mon–Wed 9.30am–6.30pm, Thur 9.30am–8pm, Fri 9am–6.30pm, Sat 10am–6pm, Sun 11am–5pm; tube: Piccadilly Circus; map p.148 A3

This Savile Row institution has moved on from its 18th-century beginnings and now has a directional diffusion line, Gieves, in addition to the more traditional ranges of classic tailoring. Bespoke two-piece suits range in price from £700–1,600, depending on the fabric used. This store has a wonderfully grand interior.

The Library
268 Brompton Road, Chelsea; tel: 020-7589 6569; Mon–Sat 10am–6.30pm (Wed until 7pm), Sun 12.30–5.30pm; tube: South Kensington; map p.156 B2

A small, independent boutique, The Library specialises in men's designer clothing both by up-and-coming designers and by more established names such as Alexander McQueen and Helmut Lang. There is also an alteration service available.

Paul Smith
40–44 Floral Street, Covent Garden; tel: 020-7379 7133; www.paulsmith.co.uk; Mon–Wed 10.30am–6pm, Thur 10.30am–7pm, Fri 10.30am–6.30pm, Sat 10am–6.30pm, Sun 12.30–5pm; tube: Covent Garden; map p.149 C4

One of Britain's best-known fashion designers, Sir Paul's Covent Garden empire is made up of four wood-panelled outlets, linked by one long passage. The clothes are beautifully tailored with innovative twists and great attention to detail. Most of the items decorating this inviting store, such as the signature stripey rug, are also for sale.

Ted Baker
9–10 Floral Street, Covent Garden; tel: 020-7836 7808; www.tedbaker.com; Mon–Sat 10am–7pm (Thur until 8pm), Sun noon–6pm; tube: Covent Garden; map p.149 C4

This mid-range label does trendy casual and sophisticated dressy clothes for young professional-types. There's a decidedly quirky edge to some of the clothes, especially the brightly-patterned shirts, but not excessively so. Womenswear

Left: the finest tailoring on Savile Row.

is very ladylike generally but otherwise in a similar mould.

Shoes and Accessories

Anya Hindmarch
15–17 Pont Street, Chelsea; tel: 0207-838 9177; www.anyahind march.com; Mon–Sat 10am–6pm; tube: Sloane Square; map p.154 A2
The eponymous designer has expanded into shoes, clothes and beachwear, but the main attraction is still the bags, now including a bespoke line, and the iconic 'I'm Not a Plastic Bag' tote. The collection features a wide range of classic leather handbags, baskets, clutches and totes. The 'Be a Bag' range features the customer's choice of photograph, and proceeds go to charity.

Georgina Goodman
44 Old Bond Street, Mayfair; tel: 020-7493 7673; www.georgina goodman.com; Mon–Sat 10am–6pm (Thur until 7pm); tube: Green Park; map p.148 A3
Glamourous designer shoes

Left: fabulous vintage dresses at Notting Hill's Rellik.

are the order of the day here, with sexy killer heels in luxe materials a particular standout, but the bold designs don't detract from the wearability.

Mulberry
41–2 New Bond Street, Mayfair; tel: 020-7491 3900; www.mul berry.com; Mon–Sat 10am–6pm (Thur until 7pm); tube: Bond Street; map p.150 C1
This classic label is best known for its luxe leather accessories. A recent collaboration with Giles Deacon and the popularity of bags such as the 'Roxanne' and 'Bayswater' has ensured Mulberry's presence on fashionistas' wish-lists.

Office
16 Carnaby Street, Soho; tel: 020-7434 2530; www.office.co.uk; Mon–Sat 10am–8pm, Sun 11.30am–7pm; tube: Oxford Circus; map p.148 A4
This is one of the most reliable chains for fashion-forward footwear, ranging from ballerina pumps and on-trend boots to funky trainers and patterned wellies. They also stock shoes by sister label, Poste Mistress, trainers by Converse and flip-flops by Haviana.

Orla Kiely
31 Monmouth Street, Covent Garden; tel: 020-7240 4022; www.orlakiely.com; Mon–Sat 10am–6.30pm, Sun noon–5pm; tube: Covent Garden; map p.148 C4
This flagship store in Covent Garden is decorated in Orla Kiely's signature graphic prints and stocks her popular range of handbags and luggage, alongside womens-wear and homeware. Bags come in crisp, retro-chic patterns in practical shapes and fabrics, at mid-range prices.

Above: brightly-coloured shoes at Absolute Vintage.

Vintage

Absolute Vintage
15 Hanbury Street, Spitalfields; tel: 020-7247 3883; www. absolutevintage.co.uk; daily 11am–7pm; tube: Aldgate East
In a bright, glass-fronted shop near Spitalfields, you can pick up bargains dating from the 1930s to 1980s, including dresses, clutch bags and accessories. But it's the shoe and boot collection that is especially strong, with constant turnover of stock.

Rellik
8 Golbourne Road, Notting Hill; tel: 020-8962 0089; www.rellik london.co.uk; Tue–Sat 10am–6pm; tube: Westbourne Park
This vintage shop, specialising in retro fashion from the 1920s to the 1980s, is very popular with London style-setters. Treasures abound from Pucci, Ossie Clark and Christian Dior, amongst many others.

Being able to show your green and ethical credentials is becoming increasingly more important in the fashion world. Environmentally friendly and fair-trade clothes can be found at Ecobtq (www.ecobtq.com), Equa (www.equaclothing.com) and Potassium (www.potassium store.co.uk). Currently, Marks & Spencer is leading the high-street's initiatives.

Film

Star-gazers head to Leicester Square, where crowds line behind barriers to watch stars parade along red carpets to film premieres, but London's cinematic scene involves so much more. Film festivals are held regularly, celebrating incredibly diverse cinema from around the world and energetically striving to reach new audiences. The characterful independent, repetory and arthouse cinemas also show a broad range of films, so you will never be short of something to watch. The home-grown film industry thrives too, with London continuing to be a backdrop to multiple projects.

London as Backdrop

London has long been a favoured setting for film-making. Some of the most successful spy thrillers, literary adaptations, musicals and romantic comedies ever made have been set and filmed in London. Years ago, Hollywood's vision of the city involved it being wreathed in fog, peopled by people who either spoke in clipped tones or dubious mock-Cockney; today, although there is a still a romanticised version of London popularised by Richard Curtis films such as *Notting Hill* and *Bridget Jones's Diary*, other films have gathered acclaim for their depictions of a grittier take on the city.

In the post-World War Two years, Ealing comedies such as *Passport to Pimlico* and *The Ladykillers* used atmospheric London settings to great effect, as did Hitchcock before them. The innovative 'swinging London' film makers of the 1960s (*Blowup*, *Alfie*, *Darling*) and more recently, auteurs like Mike Leigh *(Secrets and Lies)* and Gary Oldman *(Nil by Mouth)* have provided an edgier but equally evocative contribution to this tradition.

More recent popular home-grown fare, such as *28 Days Later*, *Bend it like Beckham*, *Shaun of the Dead* and *Kidulthood*, continue to prove the commercial strength of the London film-making scene. And of course, the evocative backdrops of the city continue to be used for period dramas such as *Elizabeth* and *Sweeney Todd*.

Multiplex Cinemas

Leicester Square is the spiritual home of the blockbusters and big screens but be aware that prices here are higher than in branches of the same cinemas elsewhere in London:

Cineworld
13 Coventry Street, Mayfair; tel: 0871-200 2000; www.cineworld.co.uk; tube: Piccadilly Circus; map p.148 B3; branches at Haymarket, Chelsea, Fulham Road

Odeon
24–26 Leicester Square, Soho; tel: 0871-224 4007; www.odeon.co.uk; tube: Leicester Square; map p.148 B3; branches at Covent Garden,

More than 50 film festivals are held in London every year. The biggest is the **London Film Festival** (www.lff.org.uk), held in October at the BFI, featuring a huge range of British and foreign films, plus talks by directors. The major independent film festival is **Raindance** (www.raindance.co.uk) held in late September at Cineworld cinemas.

West End, Tottenham Court Road
Vue
3 Cranbourn Street, Leicester Square, Soho; tel: 08712-240 240; www.myvue.com; tube: Leicester Square; map p.148 B3

Independent Cinemas

BFI Southbank
South Bank; tel: 020-7928 3535; www.bfi.org.uk; tube/rail: Waterloo; map p.149 E2
Recently revamped and enlarged, the BFI has a wide-ranging programme of classic films, old and new, plus research and educational facilities. It runs a 'Films for a Fiver' programme every Tuesday.
Curzon Soho
99 Shaftesbury Avenue,Soho;

Left: the BFI Southbank is a fabulous resource for film lovers.

with ruched curtains over the screen. Mostly mainstream.

Prince Charles
7 Leicester Place, Soho; tel: 0870-811 2559; www.prince charlescinema.com; tube: Leicester Square; map p.148 B3
Low prices for films you may have just missed, plus some golden oldies and the occasional singalong screening.

Renoir
Brunswick Square, Bloomsbury; tel: 0871-703 3991; www. curzoncinemas.com; tube: Russell Square; map p.151 E4
Shows excellent world and arthouse cinema.

Ritzy
Brixton Oval, Coldharbour Lane, Brixton; tel: 0871-704 2065; www.picturehouses.co.uk; tube: Brixton
The much-loved Ritzy shows a mixture of independent and mainstream films.

Riverside Studios
Crisp Road, Hammersmith; tel: 020-8237 1111; www.riversidestudios.co.uk; tube: Hammersmith
At this dynamic mixed arts centre, you can often catch double bills of films, which range from special repetory seasons and festival showings to first-run screenings.

Screen on the Green
83 Upper Street, Islington; tel: 0870-066 4777; www.screencinemas.co.uk; tube: Angel
A beautiful old-fashioned cinema, screening mainstream and independent films.

Tricycle Cinema
269 Kilburn High Road, Kilburn; tel: 020-7328 1000; www.tricy cle.co.uk; tube: Kilburn
An innovative programme of small and world films.

tel: 020-7292 1686; www.cur zoncinemas.com; tube: Leicester Square; map p.148 B4; branches at Bloomsbury, Mayfair, Chelsea, Richmond
Inventive selection of world cinema and independent films. Old movies are screened on Sundays.

Electric Cinema
191 Portobello Road, Notting Hill; tel: 020-7908 9696; www.the-electric.co.uk; tube: Notting Hill Gate; map p.157 D3
Tickets are pricey at this trendy spot, but worth it, to sit on comfortable chairs and sofas, with legs stretched out.

Everyman Cinema
5 Hollybush Vale, Hampstead;

tel: 0870-066 4777; www.everymancinema.com; tube: Hampstead
Now revamped, and just as luxurious as the Electric, with sofas in what they call the 'screening lounges'.

ICA Cinema
The Mall; tel: 020-930 3647; www.ica.org.uk; tube: Charing Cross; map p.148 B2
A great programme of world cinema, often very political.

Notting Hill Coronet
103 Notting Hill Gate, Notting Hill; tel: 020-7727 6705; www.coronet.org; tube: Notting Hill Gate; map p.157 D3
A wonderfully ornate and characterful small cinema

Left: a vision of a deserted London in *28 Days Later*.

Food and Drink

Forget the stereotypes about British food; homegrown has never been better. Visit the array of markets, delicatessens and bakeries in London and the vibrancy of this scene is apparent, with an increasing onus on organic and locally-sourced produce. Meanwhile, London's multicultural population ensures that there is a wealth of diversity when it comes to both eating out and food shopping. This influence is absorbed into British cuisine as it continually develops as both cutting-edge and proudly traditional. For more information on London's eating culture, see also *Restaurants, p.122*, and *Cafés, p.34*.

British Food

Not so long ago, British food had a very bad reputation. Lack of imagination, lack of taste and overcooked vegetables were often cited, and, with a few honourabale exceptions, any restaurant that claimed to specialise in British food would have been short of customers. But how things have changed in recent years. Partly due to the inevitable interchange of ideas now that people travel all over the globe, and partly to a huge swell of interest in

Below: bangers and mash, a perennial favourite.

locally-sourced food, British cooking is now varied, interesting and healthy.

In restaurants, shops and markets it is now common to see the exact source of the meat, fish and cheese specified, and, although compromises have to be made as business must be done all year round, many places take a pride in serving vegetables in season whenever possible.

So, if you want West Country pork, Aberdeen Angus beef, salt marsh lamb, Somerset cheese, fresh seasonal beetroot or locally grown rhubarb, you will find it in shops and restaurants smart and humble.

There has also been a somewhat nostalgic return to 'old-fashioned' food, reworked with a lot more panache than in days of old, and you will find dishes such as lamb shanks and treacle tarts turning up on the menus of smart restaurants. Meanwhile, the Sunday roast remains Britain's favourite dish.

Interest in good food has recieved an enormous boost

from 'celebrity chefs' on television and in the weekend sections of newspapers. Whether or not people use their recipes, it has created an awareness. Food has become sexy.

However, if you don't want British food, you don't have to eat it. London has restaurants serving food from all over the world, and its delicatessens and markets stock all the ingredients.

Different areas of the city have specialist food shops, depending on the ethnic mix. Soho, where Italian immigrants settled in the early 20th century, has mouthwatering all-Italian outlets; and nearby Chinatown, of course, has stores selling Chinese ingredients of all kinds. Go to Brixton, and you'll find Caribbean fruits and vegetables you may never have seen before; in Dalston (northeast London) you might think you were in a Turkish bazaar; while Brick Lane is lined with Bengali outlets and a bit further out, Wembley boasts many Indian and Sri Lankan shops.

Left: the bountiful produce of Borough Market.

all kinds is arrayed in such splendour that you feel as if you have walked into Aladdin's Cave.

Harrods

87–135 Brompton Road, Knightsbridge; tel: 020-7730 1234; www.harrods.com; Mon–Sat 9am–8pm, Sun 11.30am–6pm; tube: Knightsbridge; map p.154 A3

Rivals Fortnum & Mason in its opulent array of foodstuffs, sweet and savoury, fresh and preserved. Harrods is famous for its food hampers, which make decadent (but expensive) presents.

Harvey Nichols

109–125 Knightsbridge; tel: 020-7235 5000; www.harveynichols.com; Mon–Sat 10am–9pm, Sun 11.30am–6pm; tube: Knightsbridge; map p.154 A3

Another treasure trove of gourmet goodies, stylishly arranged, including their own-label products.

Partridges

2–5 Duke of York Square, Chelsea; tel: 020-7730 0651; www.partridges.co.uk; daily 8am–10pm; tube: map p.154 A1

Take a step back in time and pay a visit to this traditional

Fair trade battles for news attention with environmental concerns, but it is still one of the issues that continues to drive Britain's new foodie culture (though critics, rightly, point out that this is still very much a preoccupation of the wealthy). However, this much vaunted foodie revolution should not be allowed to disguise the fact that much of the British diet consists of unhealthy and over-processed cheap food, and the current economic climate may force the healthy eating movement to take a few steps back.

British Drink

British beers have always been popular and, despite a fashion for continental lagers, many drinkers insist on 'real ale' and have an extremely vocal pressure group, CAMRA (Campaign for Real Ale), to make sure it stays the course.

English wines, especially whites, are becoming more popular, and can be found in specialist shops and farmers' markets, but you rarely see them on restaurant menus.

Buying Food and Drink

There is so much food on offer in London's shops and markets that visitors staying in hotels and eating in restaurants may regret the few opportunities they have to sample it. However, putting together the ingredients for a picnic to take to a park, or buying preserved goods to take home, couldn't be easier. The following listings suggest some of the best places to go to stock up or just admire what's on offer.

Food Halls

Many of the large department stores have well-stocked and tempting food halls, while there are also a couple of fantastic dedicated food department stores worth a trip in their own right.

Fortnum & Mason

181 Piccadilly, Mayfair; tel: 020-7734 8040; www.fortnumandmason.com; Mon–Sat 10am–8pm, Sun noon–6pm; tube: Piccadilly Circus, Green Park; map p.148 A2

London's most glamorous grocer is the place for gourmet gifts and treats. Food of

Below: in Harrods food hall.

Right: cheeses stacked high in Neal's Yard Dairy.

purveyor of fine food and wine. A great place to buy smoked salmon, cheese, olive oil and hampers. There is an in-store café and they also run a Saturday food market outside the shop.

Whole Foods
63–97 Kensington High Street, Kensington; tel: 020-7368 4500; www.wholefoodsmarket.com; Mon–Sat 8am–9pm, Sun 10am–8pm; tube: High Street Kensington; map p.157 E1
Part of the US organic and natural-food specialist supermarket chain, this flagship UK branch caused quite a stir when it opened in the former Barkers building. The first floor is akin to an upmarket food court and there are several hot food and salad choices available downstairs to take away too.

Food Shops

& Clarke's
122 Kensington Church Street, Kensington; tel: 020-7229 2190; www.sallyclarke.com; Mon–Fri 8am–8pm, Sat 8am–4pm, Sun 10am–4pm; tube: Notting Hill Gate; map p.157 E2
A wonderful array of fresh breads, in all kinds of flavours. The shop also sells fresh fruit and veg, Neal's Yard cheese, Monmouth House coffee and various chutneys, soups and sauces from their own kitchen.

Farmers' Markets have become very popular and reflect not only a desire for fresh, organic food, but also an environmental concern over 'food miles': the distance that food is transported before it reaches the consumer. Often, the delicacies displayed in farmers' markets come from specialist, small-scale producers rather than extensive farming.

A. Gold
42 Brushfield Street, The City; tel: 020-7247 2487; Mon–Fri 9.30am–5.30pm, Sat 11am–6pm, Sun 10am–6pm; tube: Liverpool Street; map p.153 E3
This idiosyncratic village-shop-cum-delicatessan specialises in British foods, sourced from small producers working to traditional recipes. Pies, chutneys and artisan cheeses sit alongside old-fashioned sweets and meads.

De Gustibus
4 Southwark Street, Bankside; tel: 020-7407 3625; www.degustibus.co.uk; Mon–Fri 7am–5pm, Sat 7am–4pm; tube: London Bridge; map p.153 D1
This award-winning artisan bakers specialises in traditional handmade breads, offering varieties from 'Latvian Rye' to 'Parisienne'.

Drury Teas & Coffees
3 New Row, Covent Garden; tel: 020-7836 1960; www.drury. uk.com; Mon–Fri 9am–6pm, Sat 11am–5pm; tube: Leicester Square; map p.149 C3
Old-fashioned coffee grinders, espresso machines, cafetières, teapots and infusers are just some of the accessories sold alongside this shop's many fine-quality teas and gourmet coffees. You can even mix your own blend, known as 'Bob'

(buyer's own blend).

Hope & Greenwood
1 Russell Street; Covent Garden; tel: 020-7240 3314; www.hope andgreenwood.co.uk; Mon–Sat 10.30am–7.30pm, Sun 11.30am–5.30pm; tube: Covent Garden; map p.149 D4
This retro 'confectionery' is styled as if it were the 1950s, with vintage-styled sweeties and chocolate on offer.

Monmouth Coffee Company
27 Monmouth Street, Covent Garden; tel: 020-7379 3516; www.monmouthcoffee.co.uk; Mon–Sat 8am–6.30pm; tube: Covent Garden; map p.148 C4
The coffees here are sourced directly from an increasing variety of farms and cooperatives across the coffee-producing world, to aid fair trade. At this branch, where the beans are roasted, there is a sample room and a café where you can enjoy Villandry and Paul pastries alongside a strong and delicious coffee. (Another branch by Borough Market, 2 Park Street.)
SEE ALSO CAFÉS, P.36

Neal's Yard Dairy
17 Shorts Gardens, Covent Garden; tel: 020-7240 5700; www.nealsyarddairy.co.uk; Mon–Thur 11am–7pm, Fri–Sat 10am–7pm; tube: Covent Garden; map p.149 C4

Right: fungi galore in Borough Market.

At this specialists in British and Irish farmhouse cheeses, the huge truckles lining the shop's wooden shelves are a wonderful sight and the smells are overwhelmingly ripe. Employees are extremely helpful and really know and care about the produce. Good bread, too. (Another branch at 6 Park Street, Borough Market, Bankside; tel: 020-7645 3554.)

Oliviers & Co.
10 Market Street, The City; tel: 020-7392 9134; www.oliviersandco.com; daily 10am–6pm; tube: Liverpool Street; map p.153 E3
This shop offers a huge range of quality olive oils that would be impossible to find in a supermarket. A selection of these is laid out for customers to sample. Beautifully smooth pestles and mortars made out of olive wood are also on sale.

Rococo
321 King's Road, Chelsea; tel: 020-7352 5857; http://rococochocolates.com; Mon noon–5pm, Tue–Sat 10am–6.30pm, Sun noon–5pm; tube: Sloane Square; map p.154 A1
For chocolate connoisseurs and chocoholics, this tiny shop, with its lovely displays

Below: British foods from A. Gold.

and curving, antique counter, sells a fine selection of chocolates and sweets. Look out for the titchy Rococo delivery van.

Verdes
40 Brushfield Street, Spitalfields, The City; tel: 020-7247 1924; www.verde-and-company-ltd.co.uk; Mon–Fri 8am–8pm, Sat–Sun 11am–5pm; tube: Liverpool Street; map p.153 E3
Specialises in organic produce and fresh pasta, imported from Italian family firms and cooperatives. Literary fans should note that it's owned by Jeanette Winterson.

Markets

London is a great place for food markets, all with their own individual characteristics. Some to tantalise your taste buds are listed below:

Berwick Street Market
Soho; Mon–Sat 9am–5pm; tube: Piccadilly Circus; map p.148 B4
Good-value fruit, vegetables, cheese, bread, spices, dried fruits and nuts in what is still a very down-to-earth market.

Borough Market
Southwark Street, Bankside; Fri noon–6pm, Sat 9am–4pm; tube: London Bridge; map p.153 D1
Operating from its original site, adjacent to London Bridge, which once sold live animals, then became a wholesale fruit and vegetable

market, today Borough Market is still busy and buzzing, and has become very trendy.

Producers from all over the country and further afield sell goods that range from free-range pork, wild boar and ostrich to fish, cheeses, preserves and organic vegetables, including a huge variety of mushrooms. There's also a strong Spanish influence, with good-quality oils, chorizo, ham, wine and much more. Many stalls offer tastings. Lunchtime browsers can pick up sandwiches or wraps with mouthwatering roast meat or veggie fillings.

Brixton Market
Electric Avenue, Brixton; Mon–Sat 10am–6pm; tube: Brixton
A great range of African and Caribbean produce, as well as the herbs and spices to cook them with.

Spitalfields Fine Foods Market
Crispin Place, off Brushfield Street, Spitalfields, The City; Thur–Fri, Sun 10am–5pm; tube: Liverpool Street; map p.153 E3
In a recent extension to the main market, this gourmet quarter represents the area's multicultural aspects; traditional British meats, pies, pâtés and cakes sit alongside Indian sauces, chutneys and teas.

63

Gay and Lesbian

London is rightly famed as being one of the most gay-friendly cities in the world, with a vibrancy and nightlife to match. The gay male scene is booming, with new cafés, bars and clubs springing up all the time. The lesbian scene still lags behind a little, though the Candy Bar is going strong and there are some fabulous club nights dotted around. The centre of gay life in the city is still Soho and, in particular, Old Compton Street, though Vauxhall has become a male gay mecca and in ever-changing East London new haunts are springing up all the time.

Cafés and Bars

Bar Code

3–4 Archer Street, Soho; tel: 020-7734 3342; www.bar-code.co.uk; Mon–Sat 4pm–1am, Sun 4–11pm; tube: Piccadilly Circus; map p.148 B3

A very popular, and cruisey, Soho bar with a club downstairs. On Tuesdays it hosts Comedy Camp (8.30pm; www.comedycamp.co.uk), an excellent gay comedy club open to all. (Also at Arch 69, Albert Embankment, Vauxhall; tel: 020-7582 4180.)

Candy Bar

4 Carlisle Street, Soho; tel: 020-7287 5041; www.candybar soho.com; Mon–Thur 5–11.30pm, Fri–Sat 5pm–2am, Sun 5–11pm; tube: Tottenham Court Road; map p.148 B4

Love it or loathe it – it is not noted for its charming service – the Candy Bar is still the most lasting fixture on the lesbian scene. Upstairs the small bar area means it gets pretty crowded by closing time; downstairs is the more roomy DJ bar with pole dancing on Thursdays.

Dalston Superstore

117 Kingsland High Street, Dal-

Above: laughs and a friendly crowd at Comedy Camp.

ston; tel: 020-7254 2273; Mon–Fri noon–2am, Sat–Sun 11am–2am; rail: Dalston Kingsland

Glamorous East-End party-goers flock to this chic but welcoming venue by day for brunch, burgers and cakes, and by night to enjoy decent drinks amid disco, electro and house beats.

The Edge

11 Soho Square, Soho; tel: 020-7439 1313; www.edge soho.co.uk; Mon–Sat 11am–1am, Sun 2–11.30pm; tube: Tottenham Court Road; map p.148 B4

Four floors of varied fun on Soho Square. The Hygge Bar

on the first floor is good for a relaxed drink while the 3rd level dance floor offers a lively polysexual experience.

First Out

52 St Giles High Street, Holborn; tel: 020-7240 8042; www.firstoutcafebar.com; Mon–Sat 10am–11pm, Sun 11am–10.30pm; tube: Tottenham Court Road; map p.149 C4

Decent, cheap veggie food, friendly staff and a relaxed bar downstairs, these are what have made London's oldest gay and lesbian café-bar a winner for over 20 years. Girl Friday (7–11pm) is a favourite gathering for women, while things liven up for a pre-club DJ on Saturdays (7–11pm).

G-A-Y Bar

30 Old Compton Street, Soho; tel: 020-7494 2756; www.g-a-y.co.uk; daily noon–midnight; tube: Tottenham Court Road; map p.148 B4

Although its crowd of screeching 18-year-olds might not be to everyone's taste, the fun never stops at the legendary club night's sister bar, where giant video screens blare out the latest hits across three floors. At closing the party

Left: a night out at the Candy Bar.

A glitzy gay members' club (open to non-members) which packs in the fabulous, famous and aspiring. Not a cheap night out but more glamorous than some other destinations.

The Star at Night
22 Great Chapel Street, Soho; tel: 020-7494 2488; www.thes taratnight.com; Tue–Sat 6pm–midnight; tube: Tottenham Court Road; map p.148 B4
This mixed and relaxed bar is favoured by Soho lesbians trying to avoid the Candy Bar. It has a decent tapas menu and great cocktails.

Village Soho
81 Wardour Street, Soho; tel: 020-7434 2124; www.village-soho.co.uk; Mon–Sat 4pm–1am, Sun 4–11.30pm; tube: Leicester Square; map p.148 B4
Big, brash and here to stay, this long-standing venue is ideally located in central

continues round the corner at **G-A-Y Late** (5 Goslett Yard, Soho; tel: 020-7734 9858; daily 11pm–3am).

The Green
74 Upper Street, Islington; tel: 020-7226 8895; www.the greenislington.co.uk; Mon–Wed 5pm–midnight, Thur 5pm–1am, Fri 5pm–2am, Sat noon–2am, Sun noon–midnight; tube: Angel
A stylish yet down-to-earth venue that offers a fun alternative to the Soho scene. Friendly staff, decent food and lively music keep the regulars coming back for more.

Below: pouring the drinks at First Out.

Ku Bar
30 Lisle Street, Soho; tel: 020-7437 4303; www.ku-bar.co.uk; Mon–Sat noon–3am, Sun noon–10.30pm; tube: Leicester Square; map p.148 B3
This lively drinking hole packs in a sexy international crowd over three floors, with the basement level home to energetic club nights like lesbian favourite Ruby Tuesdays and pop-fest Shinky Shonky; see website for details. (Also at 25 Frith Street, Soho).

Oak Bar
79 Green Lanes, Stoke Newington; tel: 020-7354 2791; www.oakbar.co.uk; usually Mon–Thur 5pm–midnight, Fri–Sat 4pm–3am, Sun 4pm–1am, see website for club nights; bus: 73; tube: Canonbury
This North London, predominately lesbian pub has a nicely laid-back air. The club nights (such as Salla and Hustle; see website for details) are popular.

The Shadow Lounge
5 Brewer Street, Soho; tel: 020-7287 7988; www.theshad owlounge.co.uk; Mon–Sat 9pm–3am; tube: Piccadilly Circus; map p.148 B4

London's generally easy-going attitude to lesbian and gay people can fool you into thinking there is little or no homophobia in the capital. Sadly this is not the case. The 1999 bombing of the gay pub Admiral Duncan by a right-wing extremist caused wide outrage and a call for greater resources to fight hate crimes. In 2004 a young barman, David Morley, was beaten to death after leaving the gay club Heaven. In addition there has been opposition to gay rights, especially civil partnerships which became law in 2005, from religious groups. If you decide to head to the cruising grounds of Hampstead Heath and Clapham Common do take care, and remember that sex in public can be an illegal offence if you're caught.

Soho. Its three floors get very cruisey and lively at weekends.

Clubs and Club Nights

Club Kali
The Dome, 178 Junction Road, Kentish Town; tel: 020 7272 8153; www.clubkali.co.uk; 1st and 3rd Fri in the month, 10pm–3am; tube: Tufnell Park
'The world's biggest Asian music based LGBT club'. The eclectic mix of tunes ranges from Bollywood and bhangra, to Arabic and club classics.

Code
The Enclave, 25–27 Brewer Street, Soho; tel: 07956-529 649; www.club-code.net; 1st and 3rd Fri of the month, 8pm–3am; tube: Piccadilly Circus; map p.148 B3
This twice-monthly lesbian night is the place to go for gorgeous gay girls and an uplifting musical cocktail of funky house, electro and dance.

Duckie
Royal Vauxhall Tavern, 372 Kennington Lane, Vauxhall; tel: 020-7737 4043; www.duckie.co.uk; Sat 9pm–2am; tube/rail: Vauxhall; map p.155 E1
Burlesque, camp, arty and polysexual goes some way to describing Duckie. Now an institution, it's a great night out and these 'Post-Poofter Purveyors of Progressive Working Class Entertainment' are not to be missed.

Fire
38–42 Parry Street, Vauxhall; tel: 020-7582 9890; www.fire club.co.uk; Thur–Sun, see website for times and events; tube/rail: Vauxhall
Vauxhall means muscles, and this place packs them in like no other. Fire's nights attract the dedicated party crowd, often continuing well beyond the weekend. Orange (Sun 11pm–9am) Juicy (Sat 11pm–8am) are near legendary.

Above: London's gay and lesbian scene is wide and inclusive.

Ghetto
58 Old Street, The City; tel: 020-7287 3726; www.ghetto-london. co.uk; daily, see website for times and events; tube: Old Street; map p.153 C4
Week-long fun at a noted gay venue, with a packed dance-floor downstairs and sister bar Trash Palace above. Wig Out (Sat 10.30pm–5am) is the raucous weekend blowout, playing Blondie, Britney and everything in-between.

Heaven
Villiers Street, Covent Garden; tel: 020-7930 2020; www.heaven-london.com; usually Mon, Thur–Sat, see website for times; tube: Charing Cross, Embankment; map p.149 C2
Famous beyond these shores and still a good night out, even if it is a bit worn around the edges. There is generally plenty of flesh on show and a good range of music, and since 2008 it's been home to legendary cheese-fest G-A-Y club nights (www.g-a-y.co.uk; Thur–Sat).

Horse Meat Disco
Eagle London, 349 Kennington Lane, Vauxhall; www.myspace. com/horsemeatdiscolondon; Sun 8pm–3am; tube/rail: Vauxhall; map p.155 E1

Serving up disco, techno and electro tunes to a mixed crowd of revellers, this Vaux-hall institution is guaranteed to bring any weekend to a suitably debauched close.

Popstarz
The Den, 18 West Central Street, Soho; www.popstarz.org; Fri 10pm–4am; tube: Tottenham Court Road; map p.151 E2
Attracting indie guys, girls and others in equal measure, this is the original, inclusive London night out. Pop, R&B and indie tunes across three rooms.

Shops

Clonezone
64 Old Compton Street, Soho; tel: 020 7287 3530; www.clonezone direct.co.uk; Mon–Sat 11am–9pm, Sun noon–8pm; tube: Leicester Square; map p.148 B4
Underwear, books, maga-zines, DVDs and fetish wear, unintimidating Clonezone has plenty to intrigue and tempt. (Also at 266 Old Brompton Road, SW5 9HR; tel: 020-7373 0598.)

Gay's the Word
66 Marchmont Street, Blooms-bury; tel: 020-7278 7654; www.gaystheword.co.uk; Mon–Sat 10am–6.30pm, Sun 2–6pm; tube: Russell Square;

map p.151 E4
London's heroic gay and lesbian bookshop, currently battling closure due to rising rents and competition from the internet. However, nowhere else will you find such a broad selection of literature, readings and events. Support it while you can.

Prowler

5–7 Brewer Street, Soho; tel: 020-7734 4031; www.prowlerdirect.co.uk; Mon–Fri 11am–10pm, Sat 10am–10pm, Sun noon–8pm; tube: Leicester Square; map p.148 B4
Good for fashion, with the inevitable Calvin Kleins, but also an interesting selection of books, dildos and rubber and leather gear.

Sh! Women's Erotic Emporium

Below: frilly and minimal undies at Sh!

57 Hoxton Square, Shoreditch; tel: 020-7613 5458; www.sh-womenstore.com; daily noon–8pm; bus: 242, 243
Need a corset or well-engineered German vibrator? Look no further, Sh! has it all and more. Friendly and helpful staff will guide you round the goodies on offer.

Events

Pride London

June–July; www.pridelondon.org
London's very own Gay Pride event with a parade and rally in Trafalgar Square. Expect floats, costumes, music, entertainers and speakers.

Soho Pride

July–August; www.realsoho.co.uk
In case you didn't get enough of being out, proud and partying at London Pride, just a little later in the year is this street party in central Soho.

Information and Contacts

NEWSPAPERS, MAGAZINES AND LISTINGS

Boyz

www.boyz.co.uk
Weekly free mag with invaluable bar and club listings.

Diva

www.divamag.co.uk
Glossy lesbian monthly.

g3

www.g3mag.co.uk
Free lesbian magazine; download the pdf on-line.

Gay Britain Network

www.gaybritain.co.uk
A predominately male site with listings, chat room and on-line shopping.

Gay Times

www.gaytimes.co.uk
Does for gay men what Diva does for lesbians.

Gingerbeer

www.gingerbeer.co.uk
An online lesbian guide to London.

Gaydar

www.gaydar.co.uk and www.gaydargirls.co.uk
Meet your dream guy or girl at these dating sites.

The Pink Paper

www.pinkpaper.com
Weekly free newspaper with news, views and listings.

HELPLINES AND CAMPAIGNING

London Lesbian and Gay Switchboard

Tel: 020 7837 7324; www.llgs.org.uk
Helpline with advice and support on everything from coming out to sexual health.

Outrage

www.petertatchell.net
High profile human rights campaigning by the indefatigable Peter Tatchell.

Stonewall

www.stonewall.org.uk
An LGB rights organisation that grew out of the 1980s anti-Clause 28 campaign.

Terrence Higgins Trust

Tel: 0845 1221 200; www.tht.org.uk
Sexual health awareness, particularly of HIV, support and advice.

Below: a quick browse at Clonezone.

History

AD 43
Londinium settled during second Roman invasion; a bridge is built over the Thames.

61
Boudicca, Queen of the Iceni tribe in East Anglia, sacks the city before being defeated.

c. 200
5-km city wall built, encompassing fort, forum, amphitheatre and temple.

410
Troops are withdrawn to defend Rome.

449–527
Peoples from northern Germany arrive in Britain, dividing it into separate kingdoms.

604
The first St Paul's Cathedral founded by King Ethelbert.

c. 750
Monastery of St Peter is founded on Thorney Island, to become Westminster Abbey.

8th century
Shipping and manufacturing flourish on the riverbank near today's Strand.

884
London becomes capital under Alfred the Great.

1042
Edward the Confessor moves his court from the city to Westminster and rebuilds the Abbey.

1066
William I, Duke of Normandy, conquers Britain. He introduces French and the feudal system.

1191
The City elects its first mayor.

1240
First parliament sits in Westminster.

1290
Jews are expelled from the city; a ban not lifted until the 17th century.

1381
Much of London is laid waste by the Peasants' Revolt as 60,000 people protest against taxes.

1534
Henry VIII declares himself head of the Church of England and dissolves monasteries.

1588
William Shakespeare (1568–1616) begins his dramatic career in London. The English Renaissance thrives under Elizabeth I.

1605
Guy Fawkes tries to blow up Parliament.

1642–49
Civil war between Royalists (Cavaliers) and Republicans (Roundheads). Charles I is executed in 1649.

1660
Monarchy is restored under Charles II.

1660–9
Samuel Pepys (1633–1703) writes his diary.

1664–6
Great Plague kills one-fifth of London's 500,000-strong population.

1666
The Great Fire destroys 80 percent of London's buildings.

1714
The House of Hanover is ushered in by George I.

1732
George II makes 10 Downing Street available to Sir Robert Walpole, Britain's first Prime Minister.

1783
Last public execution at Tyburn.

1829
Prime Minister Robert Peel establishes a police force (still nicknamed 'bobbies').

1851
The Great Exhibition held in Hyde Park.

1863
First section of the Underground built between Paddington and Farringdon Street.

1888
Jack the Ripper strikes in Whitechapel.

1890
First electric railway to be built in deep-level tunnels, between the City and Stockwell.

1914–18
During World War I, Zeppelins and Gotha aeroplanes begin dropping incendiary and explosive bombs on the city.

1939–45
World War II. Children evacuated as London is heavily bombed. 29,000 civilians are killed and 1.75 million homes destroyed.

1960s
During the 'Swinging 60s' London becomes the world centre of fashion and pop music industries

1982
The Thames Barrier is completed.

1994
The first Eurostar trains run from Waterloo to Paris and Brussels.

2001
Greater London Authority is set up under mayor Ken Livingstone.

2003
Congestion charge imposed on cars entering central areas during the working week.

2005
London is chosen to stage the 2012 Olympic Games. On 7 July, bombs explode on three tube trains and a bus, killing more than 50 people.

2007
The new Eurostar terminal at St Pancras opens.

2008
Boris Johnson becomes mayor of London.

2009
London's financial sector is rocked by the global economic crisis. At April's G20 summit, the City sees mass protests against banking practises.

Hotels

London's hotels range from luxurious landmarks to family-run B&Bs, with a number of exciting design hotels across the price spectrum in-between. There's no denying that the cost of a decent hotel room in London is high, but there are surprisingly affordable options out there, particularly away from the West End, where budget does not mean compromising on style. Smaller guest houses can also be a good option for a more relaxed stay. If you do choose to splash out on one of the city's top-end hotels, however, the options are varyingly cutting-edge, gracious, traditional and highly glamourous.

Westminster and St James's

B&B Belgravia
64–66 Ebury Street; tel: 020-7259 8570; www.bb-belgravia.com; ££; tube: Victoria; map p.154 B2
Highly chic, modern B&B that's good value for the style and facilities it offers, including a communal area with free dvds and internet access, a choice of organic breakfasts and free bicycle hire.

The Goring Hotel
15 Beeston Place, Grosvenor Gardens; tel: 020-7396 9000; www.thegoringhotel.co.uk; £££–££££; tube: Victoria; map p.154 B3
Family-owned, elegantly traditional hotel close to Buckingham Palace, with excellent-quality service.

Prices per night for a double room with bathroom in high season, with tax but without breakfast unless otherwise stated. Prices are liable to change so always check before you book:
££££	over £200
£££	£150–200
££	£100–150
£	under £100

New England Hotel
20 St George's Drive; tel: 020-7834 8351; www.newenglandhotel.com; £–££; tube: Victoria; map p.154 C1
Set in an elegant stucco-fronted Georgian building, this friendly B&B has been in business for 25 years.

The Rubens
39–41 Buckingham Palace Road; tel: 020-7834 6600; www.rubenshotel.com; ££££; tube: Victoria; map p.154 C3
A traditional hotel with very modern amenities. The closest hotel to Buckingham Palace; some rooms have particularly good views overlooking the Royal Mews.

Sanctuary House Hotel
33 Tothill Street; tel: 020-7799 4044; www.fullershotels.co.uk; £££; tube: St James's Park; map p.155 D3
Handy for St James's Park and even handier for the Fullers pub situated beneath this small hotel.

Windermere Hotel
142–144 Warwick Way; tel: 020-7834 5163; www.windermere-hotel.co.uk; £–££; tube: Victoria; map p.154 B1
Characterful hotel on the site

Almost all hotels offer special deals that are cheaper than the published 'rack rate', particularly at weekends and outside peak season, so it is always worth checking. Hotel bills usually include service and no extra tip is needed, but if you wish to repay good service, 10 percent split between the deserving staff is the custom.

of London's first ever B&B, with a clutch of awards and a good restaurant attached.

Soho and Covent Garden

Covent Garden Hotel
10 Monmouth Street; tel: 020-7806 1000; www.firmdale.com; ££££; tube: Covent Garden; map p.148 C4
Understatedly glamourous boutique hotel, popular with visiting film stars, with a contemporary English aesthetic in the stylish bedrooms and a luxurious film screening room in the basement.

Hazlitt's
6 Frith Street; tel: 020-7434 1771; www.hazlittshotel.com; £££; tube: Tottenham Court Road; map p.148 B4

8860; www.savoygroup.com; ££££; tube: Bond Street; map p.150 B1

For many the embodiment of English hotel gracious-ness, with elegant Victorian and Art Deco design in the rooms and famed restaurants.

Cumberland Hotel
Great Cumberland Place; tel: 0871-508 8768; www.guoman.com; ££–£££; tube: Marble Arch; map p.150 A2

Highly modern decor in the public rooms and minimal-ism in the hi-tech designer rooms, where individual works of art adorn the walls.

The Dorchester
Park Lane; tel: 020-7629 8888; www.thedorchesterhotel.com; ££££; tube: Hyde Park Corner; map p.154 B4

The ultimate in luxury. Rooms have traditional but stylish decor and some have views over Hyde Park. The spa, afternoon tea and hip restau-rants are also a big draw.

Duke's Hotel
35 St James's Place; tel: 020-7491 4840; www.dukeshotel.com; £££–££££; tube: Green Park; map p.148 A2

Traditional hotel with gas-lamps lighting the courtyard, and an intimate atmosphere.

In the heart of Soho, this converted 1718 house boasts several impressive literary connections. Rooms are period style and modern lux-uries subtly tucked away.

One Aldwych
1 Aldwych; tel: 020-7300 1000; www.onealdwych.com; ££££; tube: Temple, Covent Garden; map p.149 D4

Achingly stylish, in an excel-lent location, with a cosmo-politan, refined atmosphere. A showcase of modernity, the walls are lined with contem-porary art and the gorgeous pool plays underwater music.

The Savoy
Strand; tel: 020-7836 4343; www.fairmont.com/savoy; ££££; tube: Charing Cross; map p.149 D3

Landmark hotel with a long-established reputation for comfort and personal service (if a little formal by today's standards). There's a rooftop gym and pool and smart, renowned eating options. Following a thorough refur-bishment, it is due to open it's doors again in early 2010.

Soho Hotel
4 Richmond Mews; tel: 020-

7559 3000; www.firmdale.com; ££££; tube: Tottenham Court Road; map p.148 B4

With bold, modern design touches giving an edge to Kit Kemp's signature style, the Soho Hotel feels luxuriously urban, with dramatic drawing rooms and a buzzing bar.

St Martin's Lane
45 St Martin's Lane; tel: 020-7300 5500; www.stmar tinslane.com; ££££; tube: Leicester Square; map p.148 C3

This Starck/Schrager collab-oration is one of the most stylish and stylised hotels in town. The rooms have high windows and mood-lighting choices. Particularly well placed for West End theatres.

Oxford Street, Mayfair and Marylebone

Brown's Hotel
30 Albemarle Street; tel: 020-7493 6020; www.brownshotel.com; ££££; tube: Green Park; map p.148 A3

A distinguished and classic British hotel, now owned by Rocco Forte and with a con-temporary, elegant look.

Claridge's
Brook Street; tel: 020-7629

Below: glamour at The Ritz.

Left: the calm and minimalist
Halkin Hotel.

Sherlock Holmes Hotel

108 Baker Street; tel: 020-7486
6161; www.parkplazasherlock
holmes.com; ££; tube: Baker
Street; map p.150 A3
Ignore the connotations of
the name; this is a boutique
hotel with a gym, steam room
and sauna. Rooms are decorated in warm, modern
colours, with chic bathrooms.

Kensington and Chelsea

Base2Stay
25 Courtfield Gardens; tel: 0845-
262 8000; www.base2stay.com;
£–££; tube: Earl's Court
Taking the principles and
style of boutique hotels to the
budget market, this hotel
innovator offers a wide variety of 'studios', all with their
own fridges, microwaves and
media facilities, to provide
the freedom of a flat with the
ease and style of a hotel.

Beaufort Hotel
33 Beaufort Gardens; tel: 020-
7584 5252; www.the
beaufort.co.uk; £££; tube:
Knightsbridge; map p.156 C3
Soft, neutral colours prevail
at this small, luxury design
hotel. Good for personal
attention and the cream teas
that are included in the rate.

Berkeley Hotel
Wilton Place; tel: 020-7235
6000; www.theberkeley.co.uk;
££££; tube: Knightsbridge, Hyde
Park Corner; map p.154 A3

Durrants Hotel

George Street; tel: 020-7935
8131; www.durrantshotel.co.uk;
£££; tube: Marble Arch; map
p.150 A2
Period-piece hotel in Georgian terrace, 200 years old
and oozing graciousness.
Rooms are comfortable, with
largely antique furnishings.

Edward Lear Hotel

30 Seymour Street; tel: 020-7402
5401; www.edlear.co.uk; ££;
tube: Marble Arch; map p.150 A2
Friendly hotel in the the Victorian artist and versifier's former home, near Oxford Street.

Metropolitan

19 Old Park Lane; tel: 020-7447
1000; www.metropolitan.lon
don.como.bz; ££££; tube: Green
Park; map p.154 B4
Synonymous with late-1990s
celebrity hedonism, this sleek
hotel still looks fresh, with minimalist rooms shown off by big
windows and natural light.

Montcalm Hotel

34–40 Great Cumberland Place;
tel: 020-7402 4288; www.mont
calm.co.uk; ££££; tube: Marble
Arch; map p.150 A2
Quiet, comfortable and plush,
the Montcalm is in an elegant
Georgian crescent. A special
feature is the low-allergen
bedroom. Note that the hotel
does not offer single rooms.

No. 5 Maddox Street

5 Maddox Street; tel: 020-7647
0200; www.no5maddoxst.com;
££££; tube: Bond Street; map
p.150 C1

A range of suites-cum-flats
with minimalist, Eastern-
inspired decor but full facilities including an in-room
kitchen (stocked with 'good'
healthy food and 'bad' treats).

Pavilion

34–6 Sussex Gardens; tel: 020-
7262 0905;
www.pavilionhoteluk.com; £;
tube: Edgware Road
A eccentric, fun spot where
each of the rooms has a different theme, from
'Casablanca Nights', a Moorish fantasy, to the oriental-
inspired 'Enter the Dragon'.
Funky and full of character.

Piccadilly Backpackers

12 Sherwood Street; tel: 020-
7434 9009; www.piccadilly
hotel.net; £; tube: Piccadilly
Circus; map p.148 B3
For those on a very tight
budget, especially those who
want to enjoy the capital's
nightlife (or don't mind if those
around them do), this Soho
hostel is ideal. Dorm beds
start at £12, and 'pod' style
beds are available, as are
inexpensive private rooms.

The Ritz

150 Piccadilly; tel: 020-7493
8181; www.theritzlondon.com;
££££; tube: Green Park; map
p.148 A2
One of the most famous hotel
names in the world and very
swanky, with deeply ornate
decor. Men must wear jackets
and ties in the public rooms.
The teas are legendary.

If you are visiting London in
May–September, it is wise to
book ahead, but if you arrive
without a reservation, the offical
tourist board, **Visit London**, can
help. Call their accommodation
booking service on 0845-644
3010, go to **www.visitlondon
offers.com** or make your first
stop the Visitor Centre *(see
Essentials p.51)*.

Many rate the Berkeley as the best in London. Elegantly low-key, with a country-house atmosphere, a fine spa and rooftop pool, and several renowned restaurants.

Blakes Hotel
33 Roland Gardens; tel: 020-7370 6701; www.blakes hotel.com; ££££; tube: South Kensington; map p.156 A1
Anouska Hempel's original design hotel, the discreet exterior belies the splendid rooms, designed in romantic, grand and exotic styles.

Cadogan Hotel
75 Sloane Street; tel: 020-7235 7141; www.cadogan.com; £££–££££; tube: Sloane Square; map p.154 A2
An Edwardian-decorated hotel with a whiff of scandal permeating its traditional formality. Edward VII's mistress Lillie Langtry lived here and Oscar Wilde was arrested here.

Curzon House Hotel
58 Courtfield Gardens; tel: 020-7581 2116; www.curzonhouse hotel.co.uk; £; tube: Earl's Court
A renowned independent hostel in buzzy Earl's Court. The accommodation (mixture of dorms and private rooms) is basic but functional, and there's a friendly atmosphere.

The Gore
189 Queen's Gate; tel: 020-7584 6601; www.gorehotel.com; £££–££££; tube: South Kensington; map p.156 A3
Idiosyncratic hotel close to the Royal Albert Hall. Every inch of the walls is covered in paintings and prints, and the individually-themed rooms' decor is antique with eccentric touches.

Halkin Hotel
5–6 Halkin Street; tel: 020-7333 1000; www.halkin.como.bz; ££££; tube: Hyde Park Corner; map p. 154 B3

This luxuriously modern hotel is calm and cosseting, done out in shades of cream and beige, with an Italian aesthetic and huge marble bathrooms. London's only Michelin-starred Thai restaurant is attached.

My Place Hotel
1–3 Trebovir Road; tel: 020-7373 0833; www.myplacehotel.co.uk; ££–£££; tube: Earl's Court
Modern amenities combined with Victorian ambience at this recently refurbished spot. The hotel has a nightclub, to which guests have free entrance.

The Rockwell
181 Cromwell Road; tel: 020-7244 2000; www.therockwell.com; £££; tube: Earl's Court
Styled in contemporary English design, the rooms here feel cheerful and modern, with airy colour combinations.

Vicarage Hotel
10 Vicarage Gate; tel: 020-7229 4030; www.londonvicarageho tel.com; £–££; tube: Notting Hill Gate; map p.157 E2
Very friendly place, with clean, simple rooms and a renowned English breakfast.

Prices per night for a double room with bathroom in high season, with tax but without breakfast unless otherwise stated. Prices are liable to change so always check before you book:
££££ over £200
£££ £150–200
££ £100–150
£ under £100

Bloomsbury and Holborn

Academy Hotel
17–21 Gower Street; tel: 020-7631 4115; www.theetoncollec tion.com; ££; tube: Goodge Street; map p.151 D3
A welcoming boutique hotel, located in five interlinked townhouses. Georgian-style rooms, some with terraces.

Charlotte Street Hotel
15–17 Charlotte Street; tel: 020-7806 2000; www.firmdale.com; £££; tube: Goodge Street; map p.151 D3
Art by members of the Bloomsbury set nods at the area's history, and this hotel successfully walks the line between substantial class and contemporary style, with soft colours and bold

Right: Contemporary styling at the Soho Hotel.

73

Left: A room at the chic Charlotte Street Hotel.

tion.com; £££–££££; tube: Bank; map p.153 D2

Situated in a former bank building, Threadneedles blends modern comforts with Victorian splendour. There's even plasma TV in the bathrooms. Good weekend deals.

Zetter Restaurant & Rooms

86–88 Clerkenwell Road; tel: 020-7324 4444; www.thezetter.com; £–£££; tube: Farringdon; map p.152 B4

In a converted warehouse, a trendy design hotel, where champagne is dispensed from vending machines, has sprung up. Second-hand books and hot-water bottles are thoughtful extras in the chic but comfortable rooms.

touches. There are mini-TVs in the marble bathrooms.

Crescent Hotel

49–50 Cartwright Gardens; tel: 020-7387 1515; www.crescenthoteloflondon.com; £; tube: Russell Square, Euston; map p.151 D4

Set in a Georgian building in a quiet Bloomsbury crescent, this pleasant family-run hotel has access to private gardens and tennis courts.

Hotel Russell

1–8 Russell Square; tel: 020-7837 6470; www.londonrussellhotel.co.uk; £££; tube: Russell Square; map p.151 E3

In the heart of Bloomsbury, the red-brick Russell has recently undergone a £20-million refurbishment. Opulent public spaces, individually themed and stylishly decorated bedrooms in calm, understated colours.

Sanderson Hotel

50 Berners Street; tel: 020-7300 9500; www.sanderson london.com; £££–££££; tube: Oxford Circus; map p.151 D2

A Starck/Schrager creation and the apex of their modernism-meets-theatre

stylishness. The Long Bar and Spoon restaurant are destinations in themselves and the spa is fittingly opulent.

The City

Malmaison

18–21 Charterhouse Square; tel: 020-7012 3700; www.malmaison.com; ££–£££; tube: Barbican; map p.152 C3

It is part of a chain, but the atmosphere and style for the price makes this a happy choice. Set in an attractive old building, the hotel's rooms are comfortable and the brasserie is well-regarded.

The Rookery

12 Peter's Lane, Cowcross Street; tel: 020-7336 0931; www.rookeryhotel.com; £££–££££; tube: Farringdon; map p.152 B3

The atmospheric Rookery features wood panelling, stone flagged floors, and open fires. The spacious bedrooms combine the historical with the contemporary, with 18th-century beds, silk drapery and flat screen TVs.

Threadneedles

5 Threadneedle Street; tel: 020-7657 8080; www.theetoncollec

be thoughtful extras in the chic but comfortable rooms.

South Bank and Bankside

Mad Hatter

3–7 Stamford Street; tel: 020-7401 9222; www.fullers hotels.co.uk; ££; tube: London Bridge, Southwark; map p.152 B1

Large and colourful rooms, decorated in contemporary style, above a Fullers pub and just a short stroll from the Tate Modern.

Southwark Rose

47 Southwark Bridge Road; tel: 020-7015 1480; www.sterling hotels.com; ££; tube: London Bridge; map p.153 C1

Friendly, sleek and simply designed along clean, minimalist lines. The guests' bar is smart and the location handy for its proximity to Bankside.

North London

Hampstead Britannia Hotel

32 Primrose Hill Road, Hampstead; tel: 020-7586 2233; www.britanniahotels.com; £; tube: Chalk Farm, Belsize Park

Near affluent and fashionable Primrose Hill, this is a relaxed, good-value hotel.

Hampstead Village Guesthouse
2 Kemplay Road; tel: 020-7435 8679; www.hampsteadguest house.com; £; tube: Hampstead
This quirky guest house in pretty Hampstead is near the heath, and has a lot of personality. Rooms are full of character and include fridges.

East London
Hoxton Hotel
81 Great Eastern Street; tel: 020-7550 1000; www.hoxtonhotels.com; £–£££; tube: Old Street; map p.153 E4
This hotel boasts hip design to go with the trendy location, as well as luxurious bedding and bathrooms with power showers and mirrors that don't steam up, but the thoughtful touches like the free light breakfast and fresh milk in the minibar raise this from simply good value to a real find. And if you get in early enough, you may even snag one of their famed promotional £1 per night rooms.

West London
Abbey Court
20 Pembridge Gardens; tel: 020-7221 7518; www.abb eycourt.com; £–££; tube: Notting Hill Gate; map p.157 D3
This is a beautifully restored Notting Hill town house, with

Below: Cannizaro House.

Prices per night for a double room with bathroom in high season, with tax but without breakfast unless otherwise stated. Prices are liable to change so always check before you book:	
££££	over £200
£££	£150–200
££	£100–150
£	under £100

the atmosphere of a private home. The highlight has to be the Italian marble bathrooms equipped with jacuzzi baths.

The Bingham
61–63 Petersham Road; tel: 020-8940 0902; www.thebing ham.co.uk; £££–££££; tube/rail: Richmond, then bus: 65
Luxurious, romantic hotel by the river in Richmond. Rooms are stylish but cosy with sumptuous soft furnishings. Some rooms have whirlpool baths and four-poster beds. A full breakfast is included.

Cannizaro House
4 West Side, Wimbledon Common; tel: 020-8879 1464; www.cannizarohouse.com; £££; tube/rail: Wimbledon, then taxi
Set in a gracious mansion in parkland, on the edges of the common, the hotel's picturesque setting is ideal for experiencing London's relaxing side. Most of the elegant rooms have a lovely view.

Guesthouse West
163–165 Westbourne Grove; tel: 020-7792 9800; www.guest housewest.com; ££; tube: Notting Hill Gate; map p.157 E4
A boutique B&B in the heart of trendy Notting Hill, which takes its style cues from the area: hip and a bit retro.

K West Hotel & Spa
Richmond Way; tel: 0870-027 4343; www.k-west.co.uk; £–££; tube: Shepherd's Bush
Within walking distance of Notting Hill is this excellent-value, chic boutique hotel. The design is bold but comfortable and there are great spa and

nightlife facilities on-site.

Miller's Hotel
111A Westbourne Grove; tel: 020-7243 1024; www.millersuk.com; ££–£££; tube: Bayswater; map p.157 E4
Idiosyncratic and atmospheric spot, crammed with antique furniture and curios. There's a free bar in the evenings and 24-hour computer access.

Richmond Hill Hotel
146–50 Richmond Hill; tel: 0844-855 9141; www.foliohotels.com; £–££; tube/rail: Richmond
A traditional English hotel with a friendly atmosphere, and amazing views over parkland and the river. Very close to Richmond Park and handy for Kew Gardens.

For value, it's hard to beat Britain's biggest budget hotel chain. There are several **Travel Inns** in central London, including County Hall (Westminster Bridge), Euston, Kensington and Tower Bridge. It is no frills, but clean and modern. Prices are generally around £80 for a double room and it pays to book early (tel: 0870-242 8000; www.premiertravelinn.com). The expanding **Travelodge** chain does a similar job at similar prices, but booking early can result in exceptionally good deals (tel: 0870-085 0950; www.travelodge.co.uk). **Best Western** has several individual hotels under its banner (tel: 0845-773 7373; www.best western.co.uk). Other reputable chains include **Holiday Inn** (tel: 0870-400 9670; www.holiday inn.co.uk) and **Thistle** (tel: 0870-414 1516; www.thistle hotels.com), which often have hotels in prime locations. At the top end of the chain gang are the **Hiltons** (tel: 0870-590 9090; www.hilton.co.uk) and the **Marriotts** (tel: 0800-221 222; www.marriott.co.uk).

75

Literature

London has a literary tradition that permeates its streets. All over the city are blue plaques memorialising famous writers and there's barely a place that doesn't conjure up thoughts of all the Londons that have been written about; the back streets of Holborn recall Charles Dickens's novels while the genteel terraces of Bloomsbury evoke the spirit of Virginia Woolf. Pay tribute to great writers with a visit to Poet's Corner in Westminster Abbey, take inspiration from Hampstead Heath like John Keats and C.S. Lewis or just have a drink at one of Fitzrovia or Soho's many pubs that are steeped in literary history.

London In Writing

London has been a backdrop to fiction since **Geoffrey Chaucer** (1343–1400) set his pilgrims on the road from the Tabard Inn in Southwark *(The Canterbury Tales)*. **William Shakespeare** (1564–1616) wrote plays for the popular theatres on the disreputable South Bank, as did contemporaries **Christopher Marlowe** and **Ben Jonson**.

Life in Restoration London, the plague and the Great Fire are written about in **Samuel Pepys'** (1633–1703) *Diary*, a fascinating record of life at this time and further described by **Daniel Defoe** (1660–1731), one of the founders of the English novel, in his *A Journal of the Plague Year*. In the 18th century, **Dr Samuel Johnson** (1709–84) wrote the first Dictionary and hosted the illustrious Literary Club.

Romantic poet **William Wordsworth's** sonnet, *Upon Westminster Bridge* (1802), is a very popular ode to the city. **Charles Dickens** (1812–70), novels strongly evoked Victorian London. Chronicling the lives of the poor, ambitious and dispossessed, his stories mainly take place in real locations including Southwark, Holborn and the City. Along with Dickens, it is **Arthur Conan Doyle's** *Sherlock Holmes* stories that have had the most influence on the popular view of Victorian London.

In the first half of the 20th century, London was home to many modernist writers, such as **T.S. Eliot** and **Virginia Woolf**, who was a member of the intellectual and artistic Bloomsbury Group, which also included **Lytton Strachey** and **E.M. Forster**. They had fragmented by the time war-torn London was depicted by

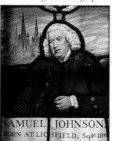
Below: the great lexicographer.

Graham Greene in *The Ministry of Fear* (1943) and *The End of the Affair* (1951).

Literature today is increasingly representative of the city's diversity, with prominent writers including **Benjamin Zephaniah**, **Hanif Kureishi** and **Zadie Smith**. Meanwhile, London's past continues to provide rich resources for fiction (**Sarah Waters's** Victorian and wartime set novels) and non-fiction (**Peter Ackroyd's** *London: The Biography*, which treats the city as a character in its own right).

London Reading List

Left: the galleried interior of Daunt Books in Marylebone.

Quaritch
8 Lower John Street, Soho; tel: 020-7734 2983; www.quaritch.com; Mon–Fri 9am–6pm; tube: Piccadilly Circus; map p.148 A3
The best known purveyor of second-hand and rare books.

Stanford's
12–14 Long Acre, Covent Garden; tel: 020-7836 1321; www.stanfords.co.uk; Mon, Wed, Fri 9am–7.30pm, Tue 9.30am–7.30pm, Thur 9am–8pm, Sat 10am–8pm, Sun noon–6pm; tube: Covent Garden; map p.149 C4
The best stocked map and travel bookshop in London, with a café and Craghoppers outdoor gear shop on site.

Waterstone's
203–206 Piccadilly, Mayfair; tel: 020-7851 2400; www.waterstones.com; Mon–Sat 9am–10pm, Sun 11.30am–6pm; tube: Piccadilly Circus; map p.148 A3
The flagship store is enormous, with sofas, in-store events and fantastic views.

WHSmith
The Plaza, Oxford Street, Marylebone; tel: 020 7436 6282; www.whsmith.co.uk; Mon–Sat 10am–7pm (Thur until 8pm), Sun noon–6pm; tube: Oxford Circus; map p.151 D2
A range of popular books and travel guides is available in their high street stores.

Below: a blue plaque marks Dickens' residence.

Two very different writers were pupils at the prestigious Dulwich College in south-east London: P.G. Wodehouse (1881–1975), author of very English comdies, and Raymond Chandler (1888–1959), American author of hard-boiled detective novels.

London: The Biography
Peter Ackroyd (2001)
White Teeth
Zadie Smith (2001)
The Night Watch
Sarah Waters (2006)

London Bookshops

Charing Cross Road is traditionally the home of bookselling. **Cecil Court** is its old-fashioned heart, selling antiquarian and rare books of all kinds. The **Riverside Walk Market** sets up on most days under Waterloo Bridge on the Southbank, selling second-hand paperbacks.

Borders
122 Charing Cross Road, Covent Garden; tel: 020-7379 8877; www.borders.co.uk; Mon–Sat 9.30am–10pm, Sun 11.30am–6pm; tube: Tottenham Court Road; map p.151 D2

Large chain with a wide selection of magazines, CDs and DVDs as well as an extensive range of books.

Daunt Books
83 Marylebone High Street, Marylebone; tel: 020-7224 2295; www.dauntbooks.co.uk; Mon–Sat 9am–7.30pm, Sun 11am–6pm; tube: Baker Street; map p.150 B3
This graceful Edwardian, galleried shop has a great mix of travel-oriented books.

Foyles
113–119 Charing Cross Road, Covent Garden; tel: 020-7437 5660; www.foyles.co.uk; Mon–Sat 9.30am–9pm, Sun noon–6pm; tube: Tottenham Court Road; map p.151 D2
This independent institution is still among the best, although its traditional eccentricities have given way to efficiency.

Hatchard's
187 Piccadilly, Mayfair; tel: 020-7439 9921; www.hatchards.co.uk; Mon–Sat 9.30am–7pm, Sun noon–6pm; tube: Piccadilly Circus; map p.148 A3
London's oldest bookshop features a huge variety of biographies and fiction.

Monuments

From the Monument itself, built to commemorate the city's rise from the ashes of the Great Fire of 1666, to the London Eye, built in celebration of the Millennium, London's iconic monuments reflect the preoccupations of the city thoughout its long and diverse history. Constructions range from the serious to the sentimental, those that can be climbed to those requiring a decorous distance, and statues of significant people to symbols representative of an age. That they also serve a practical purpose as meeting points has not dimmed the impressiveness of many of these edifices.

In Memorium

7 July Memorial
Hyde Park; tube: Hyde Park Corner; map p.154 B4
This well-judged memorial to the victims of the London bombings on July 7th 2005 was unveiled four years to the day of the attacks. Visitors can walk around and through the 52 stainless steel pillars that commemorate each person lost and are subtly grouped into clusters representative of each bomb location. A plaque at the far end of the memorial lists the victims' names.

Albert Memorial
Kensington Gardens; tours 1st Sun of month 2pm, 3pm; admission charge for tours; tube: South Kensington; map p.156 B3
Queen Victoria's most expressive tribute to her husband stands in Kensington Gardens, opposite the Albert Hall. Designed by Sir George Gilbert Scott, it depicts the prince as a glistening god or philosopher, clutching in his right hand the catalogue of the Great Exhibition of 1851, which he masterminded.

Above: Nelson on his column.

Cenotaph
Whitehall, Westminster; tube: Charing Cross; map p.149 C1
Edwin Lutyens designed this simple stone memorial to servicemen and women who have died in the two World Wars and subsequent conflicts. Originally a temporary wood and plaster structure built for the first anniversary of the Armistice in 1919, enthusiasm for the memorial led to the permanent construction, unveiled in 1920. Every year on 11 November, a service of remembrance is held here.

Eros
Piccadilly Circus, Mayfair; tube: Piccadilly Circus; map p.148 B3
Erected in 1892–3 as a tribute to Lord Shaftesbury, a prominent Victorian philanthropist, this fountain is topped by an aluminium winged statue, popularly referred to as Eros, the God of sensual love. It is in fact the Angel of Christian Charity. The fountain is one of the most popular central meeting points in London.

Monument
Monument Street, The City; daily 9.30am–5pm; admission charge; tube: Monument; map p.153 D2
Recently reopened following an extensive refurbishment, Sir Christopher Wren's commemoration of the Great Fire of London in 1666 is looking more impressive than ever. A Roman Doric column, it stands 200ft (61m) high, the same as the distance between the monument's base and the baker's house in Pudding Lane where the fire began. You can climb all 311 steps to the outdoor gallery at the top, giving you a chance to appreciate the vision Wren imposed on the City through his church

Left: the Albert Memorial in Hyde Park.

The 32 enclosed capsules take 30 minutes to make a full rotation. On a clear day, you can see for 25 miles (40km). Plan ahead if you hope to ride at busy periods.

Marble Arch
Oxford Street, Marylebone; tube: Marble Arch; map p.150 A1
In 1850, the Arch, designed by John Nash and based on the Arch of Constantine in Rome, was placed at Tyburn (where public executions used to be carried out) after being removed from the front of Buckingham Palace because it was too narrow for the state coaches to pass through. It now sits in the middle of a busy traffic island.

Wellington Arch
Hyde Park Corner, Mayfair; Apr–Oct Wed–Sun 10am–5pm, Nov–Mar Wed–Sun 10am–4pm; admission charge; tube: Hyde Park Corner; map p.154 B3
Originally designed as an outer entrance to Buckingham Palace by Decimus Burton in 1830, to celebrate Britain's Napoleonic Wars triumph, Wellington Arch was moved to its present site in 1882. It is topped with a 38-ton bronze sculpture depicting the angel of peace descending on the chariot of war.

Postman's Park, tucked between St Bartholomew's hospital and London Wall, is one of London's great hidden contemplative spots. There is a wall full of memorials to 'ordinary people' who committed acts of heroism.

spires; there are 56 of them.

Nelson's Column
Trafalgar Square; tube: Charing Cross; map p.148 C2
Trafalgar Square, laid out by John Nash on the orders of the then Prince Regent, was designed to commemorate Britain's naval might. Nelson's Column is a tribute to the great commander, who died in 1805 at the Battle of Trafalgar. Standing at 170ft (51.6m), it was built in 1840–3, although the lions, by Edwin Landseer, were not added until 1867.

Princess Diana Memorial Fountain
Hyde Park; daily 10am–dusk; tube: Knightsbridge; map p.156 B4
Opened in 2004 by the Queen, this shallow, circular fountain, designed by Kathryn Gustafson, ended up being

closed just 16 days later, when visitors walking on the granite base kept slipping. People are now encouraged to refresh their feet while sitting on the fountain edge instead.

In Celebration

Cleopatra's Needle
Embankment; tube: Embankment; map p.149 D3
The 18m monument, weighing 180 tons, stands beside Charing Cross Pier. It was carved in Aswan in around 1475 BC and presented to Britain in 1819. In 1878 it was towed in a specially constructed pontoon to London. Buried beneath it are newspapers from the day it was erected and other time capsule memorabilia.

London Eye
Westminster Bridge Road, South Bank; tel: 0870-500 0600; www.londoneye.com; daily May–Sept 10am–9pm (July–Aug until 9.30pm), Oct–Apr 10am–8pm; admission charge; tube/rail: Waterloo; map p.149 D1
The world's largest observation wheel was built to mark the turn of the millennium. At 440ft (135m), it is the fourth highest structure in London.

Below: the London Eye.

Museums and Galleries

L ondon boasts some of the greatest museums and galleries in the world and the majority of them are free to visit. In the landmark institutions such as the British Museum and the Victoria and Albert Museum, the permanent collections alone are huge and it is best to pick and choose the ones that interest you most from these and the often groundbreaking temporary shows. Meanwhile, London's position as one of the centres of the art world is demonstrated in the wealth of both established and cutting-edge art galleries on offer.

Westminster and St James's

Institute of Contemporary Arts (ICA)

The Mall; tel: 020-930 3647; www.ica.org.uk; daily noon–7pm (Thur until 9pm) during exhibitions; free; tube: Charing Cross; map p.148 B2

The two galleries in the Institute of Contemporary Arts feature temporary exhibitions that reflect the leaning of the institute to ground-breaking, political and cultural debate. Set in the somewhat incongruous Carlton House Terrace (one of John Nash's final designs), exhibitions tend towards the anti-establishment and continually challenge notions of what art is.

National Gallery

Trafalgar Square; tel: 020-7747 2885; www.nationalgallery.org.uk; daily 10am–6pm (Fri until 9pm); free; tube: Charing Cross; map p.148 C3

The National Gallery was founded in 1824, when a private collection of 38 paintings was acquired by the British Government for the sum of £60,000 and exhibited in the owner's house at 100 Pall Mall. Today, the gallery is housed in William Wilkins'

Right: the *Arnolfini Wedding* at the National Gallery.

long, low construction, with its classical facade in white Portland stone and crowned with a dome, opened in 1834. It has been remodelled in various ways over the years, notably with the three-way staircase leading to the main floor and the Sainsbury Wing.

The National Gallery displays Western European art and they are largely arranged chronologically, from the 13th century to the early 20th century, and by particular schools. Virtually all are represented here, as are most canonical artists.

The Sainsbury Wing displays paintings from 1250–1500. Among the highlights to be found here are a *Virgin and Child Enthroned with Two Angels* (1280–5), by Cimabue, and paintings by Giotto and Duccio. One of the Gallery's treasures is the *Wilton Diptych*, a beautiful, French or English portable

Left: Seurat's *Bathers at Asnières* at the National Gallery.

Left: the cavernous main hall of the Natural History Museum.

rooms in the North Wing contain paintings by the Spanish artists, Murillo, Zurbarán and Velázquez, notably the latter's sensuous nude, *The Toilet of Venus (The Rokeby Venus)* 1655–60.

Caravaggio's dramatic use of chiaroscuro, exploiting the contrasting effects of bright light and deep shadow, conveys the story of Christ's startling appearance at *The Supper at Emmaus* (1601).

In Rooms 33–46, a magnificent collection of portraits and landscapes by British artists (Gainsborough, Constable, Turner and Stubbs) is on display. Two of Turner's best-known masterpieces are hung here: *Rain, Steam and Speed* and his romantically heroic picture of the *Fighting Téméraire*. There are paintings by Hogarth; the vitality of his *Shrimp Girl* (1740s) gives as accurate a picture of

altarpiece, which is decorated with jewel-like delicacy. Also here is *The Marriage of Arnolfini*, an intriguingly realistic and ever-popular work by the early Netherlandish master, Jan van Eyck.

Paintings from 1500–1600 are found in the central hall and Rooms 2–14, and are examples of the German School. Here you can see Holbein's double portrait of *The Ambassadors*, with its sober *momento mori*, a hidden skull, in the midst of worldly success. Other

rooms are richly hung with work by El Greco, Tintoretto, Michelangelo, Bronzino, Veronese and Raphael. The large Wohl Room displays paintings by Titian, including his spirited *Bacchus and Ariadne* (1523). Also to be found here is Michelangelo's early *Manchester Madonna*, alongside work by his teacher, Domenico Ghirlandaio, and Leonardo da Vinci's celebrated *The Virgin of the Rocks* (1508).

Rooms 15–32 and 37 are home to 17th-century works, although the Turner Bequest gave the National Gallery *Dido Building Carthage* (1815) and *Sun Rising through Vapour* (exhib. 1807), on the understanding that were hung alongside two paintings by Claude, *Seaport with the Embarkation of the Queen of Sheba* (1648) and *Landscape with the Marriage of Isaac and Rebekah* (1648).

Vermeer's *A Young Woman Standing at a Virginal* is hung near Samuel van Hoogstraten's peep-box, showing realistic interiors of a Dutch house. The two largest

---

The **Cabinet War Rooms** (King Charles Street; tel: 020-7930 6961; www.iwm.org.uk; daily 9.30am–6pm; admission charge; tube: St James's Parl; map p.148 C1) are an underground bunker from which Winston Churchill directed Britain's World War Two effort, and are affiliated with the Imperial War Museum *(see p.94)*. There is claustrophobic authenticity to this wartime centre where Britian's political and military leaders worked. Displays of identity cards, ration books and newspapers evoke a further sense of wartime. Most fascinating is the converted broom cupboard housing a pioneering 'hotline' to the White House, enabling Churchill to have confidential talks with Franklin D. Roosevelt.

his times as does his satirical narrative *Marriage à la Mode*.

The most prominent pieces however, are the outstanding selection of French late 19th-century Impressionist paintings, comprising works by Seurat *(Bathers at Asnières)*, Manet, Degas, Cézanne, Monet (including the *Water Lillies* series), Renoir, Gauguin, and Dutch-born Van Gogh *(Sunflowers)*.

National Portrait Gallery
St Martin's Place; tel: 020-7306 0055; www.npg.org.uk; daily 10am–6pm (Thur–Fri until 9pm); free; tube: Charing Cross, Leicester Square; map p.148 C3
The collection is displayed broadly chronologically, from the medieval period through to work of the present day. The early part of the collection, on the top floor, contains many notable royal portraits. The large drawing of Henry VII and his son Henry VIII (1536–7) by Hans Holbein is probably the most memorable image of Henry VIII. One of the most important portraits of Queen Elizabeth I is the life-like, three-quarter length view of the Virgin Queen, sumptuous in brocade and pearls.

The Georgian and Victorian portraiture includes a superb terracotta bust of George I dressed as a Roman emperor. The official portraits of the Victorian and Edwardian periods are some of the last examples of stylish formality.

Some of the most successful 20th-century portraits are characterised by their informality, and vie with casual photographic poses. New portraits of famous figures in the arts, entertainment, sport and politics are constantly being added to the collection and a number of high-profile temporary exhibitions have been held here.

Tate Britain
Millbank; tel: 020-7887 8888; www.tate.org.uk/britain; daily 10am–5.50pm (1st Fri in month until 10pm); free; tube: Pimlico; Tate boat: from London Eye and Tate Modern; map p.155 D1
Tate Britain, the original Tate Gallery, is home to the national collection of British art. Its remit is to present the development of British art from the 16th century to the present day. From Tudor-era portraiture to the 'YBAs' (Young British Artists) of the last 15 years, the collection depicts definitive movements and figures in Britain's artistic history.

Hogarth, considered by many to be the father of Eng-

Right: the National Portrait Gallery's unassuming entrance.

Left: the National Portrait Gallery has an outstanding collection of Tudor portraiture.

lish painting, was dominant in the early 18th century and is well represented here, as are Joshua Reynolds and Thomas Gainsborough. Among the most popular 19th-century painters is John Constable, who is credited with the creation of a national landscape tradition. Some of his best-known paintings are in Tate Britain, including *Flatford Mill* (1817) and *The Opening of Waterloo Bridge* (1832).

The Pre-Raphaelites are also well-represented. The leading members were Millais, Holman Hunt, Rossetti and, later, Burne-Jones, who created sharply realistic paintings in pure, brilliant colours. Millais' *Ophelia* (1841–2), derived from Shakespeare's Hamlet, is a perennial favourite.

The Turner Galleries are home to a magnificent collection of oil paintings and works on paper by William Turner, who carried the handling of light and weather to

unmatched heights. Two paintings, *Snow Storm: Hannibal and his Army Crossing the Alps* and *Snow Storm: Steam-Boat off a Harbour's Mouth* show Turner's fascination with elemental forces.

In the 20th century, Stanley Spencer's personal and imaginative pictures, such as *The Resurrection, Cookham* (1927), are popular. Lucian Freud is celebrated, particularly his erotic nudes. Of the post-World War II painters, Francis Bacon is pre-eminent, with his three studies for *Figures at the Base of a Crucifixion* (1944). David Hockney belongs equally to this parade of prestigious British artists preferring figurative to abstract art. *Mr and Mrs Clark and Percy* (1970–1) is one of the most popular Tate paintings.

Among the British 20th-century sculptors represented are Jacob Epstein (*Doves*, 1914–15) and Barbara Hepworth (*Three Forms*, 1935); both important figures.

Queen's Gallery
Buckingham Palace,
Buckingham Palace Road;

The National Portrait Gallery has a collection of about 10,000 pictures. The person with the honour of being the subject of the most portraits is Victorian Prime Minister, William Gladstone, who is represented in no fewer than 65 of them.

tel: 020-7766 7301; www.royal collection.org.uk; daily 10am–5.30pm; admission charge; tube: Green Park; map p.154 C3
The collection is rich in royal portraits, notably by Holbein and Van Dyck. Among three early Rembrandts is a painting of the artist's mother, acquired by Charles I when the artist was hardly known abroad. Charles also commissioned the virtuoso self-portrait by Rubens. George III was an important royal collector, who commissioned around 50 landscape paintings and 100 drawings by Canaletto, including memorable views of 18th-century London.

The collection of drawings is an unrivalled selection of work by Da Vinci, Holbein, Raphael, Michelangelo and Poussin.

Below: an exhibition at Tate Britain.

Soho and Covent Garden

London Transport Museum

39 Wellington Street; tel: 020-7379 6344; www.ltmuseum.co.uk; Mon–Thur, Sat–Sun 10am–6pm, Fri 11am–6pm; admission charge; tube: Covent Garden; map p.149 D4

Reopened after a lengthy refit in the autumn of 2007, London's transport museum is better than ever. Tracing the social history of travelling within the capital, its exhibits range from early buses and tube trains, to trams and horse-drawn carriages, to posters and uniforms. The whole museum is so beautifully run and displayed in part of the old flower market that local visitors might wonder why the whole transport system couldn't receive such care and attention.

Oxford Street, Mayfair and Marylebone

Apsley House: Wellington Museum

Hyde Park Corner; tel: 020-7499 5676; Apr–Oct Wed–Sun 11am–5pm, Nov–Mar Wed–Sun 11am–4pm; admission charge; tube: Hyde Park Corner; map p.154 B4

Arthur Wellesley, the first Duke of Wellington, moved into this Robert Adam-designed house at the height of his popularity in 1817, after a dazzling military career that culminated in his victory over Napoleon Bonaparte in the Battle of Waterloo in 1815. There is a splendid collection of paintings; many from the Spanish Royal Collection. As well as works by Rubens, Bruegel, Van Dyck and an equestrian portrait of Wellesley by Francisco de Goya, the gallery features *The Con-*

> The Photographers' Gallery has one of the best photography bookshops in the country, and a friendly café selling inexpensive, wholesome food and drinks.

jurer by Caravaggio, and the evocative *The Waterseller of Seville* by Diego Velázquez.

A curious aspect of Apsley House is the recurring theme of the Duke of Wellington's arch enemy, Napoleon. Exhibits of the emperor are everywhere, and a 10ft (3m) neoclassical sculpture makes him look rather heroic.

Photographers' Gallery

16–18 Ramillies Street; tel: 0845-262 1618; www.photonet.org.uk; Tue–Wed, Sat 11am–6pm, Thur–Fri 11am–8pm, Sun noon–6pm; free; tube: Oxford Circus; map p.151 C2

The first independent gallery in Britain devoted exclusively to photography. The gallery leads the way in presenting innnovative developments in photography and new talent, and names of now-

established photographers encouraged here include Fay Godwin and Martin Parr.

Royal Academy of Arts

Burlington House, Piccadilly; tel: 020-7300 8000; www.royalacademy.org.uk; daily 10am–6pm (Fri until 10pm); charge; John Madejski Fine Rooms Tue–Fri 1–4.30pm, Sat–Sun 10am–6pm; free; tube: Piccadilly Circus, Green Park; map p.151 C1

The Academy's permanent collection is housed in the John Madejski Fine Rooms and includes masterpieces such as Michelangelo's *Taddei Tondo*, Constable's *The Leaping Horse* and Sargent's *Venetian Interior*. The gallery is best known, however, for high-profile temporary exhibitions, and for its Summer Exhibition, the world's largest open submission contemporary art exhibition.

Sherlock Holmes Museum

221b Baker Street; tel: 020-7935 8866; www.sherlock-holmes.co.uk; daily 9.30am–6pm; admission charge;

Right: long-lost glamour in the Transport Museum.

Right: the art treasures of the Wallace Collection are housed in splendid surroundings.

tube: Baker Street; map p.150 A3
The more you know about Holmes, the more you get out of the detailed exhibits, including several waxworks, which are all relevant to the stories. The house is set up as if it were the Victorian home of Arthur Conan Doyle's fictional super-sleuth. In the bedroom, atmospherically candle-lit, is a make-up case for Holmes's elaborate disguises and, in a corner, the famous violin.

Wallace Collection
Hertford House, Manchester Square; tel: 020-7563 9500; www.wallacecollection.org; daily 10am–5pm; free; tube: Bond Street, Baker Street; map p.150 B2
This remarkable display of art ranges from 17th- and 18th-century English and European paintings to Sèvres porcelain. In addition to pictures by Velázquez, Boucher and Fragonard, it contains Rembrandt's *Self-Portrait in a Black Cap*, Rubens' *Rainbow Landscape*, Franz Hals's *Laughing Cavalier*, Poussin's *Dance to the Music of Time*, and Gainsborough's *Lady Robinson as 'Perdita'*. The collection was bequeathed to the British nation by the widow of Richard Wallace, the illegitimate son of the fourth Marquess of Hertford, who originally amassed these works.

Kensington and Chelsea

Natural History Museum
Cromwell Road; tel: 020-7942 5000; www.nhm.ac.uk; daily 10am–5.50pm; free; tube: South Kensington; map p.156 B2
If any of London's museums encapsulates the Victorians' quest for knowledge and passion for sifting and cataloguing data, it's this one, with its colossal collection of 75 million plants, animals, fossils, rocks and minerals. The collection was originally a department of the British Museum, but by the mid-19th century it had outgrown the available space and in 1881 the present museum opened on Cromwell Road.

In the middle of the **Central Hall** is the cast of a **diplodocus** unearthed in Wyoming in 1899. At 26m, it is the longest complete skeleton of a dinosaur ever discovered. On the landing overlooking the hall is a statue of Richard Owen, the museum's first director and the first to recognise the existence of giant prehistoric land reptiles. He called them dinosaurs ('terrible lizards').

The **Dinosaurs** gallery is one of the busiest sections of the museum and is in the **Blue Zone**, which contains the many exhibitions concerned with animal life. Many visitors make a bee-line for the robotic dinosaurs at the far end. The full-scale animatronic T-Rex on long-term loan from Japan is responsive to human movement; the roaring, life-like model twists and turns, delighting most children.

Human Biology examines the workings behind every part of the human body, from hormones to genes. This section is packed with interactive exhibits: you can test your memory and senses or be tricked by optical illusions.

The spectacular suspension of a life-size blue whale model is the highlight of the **Mammals**, but there are many fascinating exhibits of huge

85

but now-extinct mammals. As well as displaying an astonishing array of taxidermy, these galleries contain sobering statistics on the rate at which species are becoming extinct.

The gallery of **Fish, Amphibians and Reptiles** highlights many fascinating species, including fish that live between the sea's twilight zone at 400m and total darkness at 1,000m. Next door is the contrastingly serene **Marine Invertebrates**, where cabinets of corals, shells and sea fans are enhanced by the sound of waves breaking on a shore.

The **Red Zone** is brought to life by exciting special effects and atmospheric sound and lighting. A central escalator transports visitors into a gigantic rotating globe.

Often overlooked in the Natural History Museum is the Jerwood Gallery, with a superb collection of watercolours, oils, prints and drawings, some of which are the original illustrations to books by 19th-century explorers such as Richard Burton and David Livingstone.

At the top, **Restless Surface** includes imaginative coverage of earthquakes and volcanoes: the tremors of an earthquake are simulated in a mock-up of a Japanese mini-market; a bank of TV sets next to a car covered in volcanic ash replays news reports of the 1991 eruption of Mount Pinitubo in the Philippines.

In **From the Beginning**, the gallery relates the story of the universe from the time of the big bang 15,000 million years ago to the end of the solar system, predicted 5,000 million years from now.

For sheer pleasure in the planet's beauty, the **Earth's Treasury** gallery is a treat, displaying rocks, gems and minerals glittering in semi-darkness.

For those intrigued by fossils, minerals and ecology, the **Green Zone** explores these aspects of life on Earth, along with the **Creepy Crawlies** exhibit, always popular with kids. The **Orange Zone** is home to the new **Darwin Centre**, which provides an interactive experience of natural sciences, and the **Wildlife Garden**, which opens in the summer.
Science Museum
Exhibition Road; tel: 0870-870 4868; www.science museum.org.uk; daily 10am–6pm; free; tube: South Kensington; map: p.156 B2
With more than 10,000 exhibits, plus additional attractions such as an IMAX theatre, this is a behemoth of a museum. Just about every area of science is covered and while this museum is rightly a magnet for children, the exhibits are varied and intriguing enough for anyone with an interest in scientific inventiveness and human ingenuity. The collection was developed after the success of the Great Exhibition at Crystal Palace in 1851.

Right: the V&A has an excellent fashion archive.

The ground floor is home to two of the most impressive areas of the museum: **Exploring Space** and **Making the Modern World**. The former's big attraction is a replica of the Apollo 11 lunar excursion module, but its scope encompasses videos of early rocket experiments in the 1920s. There is also a dissection of a V2 rocket, showing why it struck fear into Londoners during World War Two.

Making the Modern World brings together many of the museum's most important exhibits. 'Modern' is defined as post-1750 and stars include the world's oldest surviving steam locomotive, the coal-hauling Puffing Billy (c.1815), Stephenson's pioneering Rocket passenger locomotive (1829), a Ford Model T (1916), a Lockheed Electra airliner hanging in

splendour from the ceiling (1935) and the battered Apollo 10 command module (1969).

Dominating the third floor is the magnificent **Flight** gallery, with exhibits ranging from a seaplane to a Spitfire, from hot-air balloons to helicopters. The 1919 Vickers Vimy in which Alcock & Brown made the first non-stop transatlantic flight is here, as is Amy Johnson's Gipsy Moth Jason. There's a replica of the Wright Flyer in which Wilbur and Orville Wright pioneered powered flight at Kitty Hawk, North Carolina, in 1903. Other eye-catching exhibits include a Messerschmitt rocket-propelled fighter and the first British jet aircraft, the Gloster Whittle E28/39. Visitors can peer into the cockpit of a Douglas DC3 and participate in interactive exhibits illustrating the principles of flight. A flight simulator offers a rodeo-style ride (a fee is charged).

As well as the children oriented area, the basement contains **The Secret Life of the Home**, a collection of domestic appliances and gadgets that provoke nostalgia in adults and disbelief in children. A range of models charts the development of the electric toaster since 1923. Other items include a 1925 Sol hairdryer and a 1945 Goblin Teasmade.

Othe exhibits that are geared more towards adults include **Energy: Fuelling the Future**, **Health Matters**, **Glimpses of Medical History** and **Psychology: Mind Your Head**, while the games of **In Future** raise intriguing questions for everyone.
SEE ALSO CHILDREN P.40

Serpentine Gallery
Kensington Gardens; tel: 020-7402 6075; www.serpentine gallery.org; daily 10am–6pm; free; tube: Knightsbridge; map p.156 B4

This exhibition space for modern and contemporary art sits in a lovely location, near the Serpentine, dotted with sculptures. One of London's leading venues for contemporary work shows and retrospectives by established artists, it underwent extensive redevelopment the late 1990s and reopened as a cool white space, balancing the picturesque garden pavilion with a state-of-the-art exhibition space.

Victoria & Albert Museum
Cromwell Road; tel: 020-7942 2000; www.vam.ac.uk; daily 10am–5.45pm (Fri until 10pm); free; tube: South Kensington; floorplan p.89, map p.156 B2

With 5 million objects and almost 8 miles (13km) of galleries, the Victoria and Albert Museum, founded in 1852, is the world's largest collection of decorative and applied

The V&A's magnificent Ceramic Staircase (1869), symbolises the symbiotic relationship between art and science. The twin circular ceilings illustrate the theme, with Ceres, Mercury and Vulcan standing for agriculture, commerce and industry and Apollo and Minerva representing the arts.

arts. Its exhibits range from exquisite Persian miniatures to a whole room designed by Frank Lloyd Wright.

This immense work in the foyer of the Cromwell Road entrance is by the glass artist Dale Chihuly. The amazing accretion of blue and green glass was erected in 1999 as a spectacular talking-point for the Victorian foyer. In 2001 the sculpture doubled in size, to a height of 32ft (10m).

The **Dress** section is one of the museum's most high profile, thanks to its temporary exhibitions which are always well attended. The permanent collection looks at dress from 1600 to the present, placing trends within a historical frame of reference.

British and European neo-classical works from the late 18th and early 19th centuries are in the **Sculpture Courts**. Works by Canova (1757–1822), include *The Sleeping Nymph*, a reclining nude. Several glazed terracottas are on display, including Giovanni della Robbia's *The Last Supper*, based on Leonardo da Vinci's painting.

The vast **Raphael Cartoons** (1515–16), on loan from the Queen, are among the museum's most valuable items. These highly finished preparatory drawings were commissioned by Pope Leo X as templates for a series of Sistine Chapel tapestries.

These superb **Asian and Islamic** collections include **Indian Art** (1550–1900). Many artefacts here are from the Mughal period (1526–1707), when imperialist expansion led to immense wealth and an artistic flowering that culminated under Shah Jahan, the builder of the Taj Mahal. **Arts of the Islamic World** covers the range of decorative arts from Persia, Turkey, Iraq, Syria and Egypt. In line with Islamic prohibitions, most items do not include figurative representations, but a beautiful exception is a 10th-century ewer decorated with sensuous birds and beasts.

Highlights of the **Italian Collection** are Andrea Briosco's (1470–1532) *Shouting Horseman*; terracottas by the Florentine sculptor Andrea della Robbia (1435–1525) and the finest collection of work by Donatello (1386–1466) outside Italy.

The original **Refreshment Rooms**, now home to the V & A Café, served first, second and third-class menus before World War Two. Allusions to food and drink are worked into the decoration. The fabulously ornate **Gamble Room** (1868) is one of London's finest Victorian interiors, while the **Morris Room** (Green Dining Room), 1866–9, was designed by William Morris, Philip Webb and Edward Burne-Jones.

One of the museum's star exhibits is the stunning **Hereford Screen**, an intricate choir screen of cast iron and brass, studded with semi-precious stones and mosaics; it is 34ft (10.5m) high and 36ft (11m) wide. Designed by Sir George Gilbert Scott in 1862, it shows Christ in the centre with angels on either side welcoming his ascension.

Paintings on display range from John Constables to a superb collection of British miniatures. Also be sure to visit the **Frank Lloyd Wright Room**, the only piece of his work in Europe.

New exhibitons include the **Theatre and Performance Galleries**, which hold the national collection of live perfomance materials since the days of Shakespeare, and the **William and Judith Bollinger Jewellery Gallery**, focussing on European jewellery over the last 800 years.

Right: the Hereford Screen at the entrance of the V&A.

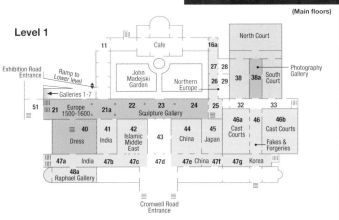

Victoria and Albert Museum

(Main floors)

Level 1

Exhibition Road Entrance — Ramp to Lower level

← Galleries 1-7

| 51 | 21 | Europe 1500-1600 | 21a | 22 | 23 Sculpture Gallery | 24 | 25 |

North Court

Cafe

11 — 16a

John Madejski Garden — Northern Europe

27 28 — 26 29 — 38 — 38a

South Court — Photography Gallery

32 — 33

| 40 Dress | 41 | 42 Islamic Middle East | 43 | 44 China | 45 |
| 46a Cast Courts | 46 | 46b Cast Courts — Fakes & Forgeries |

| 47a India | 47b | 47c | 47d | 47e China 47f | 47g Korea |

48a Raphael Gallery

Cromwell Road Entrance

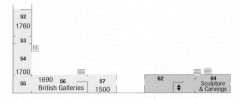

Level 2

52 1760
53
54
1700
55 1690 — 56 — 57
British Galleries — 1500

62 — 64 Sculpture & Carvings

Level 3

Seminar Room — Metalwork — Arms & Armour
Lecture Theatre

| 70a Silver 65 | 66 | 67 & 68 | 69 |

81 87 — 94 Tapestries — 95
82 88 — 96
89 88a — 105 — 97 — Textiles
— 20thC Design
103 — 98
99

John Madejski Garden — Church Plate

83 90
91
92 93 — Jewellery
84 85 — 101 100

| 74 20th Century | 76 | 77 National 78 Art Library | 85 |
109 — Leighton — 107
108

40a Musical Instruments

111 Stained Glass

113 | 114a | 114b | 114c Ironwork | 114d | 114e
116 Stained Glass | 117 — 112

up to Rooms 118-125 (British Galleries)

up to Rooms 127-131 (Architecture & Glass)

Asia — Materials and Techniques — Modern

Europe — Exhibitions — ↕ Lift

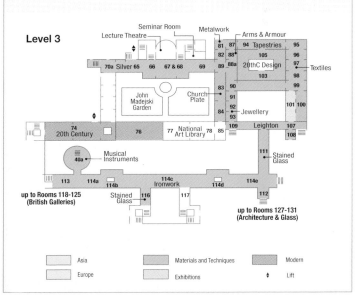

British Museum

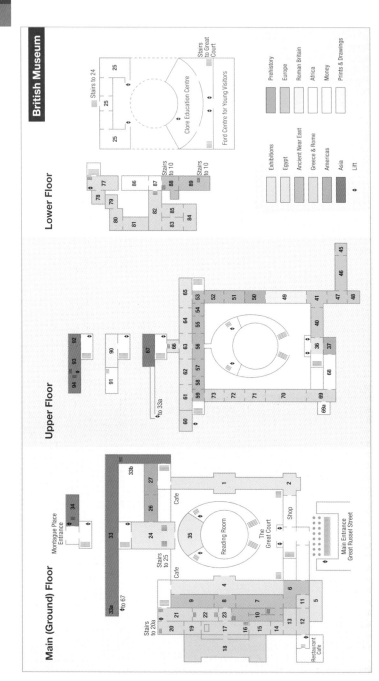

Lower Floor

Stairs to 24

25   25   25

Clore Education Centre

Ford Centre for Young Visitors

Stairs to Great Court

77   78   79   80   81   82   83   84   85   86   87   88   89

Stairs to 10

Legend:

Exhibitions

Egypt

Ancient Near East

Greece & Rome

Americas

Asia

Lift

Prehistory

Europe

Roman Britain

Africa

Money

Prints & Drawings

Upper Floor

92   93   94

90   91

67   66

to 33a

65   64   63   62   61   60

53   54   55   56   57   58   59

52   51   50   49   41   40   36   37   68

47   48   46   45

73   72   71   70   69   69a

Main (Ground) Floor

Montague Place Entrance

34

33   33a   33b

to 67

27   26   24

Cafe

Stairs to 25

Cafe

35

Reading Room

The Great Court

Shop

Main Entrance Great Russel Street

1   2

Stairs to 20a

20   21   19   17   16   15   14

18

9   8   7   4

22   23   10   13   12   11   6   5

Restaurant Cafe

Bloomsbury and Holborn

British Library

96 Euston Road; tel: 0843-208 1144; www.bl.uk; Mon, Wed–Fri 9.30am–6pm, Tue 9.30am–8pm, Sat 9.30am–5pm, Sun 11am–5pm; free; tube: King's Cross St Pancras

With more than 150 million items, in most known languages, including books, periodicals, sound recordings, newspapers, maps and stamps, this is one of the world's largest collections.

The John Ritblat Gallery houses the most valuable books and manuscripts and includes the 13th-century map of Great Britain drawn by the monk Matthew Paris. Another area houses sacred texts from around the world with a separate display of Bibles and Christian manuscripts. Among these are a 3rd-century Egyptian codex of the *Gospel of St John*, possibly the library's oldest manuscript. Alongside these are the illuminated manuscripts. Particularly fine works include the histories of the Mughal emperors Babur and Akbar, the *Baburnama* and *Akbarnama*, and 8th-century Japanese Buddhist religious texts. In the same case is a copy of the *Gutenberg Bible* (1454), the earliest European work printed using movable type.

A case dedicated to science contains Leonardo da Vinci's notebook and letters from Newton and Darwin. In the sections on literature and historical documents Shakespeare figures prominently, with a copy of the first folio of his plays (1623). There are also copies of the 1215 *Magna Carta*, Nelson's last letter, Scott's Antarctic journal and the draft of the Britain's 1939 ultimatum to Germany.

Other highlights include the first copy of *The Times*, dating from 1788, Beatles music manuscripts and the recording of Nelson Mandela's trial speech.

Cases of musical manuscripts include the autograph of Handel's oratorio *Messiah* (1741) and Beethoven's sketches for his *6th Symphony* (1808).

British Museum

Great Russell Street; tel: 020-7323 8299; www.britishmuseum.org; daily 10am–5.30pm (Thur–Fri until 8.30pm); free; tube: Russell Square, Tottenham Court Road; floorplan opposite; map p.151 E3

The British Museum contains 6.5 million objects; devote just 60 seconds to each and you'd be there for more than 12 years. Although only 50,000 objects are on display at any given time, this is not a place to rush through in a couple of hours. One of the oldest museums in the world, founded by an Act of Parliament in 1753 and opened in 1759, it is still one of the most visited attractions in London and the best time to go is soon after opening.

Thanks to enthusiastic plundering by 19th-century explorers, the **Egyptian Sarcophagi** comprise the richest collection of Egyptian funery art to be found outside Egypt.

The **Parthenon Sculptures**, commonly known as the Elgin Marbles, have been given their own spacious quarters. Carved in the 5th century BC for the Temple of Athena Parthenos, patron goddess of Athens, these are, even in their damaged state, some of the greatest sculptures ever created, their muscular detail and fluidity of movement airily transcending their origins as blocks of

marble. Understandably, the Greeks want them back.

The granite tablet from the 2nd century BC known as the **Rosetta Stone** provided the key, in the 19th century, to deciphering Egypt's hieroglyphic script. In the same room is the colossal sandstone head of the pharaoh

In 1857, the celebrated Reading Room – where Karl Marx researched *Das Kapital* – was added to the central courtyard of the British Museum to house most of its immense library. In 1997, the British Library was relocated to new premises on the Euston Road, allowing the British Museum to make major changes to its overcrowded building. The most radical was the glassing over of the Great Court, the area around the Reading Room, to create the largest covered public square in Europe, as well as a striking museum experience.

Right: the inner coffin of Henutmehyt *c.*1290 BC.

by Bernardo Daddi, a fragment from an altarpiece by Lorenzo Monaco and a predella by Fra Angelico. A triptych of the *Entombment* by the Master of Flémalle, is one of the great examples of Netherlandish Realism. A later artist of the same School, Pieter Bruegel the Elder, painted the visionary panorama, *Landscape with the Flight into Egypt*.

There are several notable works by Rubens on the first floor, among them a landscape, romantically depicted by moonlight, and a superb oil sketch for *The Descent from the Cross*.

The core collection contains works by Impressionist and Post-Impressionist artists, and includes masterpieces by Manet, Degas, Monet, Renoir, Cézanne, Seurat, Van Gogh and Gauguin. Manet's *Déjeuner sur l'herbe* (1863) is a smaller, simplified replica of the painting now in the Musée d'Orsay, in Paris; Cézanne's *Montagne Sainte-Victoire* of 1887 is the artist's most accomplished view of this stretch of Provençal landscape; and Van Gogh's famous *Self-Portrait with Bandaged Ear* is also here.

Charles Dickens Museum
48 Doughty Street; tel: 020-7405 2127; www.dickens museum.com; Mon–Sat 10am–5pm, Sun 11am–5pm; admission charge; tube: Russell Square, Chancery Lane; map p.152 A4

The world's foremost repository of Dickens documentation and memorabilia in the house where the writer and his family lived from 1837–39. The walls are adorned with numerous portraits of the

Ramesses II, said to be the inspiration for *Ozymandias*, Shelley's poetic meditation on the transience of power.

The imposing facade of the 4th-century **Nereid Monument** from Xanthos in Turkey, was destroyed by an earthquake and reconstructed by the British Museum. Another huge Turkish monument, the **Mausoleum of Halikarnassos**, a giant tomb, was finished around 351 BC in south west Turkey. This was one of the seven wonders of the ancient world.

The **Sutton Hoo Ship Burial** was the richest treasure ever dug from British soil. The early 7th-century longboat was likely to have been the burial chamber of Raedwald, an East Anglian king. The acidic sand had destroyed all organic material well before the excavation in 1939, but a rich hoard of weapons, armour, coins, bowls and jewellery has survived.

In 2001, charges to enter government-funded national galleries and musuems were scrapped. Attendance soared as a result; nearly 11 million extra visitors attended in the first two years of the scheme.

The 82 elaborately carved 12th-century chess pieces, known as the **Lewis Chessmen**, were probably made in Norway and found on the Isle of Lewis in Scotland's Outer Hebrides. The helmeted figures and faces set in curious scowls, are strangely beautiful.

In 1984, the preserved corpse of **Lindow Man**, victim of a sacrifice, was found in Lindow Moss, a peat bog in Cheshire. Scientists were able to determine what he had eaten, as well as his blood group.

In the basement are around five dozen of the 900 brass plaques found in Benin City, Nigeria, in 1897. The **Benin Bronzes** were probably cast in the 16th century to clad the wooden pillars of the palace; they depict court life and ritual in fascinating detail.

Courtauld Galleries
Somerset House, Strand; tel: 020-7848 2526; www.cour tauld.ac.uk; daily 10am–6pm, admission charge except Mon 10am–2pm; tube: Temple, Charing Cross; map p.149 D3

The gallery contains Old Master drawings and one of the world's finest collections of Impressionist paintings. The earliest works include an exquisite portable tabernacle

Somerset House, in which the Courtauld Galleries are housed, served as the Registry of Births, Marriages and Deaths until the 1970s. After renovation, it opened to the public in 2000.

author and his eccentric whiskers, as well as many delightful illustrations of his stories. The basement houses a huge collection of Dickens's books, and there is a video describing both his professional successes and his troubled personal life.

Displays on the upper floors illustrate his other great passion, the theatre. The posters and other memorabilia here give an insight into his life outside his novels and fill out the character of the man, an admired celebrity of his time.

Hunterian Museum

The Royal College of Surgeons of England, 35–43 Lincoln's Inn Fields; tel: 020-7869 6560; www.rcseng.ac.uk; Tue–Sat 10am–5pm; free; tube: Holborn; map p.152 A2

The redesigned collections of the Royal College of Sur-

geons now comprise one of the best displayed anatomical museums in the world. As well as some grisly bit and pieces pickled in bottles there is a fine collection of paintings and remarkable (if rather worrying) displays of surgical instruments.

Sir John Soane's Museum

13 Lincoln's Inn Fields; tel: 020-7405 2107; www.soane.org; Tue–Sat 10am–5pm; free; tube: Holborn; map p.152 A3

A wonderfully eclectic and eccentric collection, acquired by one of England's greatest architects, Sir John Soane (1753–1837). Items include two series of Hogarth paintings, *The Rake's Progress* and *An Election*, as well as a number of Piranesi drawings. Much of the basement is given over to the Crypt, an evocation of a Roman catacomb. The most noteworthy exhibit here is the limestone Egyptian sarcophagus of Seti I (1370 BC) acquired by Soane in 1825. The Colonnade and Dome contain a delightful confusion of fragments of sculptures, mouldings and casts of antiquity.

The City

Museum of London

London Wall; tel: 020-7001 9844; www.museum oflondon.org.uk; daily 10am–6pm; free; tube: Barbican, St Paul's, Moorgate; map p.153 C3

In the south-west corner of the Barbican complex stands this museum, fittingly overlooking the remaining fragments of the Roman London Wall, the busy city streets and the layers of history buried underneath. It is the largest museum of urban history in the world and holds more than a million objects in its store, including a vast archaeological archive and collections of Roman artefacts; costume and decorative arts and photographs. Only a small proportion of the collection are on permanent display.

The Museum of London traces the city's development chronologically, from prehistory to the modern day, with thematic threads running through each period, including architecture, trade, multiculturalism, religion and fashions. Note that a major refurbishment and development is currently underway on the galleries dealing with 1666 onwards. They are due to re-open in 2010.

Highlights include the **Great Fire Experience**, with a display of London burning playing against readings from Samuel Pepys' diaries, the recently reworked **Medieval Gallery** with weapons, ceramics and a fantastic collection of fashions from the time, and the Lord Mayor's gaudily ornate gilded coach.

Left: Hogarth's *Chairing the Member*, at Sir John Soane's Museum.

South Bank and Bankside

Design Museum

28 Shad Thames; tel: 0870-833 9955; www.designmuseum.org; daily 10am–5.45pm; admission charge; tube: Tower Hill, London Bridge

In a converted 1950s warehouse, with an elegant, layered front commanding wonderful views of the Thames and Tower Bridge, this was Europe's first museum dedicated to the exploration and study of modern design for mass production. Temporary exhibits have included subjects such as Bauhaus and alternative urban housing are staged in some of the galleries, while the permanent design collection shows thematic product displays, such as the evolution of now commonplace articles such as television sets, cameras, telephones and even plastic packaging.

Hayward Gallery

South Bank Centre, Belvedere Road; tel: 0870-380 0400; www.haywardgallery.org.uk; daily 10am–6pm (Fri until 10pm) during exhibitions; admission charge; tube/rail:

Waterloo; map p.149 E2

A large, purpose-built exhibition space which resembles a cluster of abstract blocks in reinforced concrete. Its 1960s Brutalist style is now considered an architectural classic. On the roof is the 'Neon Tower', composed of alternating coloured striplights, which has become the gallery's distinguishing sign.

Imperial War Museum

Lambeth Road; tel: 020-7416 5000; http://london.iwm.org.uk; daily 10am–6pm; free; tube: Lambeth North, Elephant and Castle

The museum is housed in the building built to house Bethlem Royal Hospital for the insane (also known as Bedlam), an inspired choice for a museum chronicling the horrors of modern war. A cinema, which shows newsreels and wartime films, is an example of the well-thought out multimedia used throughout the musuem. There are blitz and trench 'experiences'; you may have to queue for the former, where you wait in darkness for air raids to begin. The

Right: the Imperial War Museum's *HMS Belfast*.

second floor holds a splendid collection of 20th-century art. Many of the works were officially commissioned for propaganda purposes. The *London Blitz* drawings by Henry Moore are particularly evocative.

The **Holocaust Exhibition** is the largest of its kind outside Israel and the US. This is an intense and harrowing exhibition, built around the testimonies of a selection of survivors; film footage accompanies the stories, as does rare and important historical material, including a section of a deportation railcar and the entrance to a gas chamber.

On the fourth floor, a specially commissioned film entitled *Crimes Against Humanity* is a harrowing look at conflicts involving ethnic strife and genocide in recent times. Under 16s are not permitted.

The museum also owns the warship **HMS Belfast** which is anchored to the banks of the Thames near Tower Bridge (Morgan's Lane, Tooley Street; tel: 020-7940 6300; http://hmsbelfast.iwm.org.uk; Mar–Oct daily 10am–6pm, Nov–Feb daily 10am–5pm; admission charge; tube: London Bridge; map p.153 E1).

Tate Modern

Bankside; tel: 020- 7887 8888; www.tate.org.uk/modern; daily 10am–6pm (Fri–Sat until 10pm); tube: Southwark, Tate boat: from Tate Britain; map p.152 C1

Tate Modern has captured the public's imagination in a quite unprecedented way, both for its displays, presenting international modern art in an accessible way, and its

Left: the vast Turbine Hall at the Tate Modern.

building, a magnificent presence on the South Bank.

The bold decision to purchase and transform the redundant Bankside Power Station was taken in 1998, and the Swiss architects Herzog & de Meuron won an open international competition to redevelop the former electricity station. The existing brick structure, a massive horizontal block with huge central tower, has been smartened up and the monumental windows re-opened, but in other respects the industrial character of the building still asserts itself. The vast Turbine Hall hosts fascinating pieces of innovative installation art.

Definitive moments of 20th-century art history (Surrealism, Minimalism, post-war Abstraction, and the three linked movements of Cubism, Futurism and Vorticism) are arranged by theme rather than chronologically. Displays in these galleries move back and forth in time, showing how each movement developed and its role in shaping subsequent artistic developments. Their relationship to the wider social and cultural history of the 20th and early 21st century is illustrated through the juxtaposition of the pieces.

Highlights include Monet's atmospheric painting of *Water-Lilies* (after 1916), Dali's surreal vision *Autumnal Cannibalism* (1936), Jackson Pollock's entirely abstract response to the landscape outside his studio in his drip painting *Summertime* (1948) and Mark Rothko's sombre *Seagram Murals* (1958–9).

Stars among still-life painters are Picasso, Cezanne and Braque; while Pop Art is well represented by Warhol and Lichtenstein. High-profile contemporary artists on show include Rachel Whiteread and Tracy Emin.

The gallery also stages particularly exciting and bold temporary exhibitions, for which there are admission charges.

North London

The Estorick Collection
39a Canonbury Square; tel: 020-7704 9522; www.estorickcollection.com; Wed–Sat 11am–6pm, Sun noon–5pm; admission charge; tube: Highbury & Islington, bus: 19, 30
The core of this private collection comprises Futurist art by Balla, Boccioni, Carrà, Severini and Russolo, as well as figurative art of 1890–1950 by Modigliani, Campigli, de Chirico, Marino Marini and others. Displays change

every six months or so. Don't miss Boccioni's *Modern Idol* (1911), Severini's *The Boulevard* (1910–11), Balla's *Hand of the Violinist* (1912), Marini's *Quadriga* (1942) and de Chirico's *Melancholy* (1912).

East London

Dennis Severs' House
18 Folgate Street, Spitalfields; tel: 020-7247 4013; www.dennissevershouse.co.uk; Mon eve for 'Silent Night', times vary with light, booking necessary, 1st and 3rd Mon of month noon–2pm Sun noon–4pm; admission charge; tube: Liverpool Street; map p.153 E4
This is a museum quite unlike any other, an 18th-century candlelit timewarp. A life-long collector and anglophile, Dennis Severs moved from his native California in 1967. He bought this former silk weaver's house and got to know it by living in each room in turn, without benefit of electricity or modern appliances. Gradually he re-created its early 18th-century

Eric Estorick (1913–93) developed a passion for art as a student in New York. After World War II, he went to Europe and began to buy drawings by Picasso, Braque and others.

state. To give the 10-room house coherence, he invented the Jervis family, and provided evidence of their occupation in the form of a half-eaten scone and a smouldering fire.

Geffrye Museum

136 Kingsland Road; tel: 020-7739 9893; www.geffrye-museum.org.uk; Tue–Sat 10am–5pm, Sun noon–5pm; free; tube: Liverpool Street, then bus: 149, 242

The only British museum to deal with domestic interiors of the urban middle-class, the Geffrye chronicles the development of English home decoration from 1600 to the present day. The rooms are arranged chronologically and each century is preceded by a room giving background information on characteristic layouts and furniture of the century. Surrounding the museum are charming period gardens, also reflecting the prevalent styles of town gardens at different times. There is also an award-winning herb garden, which provides a valuable East End natural habitat.

Whitechapel Gallery

77–82 Whitechapel High Street; tel: 020-7522 7888; www.whitechapel.org; Tue–Sun 11am–6pm (Thur until 9pm); free; tube: Aldgate East

The Whitechapel Gallery opened in 1901, designed by Arts and Crafts architect Charles Harrison Townsend, with the aim of bringing art to the East End. It never acquired a permanent collection, but throughout its history has hosted a programme of high profile and important exhibitions, including major shows by artists such as Jackson Pollock, David Hockney and Julian Schnabel; in 1939, it was the only UK gallery to show Picasso's *Guernica* on it's tour.

In 2009, the Whitechapel opened its doors again following an extensive refurbishment and expansion to double the previous size of the gallery, through ingenious use of a former adjoining library. The new galleries will also show longer-running exhibitions than previously, making use of the gallery's extensive archive.

White Cube

48 Hoxton Square; tel: 020-7930 5373; www.whitecube.com; Tue–Sat 10am–6pm; free; tube: Old Street

Jay Jopling's famous commercial art gallery has been the nerve centre for launching 'Young British Artists' such as Tracey Emin, Jake and Dinos Chapman, Marc Quinn, Damien Hirst and many more. Along with its larger sister site at 25–26 Mason's Yard in St James's (tel: 020-7930 5373; Tue–Sat 10am–6pm; tube: Green Park; map p.148 A2), White Cube continues to mount exciting and high-profile shows by the many of the art world's biggest names. The Hoxton branch, in the heartland of the original YBA movement, is set in a 1920s industrial building.

South London

Dulwich Picture Gallery

Gallery Road; tel: 020-8693 5254; www.dulwichpicture gallery.org.uk; Tue–Fri 10am–5pm, Sat–Sun 11am–5pm, tours: Sat–Sun 3pm; admission charge; rail: West Dulwich,North Dulwich, then 10-min walk

Some 300 pictures are shown in the gallery, which is especially rich in 17th-century European painting and includes work by Poussin, Cuyp, Rembrandt, Rubens, and Van Dyck.

You can see Gainsborough's small portrait, *An Unknown Couple in a Landscape*, one of the finest of its kind. One of the highlights of the gallery is a group of seven paintings by Poussin. A group of sketches and paintings by Rubens is also worth seeing. The Dutch pictures are among the most outstanding of the collection, which includes three portraits by Rembrandt. Among the group of Dutch landscape artists, Cuyp is pre-eminent; the much-admired *A Road near a River* is one of the most beautiful of his late Italianate pastoral scenes.

Horniman Museum

100 London Road; tel: 020-8699 1872; www.horniman.ac.uk; daily 10.30am–5.30pm; free; train: Forest Hill

One of South London's

Left: the delightful grounds of the Geffrye Museum.

The **Queen's House** showcases the museum's art collections and an exhibition on **Historic Greenwich** through rotating exhibitions in this classical Renaissance building, designed as a summer palace for Queen Anne of Denmark, the wife of James I.

Founded by Charles II in 1675, the **Royal Observatory** was the centre of astronomical and other scientific research for the best part of three centuries. In the courtyard is a brass inset marking the meridian line.

Flamsteed House, designed by Sir Christopher Wren, dates from the founding of the observatory. Panels and exhibits look at the history of astronomy from its earliest origins in the ancient civilisations of Sumeria and Egypt. The **Meridian Building** houses an array of star-gazing equipment, including displays on modern astronomy.

The *pièce de résistance* is a collection of John Harrison's sea clocks, designed to remain accurate through the heat and cold, humidity and constant motion experienced on a ship at sea. These allowed mariners to determine their position as east or west.

unsung treasures, containing rich collections of ethnography, natural history and musical instruments. The **African Worlds** gallery displays objects from Africa and countries influenced by the diaspora caused by the slave trade and colonialism. A large part of the gallery is dedicated to a mask collection. Among the most valuable (and controversial) exhibits are the 16th-century bronze plaques from the royal palace of Benin.

The musical instrument collection holds a wide selection, from ancient Egyptian clappers to Western classical instruments to more recent aquisitions from Uzbekistan and Belarus; you can hear samples of them being played. There are also pleasant gardens (7.30am–dusk).

National Maritime Museum and Royal Observatory
Romney Road; tel: 020-8858 4422; www.nmm.ac.uk; daily 10am–5pm; free; DLR: Cutty Sark; rail: Greenwich, Maze Hill
The museum, the largest of its kind in the world, houses an unrivalled collection of

maritime art and artefacts in a classical palace. The vast collection comprises more than 2 million objects. Many of these can be seen in the **Upper Deck Collection**.

Arranged in and around the glass-roofed courtyard are galleries dedicated to great **Explorers**, from the Vikings, to the European explorers of the 16th and 17th centuries and the great polar expeditions of the 19th century. The **Passengers** gallery focuses on mass migrations from Europe to America during the 19th and early 20th centuries. It also celebrates the romance of sea travel with early tourism posters and models of luxury liners. This courtyard has been glazed over and provides a space for larger exhibits, including Prince Frederick's golden barge (1732).

The **Maritime London** section covers the growth of maritime trade through the port of London. Here you can also see the museum's most prized possession – the uniform coat Nelson was wearing when he was killed in the Battle of Trafalgar on board the Victory.

In May 2007, a fire ripped through the Cutty Sark in Greenwich, badly damaging it. Fortunately, as it was in the middle of a major restoration project at the time, 50 percent of the ship was being stored elsewhere, including the iconic figurehead. It will hopefully re-open in 2010, about six months behind its original restoration schedule. In the 19th-century heyday of maritime trade, clippers like the Cutty Sark ruled the oceans.

Music

L ondon's music scene is large and diverse. It ranges from one of the world's greatest opera houses, to first class orchestras, to rock and pop, to cutting edge experimental works. Music venues and performances can be found and heard all over London. The major venues are listed below, but many more concerts, amateur and professional, take place in music colleges, local halls, churches and, weather permitting, outdoors. Local press and listings magazines such as *Time Out* are a useful source of information, and keep an eye out for posters and flyers for less mainstream events.

Classical Music

The first flowering of art music in England can be heard in the early church music of composers such as John Dunstable (*c.*1390–1453). The 16th and early-17th centuries saw an indigenous madrigal style emerge in the works of John Wilbye (1574–1638) and Thomas Weelkes (1576–1623) while John Dowland (1563–1626) was noted for his compositions for lute and viols.

By the latter half of the 17th century, and through the 18th, England – and especially London – had developed a thriving music scene. Responsible in large part for this was the prolific Henry Purcell (1659–95), now best known for his stage works such as *Dido and Aeneas* and *The Fairy Queen*. London was such a commercial and artistic centre during the 18th century that it attracted musicians from abroad such as Handel (who settled here), and Mozart and Haydn, who both visited.

In the 19th century, the seeming lack of an indigenous art music tradition only abated with the emergence of figures

Above: the Royal Albert Hall.

such as Hubert Parry, (1848–1918) Charles Stanford (1852–1924) and, above all, Edward Elgar (1857–1934). At the Royal College of Music, Stanford and Parry trained most of the next generation of composers, who represented the 'English Renaissance'. Drawing on sources like early English polyphony and folk song, composers such as Gustav Holst (1874–1934) and Ralph Vaughan Williams (1872–1958) set about creating a new national style.

In doing so they laid the ground for major English composers of the mid-20th century such as William Walton (1902–83) and Benjamin Britten (1913–76).

The 21st century has seen composers such as Mark-Anthony Turnage (born 1960), Thomas Adès (born 1971) and Julian Anderson (born 1967) take centre stage, each displaying an eclecticism which distinguishes their music from that of the older generation.

CLASSICAL VENUES

Barbican Centre
Silk Street, The City; tel: 020-7638 8891; www.barbican.org.uk; tube: Moorgate, Barbican; map p.153 C3
Home to one of London's main large concert halls, this modern arts complex hosts concerts by the **London Symphony Orchestra** (www.lso.co.uk) and the **BBC Symphony Orchestra** (www.bbc.co.uk/orchestras/symphonyorchestra), as well as numerous international soloists and orchestras.
Cadogan Hall
5 Sloane Terrace, Chelsea; tel: 020-7730 4500; www.cadoganhall.com; tube: Sloane Square; map p.154 A2
London's youngest concert hall (built in 1972) is home to the **Royal Philharmonic**

bankcentre.co.uk; tube/rail: Waterloo; map p.149 D2

Vying with the Barbican as London's top arts venue, the Southbank Centre is home to three separate concert halls.

The **Royal Festival Hall**, reopened after extensive renovated in 2007, has had its acoustics enhanced to make it one of the finest halls in the country. It is home to a number of world class ensembles: the **London Philharmonic Orchestra** (www.lpo.co.uk) with principal conductor Vladimir Jurowski, the **Philharmonia** (www.phil harmonia.co.uk) under principal conductor Esa-Pekka Salonen, contemporary music ensemble the **London Sinfonietta** (www.londonsinfonietta. org.uk) lead by conductor and composer Oliver Knussen, and the period instrument ensemble, the **Orchestra of the Age of Enlightenment** (www.oae.co.uk).

The **Queen Elizabeth Hall**, to the side of the Festival Hall,

Orchestra (www.rpo.co.uk). It also hosts the chamber music concerts of the BBC Proms.

English National Opera
London Coliseum, St Martin's Lane, Covent Garden; tel: 0870-145 0200; www.eno.org; tube: Charing Cross; map p.149 C3
Britain's national repertory company stages a wide range of operas, including both classics and new works. Productions are sung in English with surtitles.

Fairfield Halls
Park Lane, Croydon; tel: 020-8688 9291; www.fairfield.co.uk; rail: East Croydon
South London's major concert hall with a season of regular visits from orchestras such as the Royal Philharmonic. It is also home to the **London Mozart Players** chamber orchestra (www.lmp.org).

LSO St Luke's
161 Old Street, The City; tel: 020-7490 3939; www.lso.co.uk; tube: Old Street; map p.153 C4
The London Symphony Orchestra converted this Hawksmoor church and now the Jerwood Hall holds recitals of chamber music, including BBC lunchtime concerts.

Royal Albert Hall
Kensington Gore, Kensington; tel: 0845-401 5045; www.royal alberthall.com; tube: South Kensington; map p.156 B3
This huge circular arena hold concerts and events throughout the year but is chiefly famous as being the location of the yearly Proms season of concerts *(see box, below)*.

Royal Opera House
Bow Street, Covent Garden; tel: 020-7304 4000; www.roh.org.uk; tube: Covent Garden; map p.149 C4
One of the world's great opera houses with a long and illustrious history. The productions are lavish and the orchestra is one of the best in the country. The house was completely renovated in 1999 and the Paul Hamlyn Hall (part of Covent Garden's old flower market) is a spectacular, if expensive, space for pre- and post-performance dining and interval drinks. The Royal Opera House is also the home of the Royal Ballet.
SEE ALSO DANCE P.46

Southbank Centre
Belvedere Road, South Bank; tel: 0871-663 2500; www.south

The best known of London's classical music festivals is the **BBC Proms** (www.bbc.co.uk/proms) which runs from July to September. Started by Henry Wood and Robert Newman in 1895, the nightly concerts by major national and international orchestras are held in the Albert Hall. There are also late night Proms starting at 10pm, childrens events and a chamber music season at the Cadogan Hall. 'Promming', standing in the centre of the hall in front of the orchestra, is the cheapest way to get a ticket. These standing tickets cannot be booked in advance and go on-sale one hour before the concert starts.

is a smaller venue used for solo recitals, chamber orchestra and chamber music concerts. A smaller hall, the **Purcell Room**, used for chamber and solo recitals, is also part of the QEH complex.
St John's, Smith Square
Smith Square, Westminster; tel: 020-7222 1061; www.sjss.org.uk; tube: Westminster; map p.155 D2
This fine Baroque church was converted into a concert hall following restoration from bomb damage during World War II. It holds many concerts throughout the year, especially chamber music, performances on period instruments and of Early and Baroque music. It is the main venue of the **Lufthansa Festival of Baroque Music** (www.lufthansafestival.org.uk).
The Wigmore Hall
36 Wigmore Street, Marylebone; tel: 020-7935 2141; www.wigmore-hall.org.uk; tube: Bond Street; map p.150 B2
The country's top solo recital and chamber music venue, with an impressive series of recitals and concerts throughout the year. The Wigmore attracts top names – many famous musicians have performed here – and tickets can sell out quickly.

Contemporary

Having produced or been home to more internationally successful artists than perhaps any other city in the world is a fact that isn't lost on the London music scene. There is a pride almost to the point of snobbishness in the city's continuing musical heavyweight status.

British pop music stirred in London in the late 1950s as Cliff Richard and Lonnie Donegan imported American teenage culture with skiffle shows in Soho coffee bars.

Right: the vinyl selection at Rough Trade East Records.

When the Beatles recorded at Abbey Road Studios in St Johns Wood (still a pilgrimage to some) they swung the focus of the musical world on London. The Rolling Stones (associated with Richmond and Twickenham), The Who (Chiswick), The Kinks (Muswell Hill) and David Bowie (Brixton) all followed. By the end of the 1960's London was perhaps only matched by Nashville or San Francisco as the heart of popular music.

The economic downturn of the 1970's ignited punk and the Mohican became as much a symbol of London as Big Ben (as many postcards will testify). The hairstyle is more for pantomime these days but the DIY ethic of punk survives with small clubs and promoters always striving for something edgy and unique. In the 1980s, the originally underground club scene and pirate radio stations brought dance music into the mainstream.

With US grunge dominant in the early 1990s, London hit back with the self-referential Britpop scene. Blur, Oasis, Suede and Pulp made 'cool Britannia' briefly untouchable.

Today, London remains one of the best places to catch live music in any number of contemporary genres, from indie-rock to synth-pop to grime.

CONTEMPORARY VENUES
93 Feet East
150 Brick Lane, Whitechapel; tel: 020-7247 3293; www.93feeteast. co.uk; tube: Liverpool Street
Part of the Old Truman Brewery on Brick Lane. Experience cutting edge bands and club nights until late.
SEE ALSO NIGHTLIFE, P.102
Brixton Academy
211 Stockwell Road, Brixton; tel:

0870-771 2000; www.brixton-academy.co.uk; tube: Brixton
With an interesting Art Deco interior this venue is one of the largest around drawing major rock artists.
Luminaire
311 Kilburn High Road, Kilburn ; tel: 020-7372 7123; www.thelu minaire.co.uk; tube: Kilburn
An alternative rock darling that wins awards regularly. Small, comfortable and showcasing bands on the rise most nights.
The Roundhouse
Chalk Farm Road, Camden; tel: 0844-482 8008; www.round house.org.uk; tube: Chalk Farm
A leading light in the 70's, recently re-opened and modernised and once again welcoming large acts looking for an atmospheric venue.
Shepherds Bush Empire
Shepherd's Bush Green, Shepherd's Bush; tel: 0870-771 2000; www. shepherds-bush-empire.co.uk; tube: Shepherd's Bush
A former BBC studio which attracts large international acts such as Björk, The Dixie Chicks and Radiohead, while retaining a degree of intimacy.
The Underworld
174 Camden High Street, Camden; tel: 020-7482 1932; www.theunderworldcamden.co. uk; tube: Camden Road

If you like music deafeningly loud, fast and sweaty then this basement venue will more than suffice.

Jazz

Jazz gigs take place all over the city (see www.jazzin london.net for listings), but below are the main venues. The **London Jazz Festival** (www.londonjazzfestival.org.uk), held annually in November, is a great time to catch exciting and high-profile acts.

JAZZ VENUES
Jazz Café
5 Parkway, Camden; tel: 020-7485 6834; www.jazzcafe.co.uk; tube: Camden Road
This venue tends to concentrate more on cross-over acts and Latin with the occasional mainstream artist.
Pizza Express
10 Dean Street, Soho; tel: 020-7439 8722; www.pizza expresslive.co.uk; tube: Tottenham Court Road; map p.148 B4
A top Soho jazz venue, downstairs from one of the ubiquitous restaurants. The intimate basement club is good place to catch well-known UK and American musicians.
Ronnie Scott's
47 Frith Street, Soho; tel: 020-7439 0747; www.ronnie

scotts.co.uk; tube: Tottenham Court Road; map p.148 B4
The doyen of London jazz clubs. Founded by the eponymous tenor sax player in 1959, many big names have played here, from Dizzy Gillespie to Ella Fitzgerald.
Vortex
11 Gillett Street, Dalston; tel: 020-7254 4097; www.vortex jazz.co.uk; train: Dalston Kingsland, bus: 243
This club moved into new, purpose-built premises a few years ago. The eclectic mix of artists means you are likely to hear something interesting.

CD and Record Shops
Fopp
1 Earlham Street, Covent Garden; tel: 020-7845 9770; www.foppreturns.com; Mon–Sat 10am–10pm, Sun noon–6pm; tube: Leicester Square; map p.151 D2
Pile 'em high and sell 'em cheap on a rotating stock of popular artists. The dvds and books are also worth a look.
HMV
150 Oxford Street, Marylebone; tel: 0845-602 7802; www.hmv. co.uk; Mon–Wed, Fri–Sat 9am–8.30pm, Thur 9am–9pm, Sun 11.30am–6.30pm; tube: Oxford Circus; map p.148 A4
The basement has one of the city's best classical sections.
Intoxica
231 Portobello Road, Notting Hill; 020-7229 8010 www.intoxica. co.uk Mon–Sat: 10.30am–6.30pm, Sun noon–4.30pm; tube: Ladbroke Grove; map p.157 C4
A must for fans of 1960's Beat, Psychedelia, Garage and Exotica. Vinylheaven.
MDC
31 St Martin's Lane, Covent Garden; tel: 020 7240 0270; www.mdcmusic.co.uk; Mon–Sat 10am–6.30pm, Sun noon–6pm; tube: Leicester Square; map p.149 C3
Independent opera special-

ists next to ENO. (Also at: Royal Festival Hall, South Bank; tel: 020-7620 0198; daily 10am–10pm.)
Pure Groove
6–7 West Smithfield, The City; tel: 020 7778 9278; www.pure groove.co.uk; Mon–Fri 10am–11pm; tube: Farringdon; map p.152 B3
Almost a gig venue that also happens to sell records. Check the website for events.
Rough Trade East
Truman Brewery, Dray Walk, Whitechapel; tel: 020-7392 7788; www.roughtrade.com; Mon–Thur 8am–9pm, Fri 8am–8pm, Sat 10am–8pm, Sun 11am–7pm; tube: Liverpool Street; map p.153 E4
A byword for all things alternative, this enormous newly-opened branch has in-store performances, latest releases and imports.

Searching out live music is usually quite simple. Check the listings magazines such as *Time Out*, who provide a useful starting point. It may be worth browsing on-line ticket agents before you arrive. www.ticket-master.co.uk has the larger venues but high service charges. www.wegottickets.com and www.ticketweb.co.uk have reasonable charges and service smaller venues and acts.

Below: London is bursting with musical history.

101

Nightlife

Whatever your after-dark tastes, you stand an excellent chance of finding nightlife in London that appeals to you. Central London is brimming with clubs of all descriptions which play a hugely eclectic range of music and you are unlikely to ever be stuck if you want a night out. DJs clamour to play in the ever-changing rota of trendy clubs; there is always a new hot destination to head to. Those who want to do some salsa or retro-style dancing are also in the right place, but for those not so keen on dancing, comedy venues and cabarets provide great alternative night-time entertainment.

The Clubbing Map

The main hub of trendy nightlife is to the east in **Shoreditch** and **Hoxton**, but hot clubs are found all over. The West End still boasts some great spots in the **Soho** area, but much of what's on offer around **Leicester Square** is dangerously close to perv territory. Some of the most exclusive and expensive spots can be found in **Mayfair** and **Kensington**; the rich and famous party here. **Camden** is still lively for the indie crowd, **Vauxhall** has a vibrant gay scene and **Brixton** has some good hard-partying options.

The quirky, installation and cabaret-influenced club nights have been a visible trend recently; club promoters have found London's night-time revellers enthusiastic about more unusual club nights, often held in innovative spaces such as under railway arches in the City, or in DJ bars. At the other end of the spectrum,

London is renowned world-wide for its superclubs like Fabric and Ministry of Sound. Located in **Farringdon** and **Elephant and Castle** respectively, these are destination clubs for hardcore dancers.

The recent change in legislation which allowed venues to apply for 24-hour licences has led to an increase in the variety of party options out there. After-hours and daytime clubbing are on offer for the hardcore who know where to go; to find out what's happening, keep an eye on these websites dedicated to clubbing:
www.4clubbers.net
www.timeout.com/london/clubs
SEE ALSO GAY AND LESBIAN, P.64

Clubs

93 Feet East

150 Brick Lane, Whitechapel; tel: 020-7247 3293; www.93feet east.co.uk; Mon–Thur 5–11pm, Fri 5pm–1am, Sat noon–1am, Sun 11am–10.30pm; admission charge; tube: Aldgate East

With a large amount of flexible space, including a wrap-around outdoor courtyard for afternoon lounging, 93 Feet East is ideal for all sorts of live and club events. Music could be anything from indie to hip-hop to retro. The crowds tend to be trendy east Londoners, but the vibe is relaxed and music loving.

333 Mother

333 Old Street, Shoreditch;

Right: the sophisticated Kensington Roof Gardens.

Left: things heat up at Fabric.

considered one of the top in the world, plays host to innovative and edgy acts and DJs every weekend, with a hip-hop and drum 'n' bass emphasis on Fridays and a more minimal, techno sound on Saturdays. Dance 'til dawn in one of the three pumping rooms, or just hang out on a staircase making new friends.

Guanabara
Parker Street, Corner Drury Lane; tel: 0207 242 8600; www.guan abara.co.uk; Mon–Sat 5pm–2.30am, Sun 5pm–midnight; Mon–Tue free, Wed–Fri Sat charge after 9pm, Sat–Sun charge after 8pm; tube: Holborn; map p.151 E2
This fabulous Brazilian themed space features a very modern, circular dance-floor. The atmosphere is kept up with hard-to-resist Latin drum beats and a vast list of caipir-inhas and mojitos.

Kensington Roof Gardens
99 Kensington High Street, Kensington; tel: 020-7368 3992; www.roofgardens.com; Fri–Sat 10pm–3am; admission charge; tube: Kensington High Street; map p.157 E1
This sophisticated club, set in 1.2 acres (0.5 hectares) of rooftop gardens, is beautifully

tel: 020-7739 5949; www.333 mother.com; Mother bar: daily 8pm–3am, free; 333 club: Fri–Sat, times and charges vary, see website for details; tube: Old Street
333 is a hip club, while the adjoining lively Mother bar hosts live music at weekends and a free party on Tuesdays. The basement 333 club sees electro, disco, dancehall and grime beats among others. A Hoxton stalwart that's maintained its popularity and offers highly eclectic music.

Bethnal Green Working Men's Club
42–44 Pollards Row, Bethnal Green; tel: 020-7739 2727; www.workersplaytime.net; days and charges vary depending on event, see website for details; tube: Bethnal Green
In an unreconstructed school-hall-type space, the most kooky and inventive happenings take place: think jiving, swing dancing, burlesque competitions, cabaret performances, bellydancing, inter-art and lots of quirky homages to retro. Impressive costumes will often get you money off the door entry.

Cargo
Kingsland Viaduct, 83 Rivington Street, Shoreditch; tel: 020-7739 3440; www.cargo-lon don.com; Mon–Thur 11–1am, Fri 11–3am, Sat 6pm–3am, Sun 1pm–midnight; admission charge varies; tube: Old Street
Underneath this railway arch in Shoreditch live bands, DJs and a great café vie for space.

Crazy Larry's
533 King's Road, Fulham; tel: 020-7376 5555; www.crazy larrys.co.uk; Thur–Sat 10pm–3am; admission charge; tube: Fulham Broadway
Longstanding Chelsea nightspot with a lively atmosphere and compact dance-floor, where mainstream dance, pop and r&b tunes are spun to the delight of the local young party crowds. One of the more relaxed clubs in the area, in spite of its 'hooray Henry' reputation.

Fabric
77a Charterhouse Street, Farringdon; tel: 020-7336 8898; www.fabriclondon.com; Fri 10pm–6am, Sat 11am–8pm; admission charge; tube: Farringdon; map p.152 B3
London's hottest superclub,

London is not brilliant for all-night eateries, but there are a few gems out there. **Vingt-Quatre** (325 Fulham Road; tel: 020-7376 7224; www.vingtquatre.co.uk; tube: Gloucester Road) is a smart spot for posh post-clubbing food. **Bar Italia** (see *Cafés*, p.34) in Soho serves sandwiches and coffee all night and the legendary **Brick Lane Beigel Bake** (see *Cafés*, p.37) is a godsend to hungry clubbers out in Shoreditch.

Central London has a comprehensive network of night buses *(see Transport p.147)* but the safest way to get home, especially if you're somewhat inebriated, is to take a licensed taxi. Never get in an unlicenced minicab; they can potentially be unreliable and dangerous. You can text the word HOME to 60835 on your mobile phone; the numbers of one taxi and two licensed minicab firms local to the area you are in are texted back to your mobile. The technophobic or too-drunk can just call **Radio Taxis** (tel: 020-7272 0272), **Dial-a-Cab** (tel: 020-7253 5000) or **Addison Lee** (tel: 020-7387 8888).

decorated and caters to a good-looking and glamourous crowd, who sip champagne and cocktails and party to club classics, soul and dance tunes.

KOKO

1a Camden High Street, Camden; tel: 0870-432 5527; www.koko.uk.com; Fri, Sat, times and other nights vary, check website for details; admission charge varies; tube: Mornington Crescent

The faded opulence of the former Camden Palace quirkily suits its NME live music nights, famed for pulling in names from Madonna and Prince to Babyshambles and Dizee Rascal. Club nights play dance, indie and everything in between to a lively young crowd.

Madame JoJo's

8–10 Brewer Street, Soho; tel: 020-7734 3040; www.madamejojos.com; Tue 8pm–3am, Thur 9pm–3am, Fri, Sun 10pm–3am, Sat 7pm–3am; admission charge; tube: Piccadilly Circus; map p.148 B4

This Soho institution is home to a number of popular club

nights, covering everything from indie and funk to cheesy pop, but its the Kitsch Cabaret shows every Saturday that are really special, involving a music-hall style show hosted by 'Miss Terri', great entertainment, dinner and dancing.

Mass

St Matthew's Peace Garden, Brixton; tel: 020-7738 7875; www.mass-club.com; Fri–Sat 10pm–6am; admission charge; tube: Brixton.

Atmospheric Brixton venue in the bowels of a converted church. Wide range of music, with great R&B in the Friday Night Mass.

Matter

02 Arena, Peninsula Square, North Greenwich; tel: 020-7549 6686; www.matterlondon.com; days and times vary, see website for details; admission charge; tube: North Greenwich

Fabric's sister venue, under the O2, burst onto the London scene in 2008. With 2,600 capacity, it is as much a live performance venue as a superclub, but with its eclectic programme of music, top-notch sound and sci-fi cool design, it works well whatever's on the bill.

Ministry of Sound

103 Gaunt Street, Elephant and Castle; tel: 0870-060 0010; www.ministryofsound.com; Fri 10.30pm–late, Sat 11pm–7am; admission charge; tube: Elephant and Castle

The famed Ministry was key in the development of dance music and superclubs back in the 1990s. Today, it still draws in big name DJs and boasts an astonishingly good sound system.

Pacha London

Terminus Place, Victoria; tel: 0845-371 4489; www.pachalondon.com; Fri–Sat

10pm–5am; admission charge; tube: Victoria; map p.154 C2

Part of the global franchise of sexy superclubs, Pacha London is a well-designed space for glitzy nights of house music and popular with a glamorous clubbing crowd.

Proud Galleries

Horse Hospital, Stables Market, Chalk Farm Road, Camden; tel: 020-7482 3867; www.proudcamden.com; Mon–Wed 7.30pm–1am, Thur–Sat 7.30pm–2am, Sun 7.30pm–midnight; tube: Chalk Farm

This multi-purpose venue beloved of trendy Camden indie kids is a contemporary photography gallery during the day, but night sees dancing to hot electro sounds, live rock performances and relaxed lounging in the booths.

Scala

275 Pentonville Road, King's Cross; tel: 020-7833 3022; www.scala-london.co.uk; events vary, see website for details; admission charge; tube: King's Cross

Large, multi-purpose venue that hosts live acts (including big names like the Scissor Sisters and Coldplay) but is otherwise home to big club nights.

Right: Soho's Comedy Store remains very popular.

seOne

41–43 St Thomas Street, Bankside; tel: 020-7407 1617; www.seone-london.com; dates and times vary, see website for details; admission charge; tube: London Bridge; map p.153 D1

London's largest dedicated nightclub (capacity, 3,000) is based under the railway arches of London Bridge station. The underground feel sets up the hard-dancing rave atmosphere perfectly and there's a chill-out room where huge fans cool down hot dancers.

Comedy

Amused Moose

Moonlighting, 17 Greek Street, Soho; tel: 020-7287 3727; www.amusedmoose.com; shows: Sat 8.30pm, for additional dates see website; admission charge; tube: Tottenham Court Road; map p.148 B4

New acts are encouraged at the two branches of Amused Moose (there's a second venue in Camden); many big-names like Harry Hill and Bill Bailey have also played here in the past. It's a popular preview spot for those about to hit the Edinburgh Fringe Festival too. Saturday nights morph into club nights after the comedy, with dancing and a late bar.

Canal Café Theatre

Bridge House, Delamere Terrace, Maida Vale; tel: 020-7289 6054; www.newsrevue.com; shows: Thur–Sat 9.30pm, Sun 9pm; charge; tube: Warwick Avenue

Newsrevue, comprised of topical comedy sketches, has been running for 28 years and is updated weekly. Other comedy stylings and plays also feature on the line-up.

Comedy Store

1A Oxendon Street, Soho; tel: 0870-060 2340; www.thecomedystore.co.uk; shows: Tue–Thur, Sun 8pm, Fri–Sat 8pm, midnight; admission charge; tube: Leicester Square; map p.148 B3

The Comedy Store was the breeding ground for some of the most influential alternative comedians of the 1980s and its legacy has ensured that it continues to pull in big names and pack out shows. It is still the only fully-dedicated comedy venue in the UK.

The Fym Fyg Bar

231–237 Cambridge Heath Road, Bethnal Green; tel: 020-7613 1057; www.thefymfygbar.com; Tue doors 7.30pm (music), show 8pm, Fri–Sat doors 7pm, show 8pm; charge; tube: Bethnal Green

Formerly, Lee Hurst's Backyard club, the man himself comperes most Saturday nights, followed by the 'Cheese on Toast' disco, while other sets belong to a range of stand-ups. There's live music on Tuesdays.

Headliners

George IV, 185 Chiswick High Road, Chiswick; tel: 020-8566 4067; www.headlinerscomedy.com; shows: Fri–Sat 9pm; admission charge; tube: Turnham Green

Headliners plays host to the cream of British comedians; entrance is through the pub.

Cabaret

The Pigalle Club

215 Piccadilly, Mayfair; tel: 020-7734 8142; www.vpmg.net/pigalle; Mon–Wed 7pm–2am, Thur–Sat 7pm–3am; free/admission charge depending on event; tube: Piccadilly Circus; map p.148 B3

This venue is designed as a 1940s style supper club, with patrons enjoying dinner to the sounds of the house band, a live set by a well-known act or visiting retro jazz or swing musicians. The emphasis is on sophisticated, vintage style.

Palaces and Houses

Many of London's palaces were designed by the great architects of their times: Inigo Jones, Sir Christopher Wren, John Nash and Robert Adam. They offer visitors a fascinating insight into the lives of the royals and aristocrats who once inhabited them – and in some cases still do – while many feature great collections of art. For those more interested in London's literary history, the homes of writers such as Thomas Carlyle and Samuel Johnson provide an intriguing view of their worlds. See also *Architecture, p.30*.

Palaces

Banqueting House

Whitehall, Westminster; tel: 0844-482 7777; www.hrp.org.uk; Mon–Sat 10am–5pm; admission charge; tube: Westminster; map p.149 C2

Still used for receptions, the Banqueting Hall was designed by Inigo Jones for James I, and has gone down in history as the place where Charles I was beheaded in 1649. It was the only part of the Palace of Westminster to survive a fire in 1698. Today, it is the Great Hall's splendid painted ceiling, the only complete project by Peter Paul Rubens still in situ, that attracts most visitors. An audioguide explains the painted panels in detail, and a video shown in the vaults fills in the historical background.

Buckingham Palace

Buckingham Palace Road, St James's; tel: 020-7766 7300; www.royalcollection.org.uk; mid-July–Sept daily 9.45am–6pm; admission charge; tube: Victoria, Green Park; map p.154 C3

The State Rooms of the palace that can be visited include the State Dining Room, resplendent with red walls and carpet, the lovely Blue Drawing Room, the gold-and-white Music Room, and the French-influenced White Drawing Room. Access to the State Rooms is via the Grand Staircase, rebuilt by John Nash (1752–1835) in gilt bronze and marble. There are good views over the gardens from all the west wing rooms.
SEE ALSO MUSEUMS AND GALLERIES, P.83

Eltham Palace

Court Yard, Eltham; tel: 020-8294 2548; www.eltham palace.org.uk; Apr–Oct Mon–Wed, Sun 10am–5pm, Nov–Dec, Feb–Mar Mon–Wed, Sun 11am–4pm; admission charge; rail: Eltham

Out of use from the time of Henry VIII, Eltham Palace was rescued from its derelict state in the 1930s by Stephen and

Hampton Court Palace is one of the most popular day trips for visitors to London. It is worth checking if any special events are being held, as there is often something on, from demonstrations of Tudor Cookery, to a music festival in June, and the July flower show.

Left: crowds gather at Buckingham Palace.

Left: skating at Hampton Court Palace's annual ice rink.

must also be purchased; tube/rail: Kew Gardens, boat: from Westminster

This recently refurbished red-brick palace was originally known as the Dutch House, as it was built in 1630 by Samuel Fortrey, a Dutch merchant, and is now the smallest of the royal palaces. Leased to the royals from 1728, the future George IV spent much of his childhood here; his father, George III, bought the house in 1781 and was subsequently locked up here when it was thought he had gone mad. The adjoining Queen Charlotte's Cottage can also be visited (June–Sept Sat–Sun 11am–4pm).

SEE ALSO PARKS AND GARDENS, P.115

Palace of Westminster (Houses of Parliament)
Parliament Square; tel: 0870-906 3773; www.parliament.uk; tours: summer recess only, admission charge; tube: Westminster; map p.155 E3

This splendid Gothic building is the home of the Houses of Parliament. Most of the original royal palace on this site, home to Henry VIII as a young man, burned down in 1834. The Jewel Tower and medieval Westminster Hall

Virginia Courtauld, who built an exemplary Art Deco mansion alongside the former Great Hall. The remains of the former medieval palace contrast beautifully with the sumptuous interior of the mansion; the Art Deco opulence is shown off at its best in the glamourous, silver-ceilinged dining room and the ornate bathroom. Surrounding the palace are 19 acres (7.7 hectares) of gardens in 20th century and medieval styles.

Hampton Court Palace
East Molesey; tel: 0870-751 5175; www.hrp.org.uk; Apr–Oct daily 10am–6pm, Nov–Mar daily 10am–4.30pm; admission charge; rail: Hampton Court, boat: from Westminster or Richmond

It would take several hours to see everything Hampton Court has to offer. The earliest section of the palace is Tudor, built in the 16th century by Cardinal Thomas Wolsey who presented it to Henry VIII. Highlights are the King's Apartments, the Renaissance Picture Gallery and the Tudor Kitchens, the most extensive in Europe. The gardens are magnificent, and the Great

Vine, the oldest in the world, and the Maze, are famous.

Kensington Palace
Kensington Gardens; tel: 0844-482 7777; www.hrp.org.uk; Mar–Oct daily 10am–5pm; Nov–Feb daily 10am–4pm; admission charge; tube: High Street Kensington; map p.156 A4

Built in 1605 and remodelled by Sir Christopher Wren, this was the childhood home of Queen Victoria. The highlights of the State Apartments are the Cupola Room, with a coffered dome, the King's Drawing Room and Queen Victoria's Bedroom. The former apartments of Princess Diana, who lived here until her death in 1997, are off-limits to the public, as are other parts of the palace that are home to minor members of the royal family.

Kew Palace
Royal Botanic Gardens; tel: 0844-482 7777; www.hrp.org.uk/kewpalace; Apr–Sept Mon 11am–5pm, Tue–Sun 10am–5pm; admission charge, Kew Gardens ticket

Right: luxurious Art Deco design at Eltham Palace.

107

were saved. The latter is open to the public as well as being used for ceremonial events. The layout of the palace, which was completed in 1860, is intricate, with the existing buildings containing nearly 1,200 rooms, 100 staircases and well over 2 miles (3km) of passages.

Tower of London

Tower Hill, The City; tel: 0870-950 4488; www.hrp.org.uk; Mar–Oct Tues–Sat 9am–5.30pm, Sun–Mon 10am–5.30pm, Nov–Feb Tue–Sat 9am–4.30pm, Sun–Mon 10am–4.30pm; admission charge; tube: Tower Hill; map p.153 E1

Encircled by a dry moat, the Tower of London was begun by William the Conqueror in 1078 and is Britain's most celebrated military monument, which has at times served as a fortress, palace and prison. The most famous highlight is Traitor's Gate, now half-submerged in the river but once the way by which doomed prisoners such as Anne Boleyn and Sir Thomas More entered the Tower. By contrast, the former entrance to the medieval palace, where monarchs once lived, is positioned just before Traitor's Gate. The oldest part of the fortress, the White Tower, was probably designed in 1078 by a Norman monk, Gandulf.

Seeing all the Tower of London's sights could easily occupy three hours, so you may prefer to skip the one-hour Beefeater-led tour (although children like it) and strike out on your own, relying on the comprehensive official guidebook, audio guide, or free map. In summer, arrive early, giving priority to the Crown Jewels and the Bloody Tower, which can attract long queues later in the day.

Right: the Palace of Westminster *(see p.107)* looms over the Thames.

The Bloody Tower is so-named because the young sons of Edward IV were allegedly murdered there during the reign of their uncle, Richard III; many of the most famous inhabitants of the Tower were held prisoner here.

Visitors snake slowly through airport-style barriers, entertained by footage of the Queen's coronation in 1953, to see the Crown Jewels. At the centre of the display are a dozen crowns and a glittering array of swords, sceptres and orbs used on royal occasions.

Houses

2 Willow Road

Hampstead; tel: 020-7435 6166; www.nationaltrust.org.uk; late Mar–Oct Thur–Fri noon–5pm, Mar–Nov Sat 11am–5pm; admission charge; tube: Hampstead

The former home of architect Ernö Goldfinger, this custom-designed and built house is exemplary of modernist design, from the original furnishings and fixtures to the art by Max Ernst, Bridget Riley and Henry Moore. The only example of international modernism under the National Trust, this functionally-designed house uses light and space to striking effect.

Burgh House

New End Square, Hampstead; tel: 020-7431 0144; www.burghhouse.org.uk; Wed–Sun noon–5pm; free; tube: Hampstead

Erected in 1703, and tucked away in the lanes of Hampstead, this is one of the finest Queen Anne residences in London. It has a delightful Music Room (although it is a 1920s addition) and hosts musical recitals. There are also beautiful, lovingly maintained

gardens, and a terrace where you can have a cream tea.

Carlyle's House

24 Cheyne Row, Chelsea; tel: 020-7352 7087; www.national trust.org.uk; Apr–Oct Wed–Fri 2–5pm, Sat–Sun 11am–5pm; admission charge; tube: Sloane Square

The home to which the dour Scottish essayist Thomas Carlyle and his wife moved in 1834 attracted a coterie of writers and intellectuals, including Charles Dickens and Alfred, Lord Tennyson. Preserved pretty much as it looked at Carlyle's death in 1881, a strong sense of how lives were lived at this time permeates the house. The skylight-lit, attic study is where he set down his thoughts on such subjects as Chartism and the French Revolution. The paintings, including a portrait of the Carlyles, are interesting, and a walled Victorian garden can be visited.

Chiswick House

Burlington Lane, Chiswick; tel: 0208-995 0508; www.chgt.org.uk; Apr–Oct Mon–Wed, Sun 10am–5pm; admission charge; tube: Turnham Green, then bus: E3

A romantic 18th-century villa with Italianate gardens, this is

a grand house in miniature. Lord Burlington (1694–1753), who built the house, was the foremost architect of his time, and was much influenced by Italian architect Andrea Palladio. The Green, Red and Blue Velvet rooms, so-called because of their intricate wallpaper, are attractive, especially the latter, which is tiny and richly coloured, and was Lord Burlington's study.

Dr Johnson's House

17 Gough Square, Holborn; tel: 020-7353 3745; www.drjohnsonshouse.org; Mon–Sat 11am–5.30pm (Oct–Apr until 5pm); admission charge; tube: Chancery Lane; map p.152 B2

The City's oldest remaining residence is tucked away in a maze of winding alleyways off Fleet Street. Samuel Johnson (1709–84) lived here from 1748–59, during which time he wrote the first comprehensive dictionary of the English language. In 1911 the house was saved from dereliction by publisher Cecil Harmsworth and a refurbishment in 2001 reinstated authentic colour schemes: chocolate brown woodwork was fashionable in Johnson's day. Most of the furniture is of the period rather than from the house itself. The walls are lined with portraits by Joshua Reynolds and the top floor of the house is the Dictionary Garret, where Johnson carried out his research. Copies of the two volumes of his dictionary can be leafed through on the ground floor.

Ham House

Ham, Richmond; tel: 020-8940 1950; www.nationaltrust.org.uk/hamhouse; late Mar–Oct Sat–Wed noon–4pm, gardens: all year Sat–Wed 11am–6pm; admission charge; tube/rail: Richmond, then bus: 371

Built in 1610, this is an unusually well-preserved Stuart House. The Great Hall, with a chequerboard floor, is part of the original building. The first floor State Apartments are the finest rooms in the house. The Long Gallery, the Library and the Green Closet are particularly rich in decoration, and the gardens are a delight.

Kenwood House

Hamptead Lane, Hampstead; tel: 020-8348 1286; www.english-heritage.org.uk; daily 11.30am–4pm; free; tube: Hampstead

Standing on the northern slopes of Hampstead Heath like a dazzling white wedding cake, Kenwood House is one of the flagship buildings of English Heritage, and home to the fine art collection of the Iveagh Bequest, with works by Rembrandt, Vermeer, Reynolds, Turner and more. The original building dates from 1700 and was remodelled by Robert Adam in the 1770s. The rooms have been beautifully maintained, while the Library is lined wth gilt-panelled walls and has splendid ceiling murals of classical mythological themes.

Leighton House

12 Holland Park Road, Kensington; tel: 020-7602 3316; www.rbkc.gov.uk/Leighton housemuseum; Wed–Mon 11am–5.30pm; admission charge; tube: High Street Kensington; map p.157 D1

The plain red-brick exterior of this house conceals one of the most extraordinary interiors in the city. The home of Victorian artist Lord Frederic Leighton is a mix of lavish middle-Eastern and conventional Victorian comfort, a private palace done out in jewel colours. Leighton's paintings hang in the Dining Room and Drawing Room. The *pièce de résistance* is the Arab Hall (1877–9), to the left of the entrance. Inspired by a Moorish palace in Palermo, it was originally conceived as a setting for Leighton's collection of Damascene and Isnik tiles, many given to him by the traveller Richard Burton.

Right: Kenwood House's ornate library.

Pampering

If sightseeing and shopping, late nights and just the general high-level hustle and bustle of London make you feel in need of pampering, there are plenty of places to find it. Indulgence doesn't come cheap, but it can be well worth it, especially with the range and quality that's on offer. Day spas and wellness centres have proved extremely popular with both women and men and as awareness of beauty treatments has improved, the options and quality out there has increased. Meanwhile, London's range of beauty shops offer the best of traditional and cutting-edge products.

Indulgence Industry

While spas have been popular as health-giving centres for the wealthy for centuries, the concept of spas and 'wellness centres' purely as forms of indulgence is relatively new and London, a very hectic city, has no shortage of them. With most of them selling gift vouchers, visits to day spas have become great presents. Prices vary, although none of them are cheap, but value packages are often available.

For those unable to for reasons of money or time to visit a spa, London's beauty product stores and perfumeries offer high-quality products at a range of prices.

Day Spas and Wellness Centres

Elemis Day Spa

2–3 Lancashire Court, Mayfair; tel: 020-7499 4995; www.elemis.com; Mon–Sat 9am–9pm, Sun 10am–6pm; tube: Bond Street; map p.150 C1
Massages in the soothing surroundings of Elemis include the Aroma Stone Therapy Massage and a Deep Tissue Muscle Massage. There's a

Above: the Thai Suite, Elemis.

variety of 'advanced anti-ageing' facials on offer as well.

Groom

49 Beauchamp Place, Knightsbridge; tel: 020-7581 1248; www.groomlondon.com; Tue–Wed, Fri 10am–7pm, Thur 11am–8pm, Sat 9am–6pm; tube: Knightsbridge; map p.156 C2
'One chair, two therapists' is Groom's claim, and that is what you get: one comfortable chair and two people pampering you at the same time during a 90-minute treatment package.

Ironmonger Row Baths

1–11 Ironmonger Row, The City; tel: 020-7253 4011; www.

aquaterra.org; Mon 2pm–9.30pm (mixed), Tue 9am–9.30pm (men), Wed 9am–9.30pm (women), Thur 9am–9.30pm (men), Fri 9am–9.30pm (women), Sat 9am–6.30pm (men), Sun 10am–6.30pm (women); tube: Old Street
These 1930s Turkish baths offer spa time on a budget; indulge in steam and hot rooms before a dip in the plunge pool and a treatment such as a Turkish body scrub.

The Porchester Spa

The Porchester Centre, Notting Hill; tel: 020-7792 3980; www.courtneys.co.uk; daily 10am–10pm (Tue,Thur, Fri, Sun until 4pm women only, Mon, Wed, Sat men only, Sun 4–10pm mixed); tube: Bayswater; map p.157 E4
This Grade II listed, recently-refurbished spa features treatments at budget prices in art deco surrounds. Facilities include steam and hot rooms, sauna and plunge pool.

The Refinery

60 Brook Street, Mayfair; tel: 020-7409 2001; www.the-refinery.com; Mon–Tue 10am–7pm, Wed–Fri 10am–8pm, Sat 9am–6pm, Sun 11am–5pm; tube: Bond Street; map p.150 B1

Left: a manicure at Groom.

Neal's Yard Remedies
15 Neal's Yard, Covent Garden; tel: 020-7379 7222; www.neal syardremedies.com; Mon–Wed, Sat 10am–7pm, Thur–Fri 10am–7.30pm, Sun 11am–6pm; tube: Covent Garden; map p.148 C4

Shop for organic wellness and beauty products at the original branch, which retains a hippyish air and friendly staff, who give advice on the various herbal remedies.

Penhaligon's
16–17 Burlington Arcade, Mayfair; tel: 020-7629 1416; www.penhaligons.co.uk; Mon–Wed, Fri 8am–6.30pm, Thur 8am–7pm, Sat 9am–6.30pm, Sun 11am–5pm; tube: Green Park; map p.148 A3

Perfumery founded in 1860, with a reputation for quality and service. Their stores (across London) offer an extensive range of scents and beauty products.

Space NK
8–10 Broadwick Street, Soho 8HW; tel: 020-7734 3734; www.spacenk.co.uk; Mon–Wed, Fri–Sat 10am–7pm, Thur 10am–8pm; tube: Oxford Circus, map p.148 B4

This cosmetics success story continues to sell cult beauty lines and ground-breaking skincare products; this store includes a separate men's department.

Many of London's top hotels boast fabulous spas in opulent surroundings and offer day membership. Some of the best are the **Dorchester Spa** (tel: 020-7319 7109; www.thedo rchester.com) and the **Spa at Mandarin Oriental** (tel: 020-7838 9888; www.mandarin oriental.com).

This men-only 'grooming emporium' bridges the gap between masculine barber's and health spa, with treatments and hairdressing available in a gentleman's club-style retreat.

The Sanctuary
12 Floral Street, Covent Garden; tel: 01442-430 330; www.the sanctuary.co.uk; Mon–Fri 9.30am–6pm, Sat–Sun 9.30am–8pm; tube: Covent Garden; map p.149 C4

The Sanctuary is an extremely popular women-only venue, offering day and half-day packages. The Atrium pool has a garlanded swing, while a proper 44ft (13.5m) pool caters to serious swimmers. Colour relaxation could be followed by visiting the steam room and sauna, or relaxing in the koi carp lounge. Many treatments and packages on offer, including massages and facials.

Urban Retreat
Harrods, 87–135 Brompton Road, Knightsbridge; tel: 020-7893 8333; harrods.urbanretreat.co.uk; daily 10am–9pm; tube: Knightsbridge; map p.154 A3

Urban Retreat, based in one of London's smartest stores, is an organisation that offers something for everyone: from a 15-minute eyebrow shaping or a 30-minute air-brush tan to hour-long sessions of numerology and intuitive healing. There are treatments for men as well as women.

Beauty Product Shops

D.R. Harris
29 St James's Street, St James's; tel: 020-7930 3915; www.drharris.co.uk; Mon–Fri 8.30am–6pm, Sat 9.30am–5pm; tube: Green Park; map p.148 A2

This pharmacy is one of the oldest in London and boasts two royal warrants. Inside the old-fashioned cabinets are a high-quality range of own-brand products, many made by traditional methods.

Below: upmarket Penhaligon's.

Parks and Gardens

London is fortunate in the number, size and beauty of its public parks and gardens. They vary from the landscaped and formal to the wooded and rural, but what they have in common is democracy; they are used by Londoners and visitors alike as places to relax, play and exercise. You can stumble on small neighbourhood green spots almost anywhere, used by office workers at lunchtime and children at the weekends. In the middle of an intense city, they provide a wonderful respite from the bustle.

Westminster and St James's

St James's Park
Tube: St James's Park; map p.148
This formal arrrangement of lakes and flowers is one of the most delightful in London. The land was acquired by Henry VIII to become a deer park in 1532, when he built St James's Palace, and it is the oldest royal park in London. The park as we see it today was designed by John Nash, at the end of the Napoleonic Wars in 1814. It has always had a collection of ducks and other water fowl, including

black swans, and there have long been pelicans in residence here. They are fed every day at 3pm. Lunchtime and early evening concerts are held in the bandstand in summer; and there's a café and restaurant at the northeast corner of the park.

Soho and Covent Garden

Victoria Embankment Gardens
Tube: Embankment; map p.149
Beside Embankment tube station, these gardens once marked the river entrance to York House, London home of the archbishops of York.

Today, despite their busy central location, they have a neighbourhood atmosphere and office workers sprawl on the grass with their sandwiches at the first hint of sun.

Oxford Street, Mayfair and Marylebone

Green Park
Tube: Green Park; map p.154
A wide green space, bordered by Piccadilly to the north, and almost joining St James's Park to the east, this is a well-used park and particularly pleasant in spring when it is bright with daffodils.

Regent's Park
Tube: Regent's Park; tube: Regent's Park, Great Portland Street, Baker Street; map p.150
An elegant 470-acre (190-hectare) space surrounded by John Nash's handsome Regency terraces. The gardens are formally planted, notably the roses in Queen Mary's Garden at the heart of the Inner Circle. In the Open Air Theatre, Shakespeare plays are put on in the sum-

Left: enjoying some sunshine in Hyde Park.

Left: the boating lake at Regent's Park.

route du roi (the King's path), which was en route to the royal hunting grounds; it is still used by well-heeled riders.

You can hire boats at the Serpentine Lake, the stretch of water that runs between Hyde Park and Kensington Gardens. On Christmas Day, dozens of people dive into the Serpentine Lake as part of an annual ritual. A bridge over the Serpentine, erected in 1826, gives fine views of Westminster Abbey and the Houses of Parliament.

Speakers' Corner, at the north-eastern corner of the park is lively on Sunday. Anybody can bring a soapbox and speak freely; the audience takes full advantage of their right to heckle them. This tradition goes back to the days when the Tyburn gallows stood here (1388–1783) and condemned felons were allowed to make a final unexpurgated speech. This corner of the park is also a starting or finishing point for many political demonstrations.

There is free music at bandstands in the park on summer Sundays, huge concerts are occasionally held here (including Live 8 and the now-demised Party in the Park) and the last night of the Proms is an annual event.
SEE ALSO SPORT, P.141

mer. The boating lake is a tranquil spot (rowing boats can be hired), and Regent's Canal runs through the north of the park. There is also an expanse of well-used playing fields. London Zoo lies at the north-eastern end of the park.
SEE ALSO CHILDREN, P.41

Kensington and Chelsea
Chelsea Physic Garden
66 Royal Hospital Road, entrance on Swan Walk; tel: 020-7352 5646; Apr–Oct Wed–Fri noon–5pm, Sun noon–6pm; admission charge; tube: Sloane Square
Founded in 1676 by Sir Hans Sloane for the study of medicinal plants, this 3.7-acre (1.5-hectare) garden is divided into four contrasting sections: a Garden of World Medicine, a Pharmaceutical Garden, and systematic ordered beds in the two southern quadrants. You will also find a pond rockery, History of Medicine beds, perfumery and aromatherapy borders, glasshouses and herb and vegetable gardens.
Holland Park
Tube: High Street Kensington, Holland Park; map p.157
A pleasant retreat, off Kens-

ington High Street, offering shady walks and attractive gardens. These are the grounds of the Jacobean Holland House, most of which was destroyed in World War II.

Peacocks screech and preen among the formal walled gardens. There is a restaurant in the beautiful Orangery and the ruins of the brick mansion provide one of the most appealing sets for open-air concerts and theatre in the city during the summer.
Hyde Park
Tube: Hyde Park Corner, Marble Arch, Knightsbridge; map p.154 A4
Only a few paces away from the most bustling parts of London lies this vast space, the largest central London park. There are lots of paths snaking through: the Ring or West Carriage Drive, which goes from Alexandra Gate at the top of Exhibition Road to Victoria Gate in Bayswater Road, officially divides Hyde Park from Kensington Gardens. South Carriage Drive runs from Hyde Park Corner to Alexandra Gate, and parallel to it is Rotten Row, originally

The Domesday Book of 1086 records that Hyde Park was inhabited by wild bulls and boars. It was first owned by the monks of Westminster Abbey, and after ecclesiastical property was confiscated in 1536 during the Reformation, Henry VIII turned it into a royal hunting ground. It was opened to the public in the 17th century.

Kensington Gardens
Tube: Lancaster Gate, High Street Kensington; map p.156 A4–C4

Kensington Gardens lie to the west of Hyde Park, and you can cross from one to the other without realising you are in a differently named park. On the south bank is a statue of J.M. Barrie's Peter Pan. In 1912, with the connivance of the local authorities, the statue was erected secretly one night so it might seem as if it had appeared by magic.

South of the statue is the Serpentine Art Gallery (daily 10am–6pm; www.serpentine gallery.org.uk; free); there is sculpture in the garden including Henry Moore's Arch.

The Princess Diana Memorial Fountain lies nearby, a circular ring of flowing water surrounding a landscaped area, designed by the Seattle-based architect Kathryn Gustafson.
SEE ALSO MONUMENTS, P.79; MUSEUMS AND GALLERIES, P.87

North London
Hampstead Heath
Tube: Hampstead, Gospel Oak, rail: Hampstead Heath

The 3 sq miles (8 sq km) Heath is a wooded, rural park which, particularly at weekends, is filled with Londoners treating it as their extended back garden. The sloping wilderness was the inspiration for C.S. Lewis's Narnia.

Parliament Hill gives splendid views across London on a clear day, as does the 111-acre (45-hectare) Primrose Hill overlooking Regent's Park to the south.

There are three swimming ponds: a mixed pond and segregated male and female ponds. The 'Ladies' Pond', in particular, surrounded by reeds and shady trees, has many passionate adherents. There is a lido at Gospel Oak.

At the north end of the park Kenwood House stands in lovely grounds, beside a lake.
SEE ALSO PALACES AND HOUSES, P.109; SPORT, P.141

Highgate Cemetary
Swain's Lane; tube: Archway, Highgate

In this quintessentially Gothic Victorian cemetery, dramatic tombs are artfully covered in creepers and set amidst wild flowers. One of the chief attractions is the stern bust of Karl Marx, who was buried in the eastern section in 1883. There are some 850 notable people buried here, among them the novelist George Eliot, Rosetti family members and the scientist Michael Faraday.

East London
Lee Valley Park
Tube: Leyton

This park stretches for 26 miles (42km) and 10,000 acres (4,048 hectares) on both sides of the River Lee, extending through East London and encompassing Tottenham Marshes. It boasts various nature reserves and many walking trails, as well as great activity facilities. These include stables, a pool, boat hire (rowboats, pedalos, canoes and motorboats) and angling. The Olympic velopark is being built here; in the meantime, the spaciousness makes it a great for cycling.

South London
Battersea Park
Rail: Battersea Park, Clapham Junction

This is a real neighbourhood park, well-used by local people. It's a great park for children, too, with ponds (boats can be hired) a small zoo, an adventure playgound and lots of open space, landscaped but not too fussy. There are also tennis courts, a small art gallery (The Pumphouse), and the Peace Pagoda, built in 1985 by Japanese Buddhist monks and nuns to commemorate Hiroshima Day.
SEE ALSO CHILDREN, P.40

Blackheath
Rail: Blackheath

The windy, wide-open heath is where Henry V was wel-

> There are many gardens in secluded squares all over London, to which only residents have a key and are allowed access. Many of these, along with other private gardens, open their gates to the public as part of the Open Gardens Weekend every June. You need to buy tickets (www.opensquares.org), and some of the most popular gardens get booked up early.

Left: the Treetop Walkway at the Royal Botanic Gardens.

9.30am–6.30pm, Sat–Sun
9.30am–7.30pm, Sept–Oct daily
9.30am–6pm, Nov–Jan daily
9.30am–4.15pm, Feb–Mar daily
9.30am–5.30pm; admission charge; tube/rail: Kew Gardens; boat: Kew Pier from Westminster
The 300-acre (120-hectare) botanic gardens at Kew are among the most extensive in the world. They were established in 1759 with the help of Joseph Banks, the botanist who named Botany Bay on Captain James Cook's first voyage to Australia. Other explorers and amateur enthusiasts added specimens over the centuries, making this a formidable repository and research centre.

The gardens feature magnificent Victorian greenhouses, including the Palm House and Waterlily House, Orangery, mock Chinese pagoda, and the 17th-century Kew Palace, built for a Dutch merchant and known until 1827 as the Dutch House. Two small art galleries focus on horticulture. The glasshouses are especially lovely on a cold winter's day.

Wimbledon Common
Tube/rail: Wimbledon, then bus: 93
A great stretch of partly wooded land (synonymous for some with the Wombles and their progressive eco-vision), Wimbledon Common feels as close to countryside as it gets in London. There are lots of paths and bridle ways to ramble on and a museum inside the old Windmill.

Nearby Cannizaro Park (free; daily 8am–dusk), the gardens of a neighbouring mansion now housing a hotel, is also a lovely place to visit, with small slopes, wooded gardens and spaces where plays and summer events are held.

comed home after beating the French at Agincourt in 1415, and it was here that James I introduced the Scottish game of golf to England in 1608. It is said that the name is derived from 'Bleak Heath' and on a gusty day this can be understandable, but it is a well-used public space, the starting point of the London Marathon and popular with kite-flyers.

West London
London Wetland Centre
Queen Elizabeth Walk, Barnes; tel: 020-8409 4400; www.wwt.org.uk; Mar–Oct daily 9.30am–6pm, Nov–Feb daily 9.30am–5pm; admission charge; tube: Hammersmith, then bus: 283, or rail: Barnes, then bus: 33, 72
A marshy piece of land transformed into a wildlife centre by naturalist Sir Peter Scott, who died shortly afterwards, in 1989. Birds, butterflies, dragonflies, trees both rare and common, and thousands of aquatic plants offer something to delight any outdoor enthusiast, and enough to keep children interested, too.
Richmond Park
Tube/rail: Richmond, then bus: 65, 371 to Richmond Gate, or

rail: Mortlake (Sheen Gate)
The park was once a royal hunting ground, but today around 650 red and fallow deer graze in peace. They enjoy the bracken thickets and gather beneath the dappled canopies of huge oaks. At 2,470 acres (1,000 hectares), this is the largest of the Royal London parks and has extensive facilities for horse riders, cricketers, golfers and footballers. Adam's Pond is used to sail model boats, and Pen Ponds are reserved for anglers. From the higher points, it is possible to see clearly to St Paul's Cathedral, 9 miles (15km) away.

Taking a break from rambling or off-road cycling, Pembroke Lodge, the childhood home of philosopher Bertrand Russell, has a charming, old-fashioned café with splendid views over the Thames Valley.

The Isabella Plantation within the park (dawn–dusk) is spectacular in spring and early summer when the rhododendrons and azaleas are flowering, but pleasant at any time, with streams and bog gardens, and meandering paths.
Royal Botanic Gardens
Kew; tel: 020-8332 5644; www.kew.org; Apr–Aug Mon–Fri

Pubs and Bars

L ondon is known for its traditional pubs, and many of these still exist, oak-panelled and cosy, and proud of the quality of their draught beer. Many, however, have been transformed into 'gastropubs'; they've knocked down walls, made light open spaces and now concentrate as much on food as on drinks, encouraged by the 2007 smoking ban. Alongside these is a plethora of bars, some loud, some glitzy, catering to all drinking tastes. Whatever your opinion of Britain's drinking culture, there's no denying that pubs and bars are the scene of much of London's recreation and the multiple options reflect this.

Westminster and St James's

5th View
5th Floor, Waterstone's, 203–206 Piccadilly; tel: 020-7851 2433; www.5thview.co.uk; Mon–Sat 9am–9.30pm, Sun noon–5pm; tube: Piccadilly Circus; map p.148 B3
For truly fabulous views while enjoying a drink, the cocktail lounge atop Waterstone's flagship bookstore is hard to beat. Several wines by the glass and a large international beer selection in addtition to the cocktails.

Albannach
66 Trafalgar Square; tel: 020-7930 0066; www.albannach.co.uk; Mon–Sat noon–1am; tube: Charing Cross; map p.148 C3
Fantastic views over Trafalgar Square and a huge choice of single malt whiskies and whiskey-based cocktails, accompanied by Scottish-themed decor.

ICA Bar
The Mall; tel: 020-7930 8619; www.ica.org.uk; Mon–Wed noon–11pm, Thur–Sat noon–1am, Sun noon–9pm; tube: Charing Cross; map p.148 B2

The ICA's bar is understatedly cool and gives off the vibe of a grown-up student canteen, quite trendy but also relaxed. It is a pleasant place to stop off for a drink or meal; the cocktails and wine are pretty decent.

Soho and Covent Garden

Cork & Bottle
44 Cranbourn Street; tel: 020-7734 7807; www.corkandbottle.net; Mon–Sat 11am–midnight, Sun noon–11pm; tube: Leicester Square; map p.148 C3
Owner Don Hewitson is rightly proud of this appealing basement wine bar. Wide range of well-chosen wines. Food available at lunch, dinner and in-between, including after-theatre meals.

Floridita
100 Wardour Street; tel: 020-7314 4000; www.floridita.co.uk/london; Tue–Wed 5.30pm–2am, Thur–Sat 5.30pm–3am; tube: Piccadilly Circus; map p.148 B4
Hugely lively spot where the music is great, the cocktails imaginative and there's a good Cuban-style menu served until 2am.

For a more sophisticated and often quieter drink than can be had in many of London's bars, try a hotel bar. **Artesian** (tel: 020-7636 1000; www.artesian-bar.co.uk) at the Langham is expensive but incredibly stylish, while the **Blue Bar** (tel: 020-7235 6000; www.the-berkeley.co.uk) at the Berkeley is highly fashionable.

Glass
9 Glasshouse Street; tel: 020-7439 7770; www.paperclublondon.com/GLASS; Mon–Fri 5–11pm, Sat 7pm–1am; tube: Piccadilly Circus; map p.148 B3
Glamourous cocktail bar, decorated stylishly in shiny monochrome and offering a sophisticated list of cocktails.

Gordon's
47 Villiers Street; tel: 020-7930 1408; www.gordonswinebar.com; Mon–Sat 11am–11pm, Sun noon–10pm; tube: Embankment, Charing Cross; map p.149 C2
Always packed out, this subterranean wine bar dates from 1890 and is chock full of atmosphere. If you can find a table in one of the dimly-lit alcoves, sample the wine,

Left: a crowded beer garden on a sunny day in east London.

cocktails. The bar is named after photographer Terence Donovan; the walls are adorned with black-and-white photos (including some rather risqué ones in the 'naughty corner', and the signature cocktail is the Box Brownie. Live jazz is performed Mon–Sat.

Ye Grapes
16 Shepherd Market; tel: 020-7499 1563; Mon–Sat 11am–11pm, Sun 11am–10.30pm; tube: Green Park; map p.154 B4
A pub with a villagey-feel, decorated with stuffed birds and, of course, carved bunches of grapes. Decently-priced Thai food is on the menu.

Kensington and Chelsea

190 Queensgate
Gore Hotel, 190 Queensgate; tel: 020-7584 6601; Mon–Wed, Sun noon–1am, Thur–Sat noon–2am; tube: Gloucester Road; map p.156 A3
This wood-panelled bar on the ground floor of the Gore Hotel has a wide range of cocktails and excellent food,

Below: some cocktails are almost works of art.

port and sherry lists, maybe with a plate of cheeses.

LAB
12 Old Compton Street; tel: 020-7437 7820; www.lab-townhouse.com; Mon–Thur 4pm–midnight, Fri–Sat 4pm–12.30am, Sun 4–11pm; tube: Leicester Square; map p.148 B4
Seventies decor, loud music, an extensive range of reasonably priced cocktails, bar snacks and a young clientele.

Lamb & Flag
33 Rose Street; tel: 020-7497 9504; Mon–Sat 11am–11pm, Sun noon–10.30pm; tube: Covent Garden; map p.149 C3
Much loved 300-year-old traditional pub that specialises in a variety of beers. Food is basic and substantial.

The Langley
5 Langley Street; tel: 020-7836 5005; www.thelangley.co.uk; Mon–Sat 4.30pm–1am, Sun 4.30–midnight; tube: Covent Garden; map p.149 C4
Try a cocktail at this retro-styled underground bar and lounge, with exposed brick walls and colourful graphic details. Bar food is available and DJs (Wed–Sat) keep the atmosphere clubby and lively.

Oxford Street, Mayfair and Marylebone

Coach & Horses
5 Bruton Street; tel: 020-7629 4123; Mon–Sat 11am–11pm, Sun 11am–10.30pm; tube: Green Park; map p.150 C1
Set in an attractive timbered building with verdant window boxes, this pub has lots of character but the small size means it gets quite crowded.

Coco Momo
79 Marylebone High Street; tel: 020-7486 5746; www.coco momo.co.uk; Mon–Thur 10am–11pm, Fri 10am–midnight, Sat 9am–midnight, Sun 9am–10.30pm; tube: Baker Street; map p.150 B3
Pretty, upbeat gastro-bar with of plenty of window seating and an extensive wine list. The lunch menu offers good value, and brunch with newspapers and a Bloody Mary is a popular at the weekend.

Donovan Bar
Brown's Hotel; tel: 020-7493 6020; www.brownshotel.com; Mon–Sat 11am–1am, Sun noon–midnight; tube: Green Park; map p.148 A3
Stained glass, black leather and excellent, if expensive,

ing a good selection of beers as well as inexpensive, classic pub grub.

Bar Polski
11 Little Turnstile; tel: 020-7831 9679; Mon 4–11.30pm, Tue–Thur 12.30–11pm, Fri 12.30–11.30pm, Sat 6–11.30pm; tube: Holborn; map p.151 E2

This tucked-away bar is a real find, with an airy atmosphere, vast list of vodkas (intended to be browsed, tapas-style) and authentic Polish food to keep the stomach lined.

Fitzroy Tavern
16 Charlotte Street; tel: 020-7580 3714; Mon–Sat 11am–11pm, Sun noon–10.30pm; tube: Goodge Street; map p.151 D3

George Orwell and Dylan Thomas were once regulars at this Victorian pub which gave its name to the surrounding area. It's been taken over by a brewery chain but still has a pleasant atmosphere as well as outside tables for warm days.

The Lamb
94 Lamb's Conduit Street; tel: 020-7405 0713; Mon–Sat 11.30am–midnight, Sun noon–10.30pm; tube: Holborn; map p.151 E3

Founded in the early 18th century, but mostly Victorian in style, The Lamb is known for its 'snob screens', panels of etched glass once used to conceal a drinker's identity. Serves excellent meaty food, is praised for the quality of its Young's beer, and makes a point of having no piped background music.

Princess Louise
208–209 High Holborn; tel: 020-7405 8816; Mon–Fri 11am–11pm, Sat noon–11pm, Sun noon–10.30pm; tube: Holborn; map p.151 E2

The food is good pub fare at

and it's very handy for a post- or pre-concert drink when going to the Royal Albert Hall.

Admiral Codrington
17 Mossop Street; tel: 020-7581 0005; www.theadmiralcodrington.co.uk; Mon–Thur 11.30am–midnight, Fri–Sat 11.30–1am, Sun noon–10.30pm; tube: South Kensington; map p.156 C2

'The Cod' has been around for a long time, but has been re-invented as a gastropub and serves good modern British cuisine as well as traditional bar food.

Cross Keys
1 Lawrence Street; tel: 020-7349 9111; www.thexkeys.co.uk; Mon–Sat noon–3pm, 7–11pm; Sun noon–4pm, 7–10.30pm; tube: Sloane Square, then bus: 11, 22

In the heart of Chelsea, this fine gastropub has a colourful and decorative main bar, with two open fireplaces, a cheerful conservatory and some

good draught beers and real ales on offer, alongside the substantial wine list.

Piano
106 Kensington High Street; tel: 020-7938 4664; www.pianokensington.com; Tue–Sun noon–midnight; tube: High Street Kensington; map p.157 E1

Pianist Bazz Norton plays popular music at this cosy bar with suitably moody lighting but merry clientele. The wine and cocktail list is extensive and the music makes this small spot great fun; it's advisable to book a table.

Bloomsbury and Holborn

Angel
61 St Giles High Street; tel: 020-7240 2876; Mon–Fri 11.30am–11pm, Sat noon–11pm, Sun 1–10.30pm; tube: Tottenham Court Road; map p.151 D2

Highly traditional pub in both decor and profferings, serv-

For those who like to combine their drinking with something more active, these Bloomsbury venues have revived bowling in London in a glamourous way, **All Star Lanes** (Victoria House, Bloomsbury Place; tel: 020-7025 2676; www.allstarlanes.co.uk) and **Bloomsbury Bowling** (Basement, Tavistock Hotel, Bedford Way; tel: 020-7691 2610; www.bloomsburylive.com) have smart cocktails on tap and good menus.

this splendidly decorated Victorian pub, which was fitted out by the master craftsmen of its day with fine mirrors and ornate plasterwork.

Seven Stars
53 Carey Street; tel: 020-7242 8521; Mon–Fri 11am–11pm, Sat noon–11pm, Sun noon–10.30pm; tube: Holborn, Chancery Lane; map p.152 A2
A great little place, tucked away in a narrow street at the side of the Law Courts. Good wholesome food, well-chosen beer and wine, and a friendly atmosphere. The walls are decorated with posters of old British films with a legal background.

Ye Old Mitre
1 Ely Court, by 8 Hatton Garden; tel: 020-7405 4751; Mon–Fri 11am–11pm; tube: Chancery lane, Farringdon; map p.152 B3
Tucked away in an alley this quaint little pub dates from the 16th century. There's a wide range of draught beers, traditional pub food, and the service is friendly.

The City

Bleeding Heart Tavern
Bleeding Heart Yard, Greville Street; tel: 020-7242 8238; www.bleedingheart.co.uk/tavern; Mon–Fri 7am–11.30pm;

tube: Farringdon; map p.152 B3
The Bleeding Heart has an extensive wine list and serves excellent, traditional British food. Tables in an outside courtyard are a pleasant place to sit in fine weather.

Jerusalem Tavern
55 Britton Street; tel: 020-7490 4281; www.stpetersbrewery.co.uk; Mon–Fri 11am–11pm; tube: Farringdon; map p.152 B4
There's a great selection of beers in this cosy little pub. The building dates from 1720, the frontage from 1810 and it is furnished in Georgian style. Mixed clientele and a good atmosphere.

Ten Bells
84 Commercial Street; tel: 020-7366 1721; Mon–Thur, Sun noon–midnight, Fri–Sat noon–1am; tube: Liverpool Street; map p.153 E3
Popular with both trendy kids and those intrigued by Jack the Ripper (the pub is thought to be where he met at least one of his victims), this Victoriana pub successfully trades on its gas-lit past.

South Bank and Bankside

Boot & Flogger
10-20 Redcross Way; tel: 020-7407 1184; Mon–Fri

11am–8pm; tube: London Bridge; map p.153 C1
This wood-panelled wine bar is a truly unique spot, and one where they really know their drinks. Quirkily old fashioned, with gentlemen's club-style leather armchairs and sawdust on the floor, the welcoming staff encourage you to relax. The food menu includes a range of light bites, such as the popular potted shrimps.

Cubana
48 Lower Marsh; tel: 020-7928 8778; www.cubana.co.uk; Mon–Tue noon–midnight, Wed–Thur noon–1am, Fri noon–3am, Sat 5pm–1am; tube: Waterloo; map p.149 E1
Always busy, Cubana is proud of its heritage and has a reputation for excellent mojitos and Cuban-style dishes. It's noisy and friendly and there's late-night salsa from Wed–Sat.

The George Inn
77 Borough High Street; tel: 020-7407 2056; Mon–Sat 11am–11pm, Sun noon–10.30pm; tube: London Bridge; map p.153 D1
This attractive, galleried building (which now belongs to the National Trust) was a 17th-century coaching inn and was mentioned by Charles Dickens in *Little Dorrit*. There are

Right: the George Inn is full of London history.

119

open fires in winter and lots of wooden benches out in the large courtyard, which fill up when the weather is warm.

The Market Porter
9 Stoney Street; tel: 020-7407 2495; www.markettaverns. co.uk/The-Market-Porter; Mon–Fri 6–8.30am, 11am–11pm, Sat noon–11pm, Sun noon–10.30pm; tube: London Bridge; map p.153 D1
Wood-panelled and rustic in decor, this pub does cater to porters from Borough Market (hence the breakfast-time opening hours), but its clientele also includes post-work office staff, so the road outside often resembles a street party. The real ale selection is particularly renowned.

Wine Wharf
Stoney Street; tel: 020-7940 8335; www.winewharf.com; Mon–Sat noon–11pm; tube: London Bridge; map p.153 C1
Part of the Vinopolis complex, the Wine Wharf offers a huge selection of wines from all over the world, many by the glass, and food to go with them. It's a cavernous place, with bare brick walls and comfy leather sofas.

On 1st July 2007, all London's bars and pubs, along with other public enclosed spaces, became subject to a smoking ban. Defying the ban can now lead to a £50 fine.

North London

Holly Bush
22 Holly Mount, Hampstead; tel: 020-7435 2892; www.hollybush pub.com; Mon–Sat noon–11pm, Sun noon–10.30pm; tube: Hampstead
This friendly pub has been a hostelry since the early 19th century. It's an unpretentious place, with oak floors, painted settles, and an open fire. It serves a variety of good draught beers.

Lockside Lounge
75–89 West Yard, Camden Lock Place; tel: 020-7284 0007; www.locksidelounge.com; Sun–Thur noon–midnight, Fri–Sat noon–1am; tube: Camden Town
Artwork on the walls and a trendy Camden vibe at this converted boat house, which boasts a fantastic deck overlooking the market and regular barbeques in the summer.

Narrow Boat
119 St Peter Street, Islington; tel: 020-7288 0572; Mon–Sat 11am–midnight, Sun noon–10.30pm; tube: Angel
Full-length windows provide fantastic views over the Regent's Canal and the interior is comfortable for enjoying a drink from the good wine list or a choice of ales.

Spaniards Inn
Spaniards Road, Hampstead Heath; tel: 020-8731 6571; Mon–Fri 11am–11pm, Sat–Sun 10am–11pm; tube: Hampstead, then bus: 210
This pretty, weatherboarded pub, with many real ales on tap, is famous and busy. The pub's age and its low ceilings and creaky floors make it easy to believe the story that highwayman Dick Turpin's ghost haunts the place. Ideal for a stopping point during a walk on the heath.

East London

Camel
277 Globe Road, Bethnal Green; tel: 020-8983 9888; www.thecamele2.co.uk; Mon–Wed 4–11pm, Fri–Sat noon–11pm, Sun noon–10.30pm; tube: Bethnal Green
A real old East End pub serving gastropub food. Its brown-tiled exterior is unchanged, though its interior has been well renovated. Serves real ales and a range of well-priced wine by the glass, and is known locally for its excellent pies.

Hoxton Square Bar & Kitchen
2–4 Hoxton Square, Shoreditch; tel: 020-7613 0709; www.hox tonsquarebar.com; Mon 11am–midnight, Tue–Thur 11am–1am, Fri–Sat 11am–2am, Sun 11am–12.30am; tube: Old Street
Three bars, a restaurant and a club room make up this very popular Hoxton stalwart,

Below: live music at the Hoxton Square Bar & Kitchen.

a good start to a night out in the area. A wide selection of bottled beers, draught lager and cocktails can be enjoyed lounging on the sofas, but arrive early as it gets busy. The food – burgers, salads, hangover-soothing brunches – is very good.

LoungeLover

1 Whitby Street, Shoreditch; tel: 020-7012 1234; www.loun gelover.co.uk; Tue–Thur 6pm– midnight, Fri 6pm–1am, Sat 7pm–1am, Sun 6–10.30pm; tube: Liverpool Street; map p.153 E4

Tucked away in Shoreditch this swanky bar is unexpected. Exotic, eclectic decor and expensive cocktails; there is a limit on numbers, which does mean it doesn't get overcrowded, but means that it's advisable to book a table ahead of going.

Prospect of Whitby

57 Wapping Wall, Wapping; tel: 020-7481 1095; Mon–Wed, Sun noon–11pm, Thur–Sat noon–midnight; DLR: Shadwell

This has been a pub since the 16th century, and its stone floors and beamed ceilings look pretty much unchanged. You can drink good beer while you drink in the history, but it is likely to be packed.

South London

Bar Estrela

111–115 South Lambeth Road, Stockwell; tel: 020-7793 1051; Mon–Sat 8am–midnight, Sun 10am–11pm; tube: Stockwell, Vauxhall

Hugely popular bar in the 'Little Portugal' area, serving authentic Portuguese beers and food to a lively crowd.

Effra

38A Kellet Road, Brixton; tel: 020-7274 4180; daily 3–11pm; tube: Brixton

A laid-back atmosphere in a long-standing venue, and live music – jazz and reggae –

most evenings. The food is mainly Afro-Caribbean.

Holy Drinker

59 Northcote Road, Battersea; tel: 020-7801 0544; www.holy drinker.co.uk; Mon–Wed 4.30– 11pm, Thur–Fri 4.30pm–mid-night, Sat noon–midnight, Sun 1–11pm; rail: Clapham Junction

Relaxed bar near Clapham Common, perfect for a chilled afternoon drink or a buzzy night with the Battersea locals.

Lost Society

697 Wandsworth Road; tel: 020-7652 6526; www.lostsociety.co.uk; Tue–Thur 5pm–1am, Fri 4pm–2am, Sat 11–2pm, Sun 11am–1pm; tube: Clapham Common

Decadent bar, spread over several rooms featuring luxurious decor and glamourous twentysomethings dancing and getting stuck into the top-notch cocktails.

West London

Crooked Billet

14–15 Crooked Billet, Wimble-don; tel: 020-8946 4942; Mon–Sat 11am–11pm, Sun noon–10.30pm; tube: Wimbledon, then bus: 93, 200, 493

At the west side of Wimbledon Village is this charming, old pub. Choices from the good wine and beer lists can be enjoyed in front of the open fire in winter, or lolling on the green outside in summer.

The Elbow Room

103 Westbourne Grove, Notting Hill; tel: 020-7221 5211; www.theelbowroom.co.uk; Mon–Sat noon–11pm, Sun noon–10.30pm; tube: Bayswa-ter; map p.157 E4

With loads of pool tables as well as good burgers and list of beers, this American-style bar attracts a pleasantly mixed crowd.

Sun Inn

7 Church Road, Barnes; tel: 020-8876 5256; Mon–Wed, Sun 11am–11pm, Thur–Sat

Above: Ye White Hart, by the river in Barnes.

11am–midnight; rail: Barnes Bridge

Embodying the affluent-village feel of Barnes is this cosy pub in a picturesque spot right by the green and pond. Belgian and real ales are on tap and the food is standard decent pub fare.

Trailer Happiness

177 Portobello Road, Notting Hill; tel: 020-7727 2700; www.trailerhappiness.com; Tue–Fri 5–11pm, Sat 7–11pm, Sun 6–10.30pm; tube: Ladbroke Grove; map p.157 C4

Retro, tongue-in-cheek chic at this tiny basement spot that seems to take its design from a 1960s bachelor pad. Good cocktails and bar food (known as 'TV dinners') in a fun atmosphere.

Ye White Hart

The Terrace, Riverside, Barnes; tel: 020-8876 5177; daily 11am–midnight; rail: Barnes Bridge

The wooden deck is the perfect spot for watching the Boat Race (see p.141) or lounging in the sun, but this old, relaxed pub is a great spot all year round, with a blazing fire in the winter, Young's ales on tap and a great wine selection.

Restaurants

London has become a gastronomic paradise in recent years. Thanks to London's diverse, international populace, the choice is vast and every cuisine imaginable is on offer. At the top end of the range there are some world-class restaurants, charging commensurately high prices; at the lower end, there are places that offer very good value without compromising on the food. With such a vibrant and competitive restaurant scene, you shouldn't ever go hungry. Gastropubs are included in this section, where they are more focussed on food than drinking; see also *Pubs and Bars, p.116*, for more options.

Westminster and St James's

The Cinnamon Club
Old Westminster Library, 30–32 Great Smith Street; tel: 020-7222 2555; www.cinnamonclub.com; Mon–Fri 7.30–9.30am, Mon–Sat noon–2.45pm, 6–10.45pm; ££; tube: Westminster; map p.155 D3
The Cinnamon Club is set in a beautifully refurbished Victorian library full of light and space. The modern Indian, haute-cuisine menu offers a fine selection of specialities, from wild African prawns to rump of water buffalo, with good vegetarian options.

Soho and Covent Garden

Andrew Edmunds
46 Lexington Street; tel: 020-7437 5708; Mon–Fri 12.30–3pm, Sat 1–3pm, Sun 1–3.30pm, daily 6–10.45pm (Sun until 10.30pm); ££; tube:

Prices for an average three course meal per person, with half a bottle of house wine:
££££	over £50
£££	£30–50
££	£20–30
£	under £20

Piccadilly Circus; map p.148 B4
A lack of signage gives an anonymous secretive feel to this romantic hideaway. Soft candlelight and wood panelling make it cosy and intimate. Dishes are European and simple but varied, ranging from beef to well-presented pasta. The staff are relaxed and friendly.

Asia de Cuba
St Martin's Lane Hotel, 45 St Martin's Lane; tel: 020-7300 5588; www.chinagrillmgt.com; daily noon–2pm, 5pm–midnight (Sun until 10pm); ££££; tube: Charing Cross; map p.148 C3
Expensive and a touch pretentious, but it does have interesting and beautifully cooked food. The decor is eccentric, with shelves laden with old radios and books, lit by low-slung naked light bulbs. The fusion menu is imaginative, and sharing is encouraged so that you get to sample more. Leave room for dessert. Reservations necessary.

Café Emm
17 Frith Street; tel: 020-7437 0723; www.cafeemm.com; Mon–Fri noon–3pm, 5.30–11.30pm, Sat noon–11.30pm,

It is becoming increasingly common for a 'service charge' of between 10 and 15 percent to be added to your bill before you receive it. This is, in effect, a tip and if the service has been bad, or even if not, you are quite within your rights not to pay it. Also note that you are not expected to pay a tip in addition to the service charge. Where no extra charge is mentioned it is customary to leave a tip of about 10–12 percent of the total bill.

Sun noon–10.30pm; £; tube: Leicester Square; map p. 148 B4
Buzzy, intimate and exceptionally good value, Café Emm is packed every night. Portions are always large, but well cooked, from calamari and salmon fish cakes to lamb shank with ratatouille and creamy mash. Be prepared to queue, and for boisterous birthday parties.

Food for Thought
31 Neal Street; tel: 020-7836 0239; Mon–Sat noon–8pm, Sun noon–5pm; £; tube: Covent Garden; map p.149 C4
An imaginative selection of

Left: casual and convivial dining at Ottolenghi.

A small, intimate restaurant with a lovely atmosphere. Friendly and unobtrusive staff serve impeccably sourced and creative French dishes, such as monkfish and black pudding mash. The wine list is also quirky and exotic. Thoroughly recommended for a slow-paced romantic meal.

L'Escargot
48 Greek Street; tel: 020-7439 7474; www.whitestarline.org.uk; Mon–Fri noon–2.15pm, Mon–Sat 6–11.30pm; ££££; tube: Leicester Square; map p.148 B4
The grand-père of French restaurants in London, L'Escargot is steeped in history with its 1920s Art Deco interior and priceless artworks. Now part of the culinary brand of Marco Pierre White, it offers a choice of à la carte and set menus (both, of course, featuring snails).

Masala Zone
9 Marshall Street; tel: 020-7287 9966; www.realindianfood.com; Mon–Fri noon–3.30pm, 5.30–11pm, Sat 12.30–11pm, Sun 12.30–3.30pm, 5–10.30pm; £; tube: Oxford Circus; map p.148 A4
Masala Zone serves an authentic thali ('tray', which comes with a number of indi-

generous, affordable vegetarian dishes. Tom yam soup might be followed by gnocchi gorgonzola with garlic roasted chestnut and oyster mushrooms. BYOB (no corkage). No credit cards and no reservations.

Gay Hussar
2 Greek Street; tel: 020-7437 0973; www.gayhussar.co.uk; Mon–Sat 12.15–2.30pm, 5.30–10.45pm; ££; tube: Leicester Square; map p.148 B4
A classic London restaurant, the Gay Hussar has a long history of political intrigue and pays tribute to its Westminster village diners with a gallery of caricatures. In polished, gentleman's club surroundings, you can treat yourself to a mix of traditional hearty British and Hungarian dishes. Pork and potatoes are prominent.

The Ivy
1–5 West Street; tel: 020-7836 4751; www.theivy.co.uk; Mon–Sat noon–3pm, 5.30–midnight, Sun noon–3.30pm, 5.30–11pm; £££; tube: Covent Garden; map p.148 C4
One of London's most famous haunts, yet it is surprisingly

unaffected. The downside is the difficulty in getting a table: you need to reserve weeks rather than days ahead. The menu is comfortingly familiar (British interjected with international favourites), the wine list strong and the star-spotting irresistible.

J Sheekey
28–32 St Martin's Court; tel: 020-7240 2565; www.j-sheekey.co.uk; Mon–Sat noon–3pm, 5.30pm–midnight, Sun noon–3.30pm, 6–11pm; ££££; tube: Leicester Square; map p.148 C3
Sister restaurant to The Ivy and Caprice, J Sheekey is set in a series of panelled rooms hung with black and white theatre prints, and is a paradise for fish lovers. Think chargrilled squid with gorgonzola polenta, Cornish fish stew and New England baby lobster, followed by Scandinavian iced berries with white chocolate sauce. Reservations necessary.

La Trouvaille
12a Newburgh Street; tel: 020-7287 8488; www.latrouvaille.co.uk; daily 6–11pm; £££; tube: Oxford Circus; map p.148 A4

Below: specials at the well-priced Café Emm.

Prices for an average three course meal per person, with half a bottle of house wine:	
££££	over £50
£££	£30–50
££	£20–30
£	under £20

vidual curries, dal and rice). The funky decor was created by artists from Central India. It can get very busy and staff may not be as attentive as you might wish. (Also at 80 Upper Street.)

Mr Kong
21 Lisle Street; tel: 020-7437 7341; www.mrkongrestaurant. com; Mon–Sat noon–2.45am, Sun noon–1.45am; ££; tube: Leicester Square; map p.148 B3
With 100 seats ranging over three floors, Mr Kong is one of the more authentic (and claustrophobic) Chinese restaurants in the area. Dishes include Kon Chi baby squid with chilli sauce or sandstorm crab. There's a lively vegetarian selection too, including fried mock pork with fresh mango.

National Dining Rooms
Sainsbury Wing, National Gallery, Trafalgar Square; tel: 020-7747 2525; www.thenationaldin ingrooms.co.uk; daily 10am–3pm, Fri 5–9pm; ££–£££; tube: Charing Cross; map p.148 C3
Excellent English food served in a large, light space. Typical dishes might be watercress, dandelion and potato salad, followed by roast loin of Suffolk lamb with purple sprouting broccoli and treacle tart.

Randall & Aubin
16 Brewer Street; tel: 020-7287 4447; www.randallandaubin. com; Mon–Sat noon–11pm, Sun 4–10pm; £££; tube: Piccadilly Circus; map p.148 B3
Named after the old deli-

catessen that inhabited this spot for 90 years, French-accented Randall & Aubin has inherited a feeling of shopping bustle. Piles of lobster, crabs and oysters greet you as you enter.

Rules
35 Maiden Lane; tel: 020-7836 5314; www.rules.co.uk; daily noon–11.30pm (Sun until 10.30pm); ££££; tube: Covent Garden; map p.149 C3
London's oldest restaurant, established 1798. The decor reflects its heritage: floor-to-ceiling prints, gently revolving fans, chandeliers and red-velvet booths. The robust cuisine has stood the test of time and ingredients remain quintessentially English, with beef, lamb and game from Rules' own estate in the Pennines. Reservations advisable.

Simpson's-in-the-Strand
100 The Strand; tel: 020-7836 9112; www.simpsonsinthes trand.co.uk; Mon–Fri 7.15–10.30am, Mon–Sat 12.15–2.45pm, 5.45–10.45pm, Sun 12.15–3pm, 6–9pm; ££££; tube: Charing Cross; map p.149 D3
Recently refurbished, this bastion of Britishness combines the grandeur of bygone days – gleaming chandeliers, oak-panelled booths and tail-coated waiters – with a relaxed atmosphere. The menu is traditional (calves liver, Dover sole) but for many

the trademark roast beef, wheeled in on a silver-domed carving trolley, is the only choice. Reservations advised.

Souk
27 Litchfield Street; tel: 020-7240 1796; www.soukrestau rant.net; daily noon–11.30pm (Fri–Sat until 2am); ££; tube: Leicester Square; map p.148 C4
Small candlelit rooms with low seats and cushions set around brass tables. Cramped but decidedly atmospheric, it's the perfect setting for a Moroccan feast. The menu offers the usual mezze starters, with a selection of couscous and tagine dishes to follow. Belly-dancing on most nights. Reservations advisable.

Stockpot
18 Old Compton Street; tel: 020-7287 1066; Mon–Tues 9am–11.30pm, Wed–Sat 9am–midnight, Sun noon–11.30pm; £; tube: Leicester Square; map p.148 B4
'The Pot' has been going for years, serving reliably good meals at extremely low prices. A variety of pasta and meat dishes, good salads, satisfying puddings and possibly the lowest-priced house wine in London. (Also at 273 King's Road and 40 Panton Street.)

Zilli Fish
36–40 Brewer Street; tel: 020-7734 8649; www.zillialdo.com; Mon–Sat noon–11.30pm; £££;

Right: service at the Gay Hussar and Zilli Fish.

Left: sweet treats at Cecconi's.

Gordon Ramsay at Claridge's

Claridge's Hotel, Brook Street; tel: 020-7499 0099; www.gordonramsey.com; Mon–Fri noon–2.45pm, 5.45–11pm, Sat noon–3pm, 5.45–11pm, Sun noon–3pm, 6–10.30pm; ££££; tube: Bond Street; map p.150 B1
Ramsay is London's most fêted chef and tables are hard to come by in this gorgeous dining room. Working under Ramsay's supervision, Mark Sargeant cooks dreamy rich, intricate dishes. A superb wine list and pampering service all add up to a memorable experience. Set lunch is a relative bargain. Booking essential.

Greens Restaurant and Oyster Bar

36 Duke Street; tel: 020-7930 4566; www.greens.org.uk; Mon–Sat 11.30am–3pm, 5.30–11pm; ££££; tube: Green Park; map p.148 A2
Clubby Mayfair stalwart and a favourite of the old school. Fabulous traditional British dishes, from potted shrimps to lemon sole with perfect hollandaise. The cheeseboard is supplied by nearby Paxton & Whitfield.

The Guinea Grill

30 Bruton Place; tel: 020-7409 1728; www.theguinea.co.uk; Mon–Fri 12.30–3pm, 6–10.30pm, Sat 6–10.30pm; £££; tube: Piccadilly; map p.150 C1
Old-world, wood-panelled pub

tube: Piccadilly; map p.148 B3
This Italian accented fish restaurant is part of a mini-Zilli empire in Soho. Try the lobster spaghetti or salmon stuffed with spinach, both fresh and delicate. Banana spring rolls with chocolate sauce are divine. Booking advisable.

Oxford Street, Mayfair and Marylebone

Cecconi's

5a Burlington Gardens; tel: 020-7434 1500; www.cecconis.co.uk; Mon–Fri 7–1am, Sat 8–1am, Sun 8am–midnight; £££; tube: Green Park; map p.148 A3
Sophisticated Italian, with a menu of classic regional gems, which attracts an impeccably dressed, lively crowd. Chef Stephen Terry's specialities include salt duck breast with raisins, pine nuts and sweet and sour pumpkin. A formidable wine list.

China Tang

The Dorchester, 53 Park Lane; tel: 020-7629 9988; www.thedorchester.com; Mon–Fri

11am–3.30pm, 5.30pm–midnight, Sat–Sun 11am–4pm, 5.30pm–midnight; ££££; map p.154 B4
Decorated with antique silks and *objets d'art*, this is one of the most fashionable spots in town. Chinese favourites sit alongside authentic specialities like shark's fin soup. Dinner prices are astronomical but the superb lunchtime dim sum menu is reasonable.

Criterion Grill

224 Piccadilly; tel: 020-7930 0488; www.criterionrestaurant.com; Mon–Sat noon–2.30pm, 5.30–11pm, Sun noon–3.30pm, 5.30–10.30pm, Thur–Sun 2.30–5.30pm (afternoon tea); ££££; tube: Piccadilly Circus; map p.148 B3
Another prizewinner in the Marco Pierre White stable, the Criterion has a simple menu of French classics, all excellently prepared. The opulent neo-Byzantine interior is wonderful, and the pre-theatre set menu is very reasonably priced.

Many of the restaurants in the Covent Garden area offer a pre-theatre set menu, which often represent very good value. The condition is generally that you must be on your way by around 7.30pm; ideal if you are actually going to see a show and cost-effective even if you're not.

restaurant in a cobbled mews. Great British dishes include steak and kidney pie, grills and oysters and a good choice of ports, beers and wines.

Le Caprice
Arlington House, Arlington Street; tel: 020-7629 2239; www.le-caprice.co.uk; Mon–Sat noon–3pm, 5.30pm–midnight, Sun noon–11pm; £££; tube: Green Park; map p.148 A2

Chic, buzzy bistro with Art Deco decor and fabulous celebrity photographs on the walls. Le Caprice's tables remain among the hottest in town, so booking well ahead is essential. Sophisticated salads, excellent seafood and a long list of creamy desserts with wine list to match. Last-minute seating at the bar may be an option.

Le Gavroche
43 Upper Brook Street; tel: 020-7408 0881; www.le-gavroche.co.uk; Mon–Fri noon–2pm, Mon–Sat 6.30–11.30pm; £££; tube: Marble Arch; map p.150 B1

This legendary restaurant still produces food of the highest order, with Michel Roux Jnr inheriting the culinary mantle from Albert Roux. Elegantly balanced French haute cuisine with hints of Asian influence. The soufflés are masterly. Polished, welcoming service.

Locanda Locatelli
Churchill InterContinental, 8 Seymour Street; tel: 020-7935 9088; www.locandalocatelli.com; Mon–Fri noon–3pm, 6.45–11pm (Fri until 11.30pm), Sat–Sun noon–3.30pm, 6.45–11.30pm (Sun until 10.15pm); £££; tube: Marble Arch; map p.150 A2

Startlingly good and fairly priced north Italian food in retro-elegant decor at this restaurant beloved of the glitterati. Try elegantly presented dishes of ravioli with pork ragout and lemon cream, the signature duck with spelt, and a degustazioni of Amedei chocolate desserts. Booking is essential.

Momo
25 Heddon Street; tel: 020-7434 4040; www.momoresto.com;

Mon–Sat noon–2.30pm, daily 6.30–11.30pm; £££; tube: Green Park; map p.148 A3

Momo's wonderfully theatrical decor and authentic Moroccan cuisine is a hit. It has a real party feel in the evening, when candles are lit and the music is upbeat. Share pastilla, couscous or tagines and linger over mint tea.

Orrery
55–57 Marylebone High Street; tel: 020-7616 8000; www.orreryrestaurant.co.uk; daily noon–2.30pm, 6.30–10.30pm (Sat until 11pm); £££; tube: Bond Street; map p.150 B3

Dinner in this elegant Conran dining room is a gastro-experience. Barbary duck with *pain d'épice*, *foie gras tarte tartin* and *banyuls jus* are typical of the intensely flavoured dishes. There is also a prize-winning cheese trolley and a definitive wine list.

The Providores and Tapa Room
109 Marylebone High Street; tel: 020-7935 6175; www.theprovidores.co.uk; daily noon–2.45pm, 6–10pm; £££; tube: Bond Street; map p.150 B3

Refreshingly different ingredients from inimitable fusion food master Peter Gordon and fellow New Zealander Anna Hansen. The downstairs Tapa Room is more informal. Well worth queuing for weekend brunch.

Rocket
4–5 Lancashire Court; tel: 020-7629 2889; www.rocketrestaurants.co.uk; Mon–Sat noon–11pm; ££; tube: Bond Street; map p.150 C1

Left (from top): the distinctive styles of Locanda Locatelli, Royal China and Momo.

Prices for an average three course meal per person, with half a bottle of house wine:	
££££	over £50
£££	£30–50
££	£20–30
£	under £20

Left: Sketch, for dazzling food and dizzy prices.

The Wolseley
160 Piccadilly; tel: 020-7499 6996; www.thewolseley.com; Mon–Fri 7am–midnight, Sat 8am–midnight, Sun 8am–11pm; £££; tube: Green Park; map p.148 A2

Housed in a stunning 1920s listed building which started life as a Wolseley car show-room, the concept is a Viennese-style grand café. Despite being very popular with London's celebrities and media folk, the atmosphere is refined but relaxed with tasty and well-presented food for breakfast, brasserie-style lunches, afternoon tea and late-night dinners.

Kensington and Chelsea
Amaya
Halkin Arcade; tel: 020-7823 1166; www.realindianfood.com; Mon–Sat 12.30–2.15pm, 6.30–11.30pm, Sun 12.45–2.45pm, 6.30–10.30pm; ££; tube: Knightsbridge; map p.154 A3

In lovely surroundings, embellished with terracotta ornaments, enjoy the special-

Lively, simply decorated modern Italian with a menu of 12-inch wood-fired pizzas, pasta and salad in a pretty enclave just off New Bond Street. Arrive early for a seat outside.

Royal China
24–26 Baker Street; tel: 020-7487 4688; www.rcguk.biz; Mon–Thur noon–11pm, Fri–Sat noon–11.30pm, Sun 11am–10pm; £££; tube: Baker Street; map p.150 B2

Invariably packed and extremely lively at weekend lunchtimes as the dim sum is regarded among the best in town. Put your name on the waiting list as soon as you cross the threshold. Crab-meat dumpling in soup is the delicious house special.

Scotts
20 Mount Street; tel: 020-7495 7309; www.scotts-restaurant.com; daily noon–10.30pm (Sun until 10pm); ££££; tube: Green Park; tube: map p.150 B1

This treasured institution has been revamped and continues to serve impeccable fish dishes, including rarities such as stargazy pie. Old-fashioned puddings get a modern twist.

Sketch
9 Conduit Street; tel: 020-7659 4500; www.sketch.uk.com; Lec-ture Room: Tue–Fri

noon–2.30pm, Tue–Sat 6.30pm–midnight, Gallery: Mon–Sat 7pm–2am; £££; tube: Bond Street; map p.148 A3

An outrageously decadent interior and dazzling, dizzily priced food by Parisian super-chef Pierre Gagnaire. Choose between the gastronomic Lecture Room and the more modestly priced Gallery.

St Alban
4–12 Lower Regent Street; tel: 020-7499 8558; www.stalban. net; Mon–Sat noon–3pm, 5.30–11pm; £££; tube: Piccadilly Circus; map p.148 B3

In a stunningly stylish dining room, St Alban is quickly establishing itself on the map for its modern southern European dishes, such as rump of lamb, charcoal-grilled sea bream or veal chop.

Truc Vert
42 North Audley Street; tel: 020-7491 9988; www.trucvert.co.uk; Mon–Fri 7.30am–10pm, Sat 9am–10pm, Sun 9am–5pm; £££; tube: Marble Arch; map p.150 B1

Informal, buzzy restaurant in a wonderful French-style deli. Exceptional salads, pâtés and pastries plus charcuterie and cheese plates made to order. Vegetarians are always well catered for. Wines are well priced.

Thanks to a seemingly insatiable interest in food-related programming, many top chefs have made the move to TV and become household names. Gordon Ramsey, Marco Pierre White and Jamie Oliver are probably the most famous, with an influence spreading well beyond the TV schedules. Oliver, in particular, has used his position to promote fresh and healthy eating for kids, with influential shows such as *Jamie's School Dinners* and *Jamie's Ministry of Food*. Ramsey and White's respective *Kitchen Nighmares* and *Hell's Kitchen* remain popular enter-tainment programmes too.

ity of kebabs cooked in a clay oven and interesting desserts. Booking advisable.

Bibendum
Michelin House, 81 Fulham Road; tel: 020-7581 5817; www.bibendum.co.uk; Mon–Fri noon–2.30pm, Sat–Sun 12.30–3pm, daily 7–11pm (Sun until 10.30pm); ££££; tube: South Kensington; map p.156 B2

Chef Matthew Harris maintains high standards. Dishes such as grilled oysters with curried sauce and courgette linguine are faultless, the wine list impressive and the service excellent. Take advantage of the reasonable lunchtime prix-fixe menus, but make sure you book at least a week in advance.

Boisdale
15 Eccleston Street; tel: 020-7730 6922; www.boisdale.co.uk; Mon–Fri noon–1am, Sat 6pm–1am; ££; tube: Sloane Square; map p.154 B2

Boisdale would actually call itself Scottish, not British, and all the fresh produce reflects this. Feast on Hebridean lobster bisque, Macsween haggis and Aberdeen Angus steaks. There is always a fresh fish and a full malt whisky line-up.

Cambio de Tercio
163 Old Brompton Road; tel: 020-7244 8970; www.cambiodetercio.co.uk; Mon–Fri noon–2.30pm, 7–11.30pm, Sat–Sun noon–3pm, 7–11.30pm (Sun until 10.30pm); ££; tube: Gloucester Road; map p.156 A1

This small restaurant has won many accolades for its exciting food and high standards, and has been called the best Spanish restaurant in London. The atmosphere is bright and cheery, the service impeccable.

Prices for an average three course meal per person, with half a bottle of house wine:	
££££	over £50
£££	£30–50
££	£20–30
£	under £20

Chelsea Bun
9a Limerston Street; tel: 020-7352 3635; www.chelseabun.co.uk; Mon–Sat 7am–6pm, Sun 8am–7pm; £; tube: Sloane Square

This small café just off the King's Road serves one of the best breakfasts in London. Whether it's waffles and maple syrup or a full English, they'll do it. In the evening, it dims its lights, puts candles on the tables and takes on a bistro feel. BYOB; corkage.

Chutney Mary
535 King's Road; tel: 020-7351 3113; www.realindianfood.com; Sat 12.30–2.30pm, daily 6–11pm (Sun until 10pm); £££; tube: Fulham Broadway

This smart Indian restaurant is in a league of its own. Stylish decor, impeccable service and exceptional food. The chefs come from across the subcontinent, so you can take your pick of regional dishes.

Right: top-notch comfort food at Tom's Kitchen.

The Ebury
11 Pimlico Road, SW1; tel: 020-7730 6784; www.theebury.co.uk; Mon–Sat noon–3.30pm, 6–10.30pm, Sun noon–4pm, 6–10pm; ££; tube: Sloane Square; map p.154 B1

The ground floor has a brasserie and seafood bar where you can have a simple salad, down a dozen British oysters or tuck into a ribeye steak and chips. The upstairs dining room offers a more sophisticated set menu.

Gordon Ramsay
68–69 Royal Hospital Road; tel: 020-7352 4441/3334; www.gordonramsey.com; Mon–Fri noon–2.30pm, 6–11pm; ££££; tube: Sloane Square; map p.154 A1

The front is unobtrusive, the decor minimalist, the gastronomic experience exquisite. Try such delights as fricassee of English snails with spinach, followed by chargrilled monkfish tail with crispy duck. The service is charming and attentive. If the price is too high, take advantage of the excellent set lunch time menu.

Hunan
51 Pimlico Road; tel: 020-7730

Right: the eye-catching window at Bibendum.

5712; www.hunanlondon.com; Mon–Sat 12.30–2pm, 6.30–11pm; ££; tube: Sloane Square; map p.154 B1

Mr Peng, the proprietor, won't hesitate to tell you where you are going wrong with your ordering and brings dishes that you didn't order as well as those you did, but those who know what's good for them don't object and just submit to the feast. Menus for a minimum of two people start at £30 per head.

Maggie Jones's

6 Old Court Place, Kensington Church Street; tel: 002-7937 6362; daily 12.30–2.30pm, 6.30–11pm (Sun until 10.30pm); ££; tube: High Street Kensington; map p.157 E2

This quirky restaurant, with paraphernalia-filled nooks and crannies, is a wonderful place. Traditional British dishes, such as guinea fowl in red wine sauce and baked mackerel with gooseberries, are beautifully cooked and portions are generous. Wine is served in huge carafes and you pay for what you drink.

Papillon

96 Draycott Avenue; tel: 020-7225 2555; www.papillonchelsea.co.uk; Mon–Fri noon–3pm, 6pm–midnight, Sat noon–4pm, 6–11pm, Sun noon–4pm; ££; tube: South Kensington; map p.156 C2

Excellent Provençal cooking includes roast scallops on parsnip purée, which is a winner. Great cheese board and a huge wine list (many available by the glass).

Racine

239 Brompton Road; tel: 020-7584 4477; Mon–Fri noon–3pm, 6–10.30pm, Sat noon–3.30pm, 6–10.30pm, Sun noon–3.30pm, 6–10pm; ££; tube: South Kensington; map p.156 B2

The beautiful glass exterior promises a classy meal. The food is innovative yet firmly rooted in the French tradition. Chilled cucumber and mint soup in summer, and warm garlic and saffron mousse with mussels are typical dishes.

Tom Aitkens

43 Elystan Street; tel: 020-7584 2003; www.tomaitkens.co.uk; Tue–Fri noon–2.30pm, Tue–Sat 6.35–10.30pm; ££££; tube: South Kensington; map p.156 C1

This modern French restaurant has a Michelin star. Intensely flavoured dishes such as frog's legs with poached lettuce, and pig's head braised with spices and ginger demonstrate Aikens' culinary craftsmanship and flair.

Tom's Kitchen

27 Cale Street; tel: 020-7349 0202; www.tomskitchen.co.uk; £ (breakfast)–£££; Mon–Fri 7–10am, noon–3pm, Sat–Sun 10am–3pm, daily 6–11pm; tube: South Kensington; map p.156 B1

Tom Aitken's more-relaxed brasserie is known for its excellent breakfasts, but also offers a full range of comfort foods like fish pie or macaroni cheese, through to roasts, salads and sandwiches.

Zafferano's

15 Lowndes Street; tel: 020-7235 5800; www.zafferanorestaurant.com; Mon–Fri noon–12.30pm, 7–11pm, Sat noon–3pm, 7–11pm, Sun noon–3pm, 7–10.30pm; £££; tube: Knightsbridge; map p.154 A3

This is Italian food at its most sophisticated, with every attention to detail taken care of, at a price. Exquisite black truffle salads, risottos, fresh pasta, sirloin steaks, and faultless tarts and homemade ice cream.

Increasingly, London's mid-priced and budget eating options belong to chains, which you will see everywhere and which are patronised by locals as reliable bets for a casual and often well-priced bite. Try **Strada**, **Pizza Express**, **Zizzi** and **ASK** for pizza and pasta, or **Giraffe** (world food), **Carluccio's** (stylish Italian) or **Wagamama** (Japanese-style noodles). Burger joints have become increasingly popular of late (**Gourmet Burger Kitchen**, **Hamburger Union**, **Tootsies**). Giraffe, Pizza Express and the burger bars are especially good for those with kids.

129

Zaika
1 Kensingston High Street; tel:
020-7795 6533; www.zaika-
restaurant.co.uk; Tue–Sun
noon–2.45pm, daily 6–10.45pm
(Sun until 9.45pm); ££–££££;
tube: Kensingon High Street;
map p.157 E1
This Indian restaurant is stylish
and luxurious, with high ceilings and beautiful furnishings.
Ground-breaking chef Vineet
Bhatia turns out imaginative
dishes that are both fragrant
and subtle. The coconut soup
is a taste sensation. Take
advantage of the good-value
set lunch, for which you
should book in advance.

Bloomsbury and Holborn
Busaba Eathai
22 Store Street; tel: 020-7255
8686; www.busaba.com;
Mon–Thur noon–11pm, Fri–Sat
noon–11.30pm, Sun noon–10pm;
££; tube: Goodge Street; map
p.151 D3
Sleek and rather quieter
replica of the Soho original
(106–10 Wardour Street), serving
fresh and well-prepared Thai
dishes with plenty of original
vegetarian options. Very reasonable prices for such chic
surroundings. No bookings.
Cigala
54 Lamb's Conduit Street; tel:
020-7405 1717;
www.cigala.co.uk; Mon–Fri

noon–2.45pm, 6–10.45pm, Sat
12.30–3.30pm, 6–10.45pm, Sun
12.30–3.30pm; ££; tube: Russell
Square; map p.151 E3
Owner-chef Jake Hodges
(ex-Moro) wins accolades for
simple, immaculately cooked
seafood, succulent meats
and well-chosen wines.
Elena's l'Etoile
30 Charlotte Street; tel: 020-
7636 7189;
www.elenasletoile.co.uk;
noon–2.45pm, Mon–Sat
6–10.30pm; ££–£££; tube:
Googe Street; map p.151 D3
A time-warp haven of old-
fashioned virtues, still presided
over by one of London's
restaurant personalities, Elena
Salvoni. The food is traditional
French bistro fare, reliably prepared, professionally presented and satisfyingly
substantial.
Hakkasan
8 Hanway Place; tel: 020-7907
1888; www.hakkasan.com;
daily noon–3pm (Sat–Sun until
5pm), 6pm–midnight (Sun until
11pm); £££; tube: Tottenham
Court Road; map p.151 D2
Glamorous, opulent designer
basement restaurant con-
cealed down an alley at the
back of Sainsbury's on Tottenham Court Road. Exquisite
dim sum (lunchtime only),
exotic and classily executed

fish and meat dishes. Prices,
though, are punishing, so it's
really a place for special occasions. Booking advisable.
Navarro's
67 Charlotte Street; tel: 020-
7637 7713; www.navarros.co.uk;
Mon–Sat noon–3pm, Mon–Sat
6–10pm; £–££; tube: Googe
Street; map p.151 C3
The bright blue frontage and
cheerily colourful interior decor
provide an appropriately
Spanish setting for a choice of
some 50 selections of tapas.
Reservations recommended.
Passione
10 Charlotte Street; tel: 020-
7636 2833;
www.passione.co.uk; Mon–Fri
12.30–2.15pm, Mon–Sat
7–10.15pm; £££; tube: Googe
Street; map p.151 D3
Delectable modern Italian in
two small but well-patronised
rooms, featuring light and
rustic southern Italian fare,
often enhanced with unusual
herbs and fungi, which, it is
said, illustrious chef Gennaro
Contaldo (who was one of
Jamie Oliver's mentors) goes
out and gathers himself.
Pied à Terre
34 Charlotte Street; tel: 020-7636
1178; www.pied-a-terre.co.uk;
Mon–Fri 12.15–2.30pm, Mon–Sat
6.15–11pm; ££££; tube: Googe
Street; map p.151 D3

Fish and chips is one of
Britain's most enduring
contributions to the canon of
classic dishes, starting life as a
cheap and filling staple for
workers in the 1850s. It is given
the upscale treatment today in
many of the fish restaurants
that have sprung up with the
increasing interest in seafood,
but lots of the traditional outlets
and take-aways do the golden-
battered pieces of fish served
with chunky chips better and
invariably cheaper.

Below: one of Britain's favourites, fish, chips and mushy peas.

Left: relaxed eating at Busaba Eathai.

Fitzrovia's most prestigious restaurant has now regained its second Michelin star, under Australian chef Shane Osborn. The two-course lunch is reasonably priced, but the eight-course tasting menu will set you back £80.

Rasa Samudra
5 Charlotte Street; tel: 020-7637 0222; www.rasarestaurants.com; Mon–Sat noon–3pm, Mon–Sun 6–11pm; ££; tube: Goodge Street; map p.151 D2

London's first Indian seafood restaurant, offering high-quality, spicy Keralan seafood and vegetarian dishes with delightful sauces, at tables in a series of highly decorated town-house rooms.

Sardo
45 Grafton Way; tel: 020-7387 2521; www.sardo-restaurant.com; Mon–Fri noon–3pm, Mon–Sat 6–11pm; ££; tube: Warren Street; map p.151 C3

Sardinian specialities, including swordfish, fregola with frutti di mare, and honey-drizzled cheese sebada, served with panache in a contemporary environment.

The City

Cicada
132–6 St John Street, EC1; tel: 020-7608 1550; www.rickerrestaurants.com; Mon–Fri noon–3pm, 6–11pm, Sat noon–11pm; ££; tube: Farringdon; map p.152 B4

A little oasis of trendy eating. A range of well-executed pan-Asian dishes like chilli-crusted tofu, and black cod, with sumptuous sorbets for dessert.

Clark's
46 Exmouth Market; tel: 020-7837 1974; Mon–Thur 10.45am–4pm, Fri–Sat 9.45am–5pm; £; tube: Farringdon; map p.152 B4

One of the few remaining pie and mash shops standing its ground among the fast-food chains. The worn wooden pews, tiled floors, low prices and no-nonsense service keep the tradition alive. Cash only.

Club Gascon
57 West Smithfield; tel: 020-7796 0600; www.clubgascon.com; Mon–Fri noon–2pm, Mon–Sat 7–10.30pm; ££–£££; tube: Farringdon; map p.152 C3

There's more to this Michelin-starred Gascon restaurant than the foie gras, cassoulet and magret de canard standards. Dishes of south-western France are lovingly prepared with an inventive modern touch and served tapas style, with a fine selection of regional wines. Booking essential.

Coach & Horses
26–8 Ray Street; tel: 020-7278 8990; www.thecoachandhorses.com; Mon–Fri noon–11pm, Sat 5–11pm, Sun noon–5pm; ££; tube: Farringdon; map p.152 B4

Of the many gastropubs trying to make their mark across the city, this one really gets it right. The scrubbed-wood decor is simple, but homely, the food inventive, but unpretentious, the wines excellent value and the service good-natured.

The Eagle
159 Farringdon Road; tel: 020-7837 1353; daily noon–3pm (Sat–Sun until 3.30pm), Mon–Sat 6.30–10.30pm; £; tube: Farringdon; map p.152 B4

It has all the outward signs of being a perfectly ordinary pub, but The Eagle is quite a lot more. The food, which has a Mediterranean bias, is complemented by an extensive range of European beers. However, it is tiny, and invariably crowded, so get there early. No bookings.

Little Bay
171 Farringdon Road; tel: 020-7278 1234; www.littlebay.co.uk; Mon–Sat noon–midnight, Sun noon–11pm; £; tube: Farringdon; map p.152 B4

For honest food honestly priced, this friendly little bistro is hard to beat. The dishes are surprisingly sophisticated, with starters such as dressed crab terrine, and mains like Barbary duck breast, red cabbage, honey and ginger.

Prices for an average three course meal per person, with half a bottle of house wine:	
££££	over £50
£££	£30–50
££	£20–30
£	under £20

131

Moro

34–6 Exmouth Market; tel: 020-7833 8336; www.moro.co.uk; Mon–Sat 12.30–2.30pm, 7–10.30pm, tapas served all day; £££; tube: Farringdon; map p.152 B4

Moro has a reputation for excellent food and friendly service. The food on the lively Spanish–North African menu includes charcoal grilled lamb and wood-roasted pork.

The Quality Chop House

94 Farringdon Road; tel: 020-7837 5093; www.qualitychophouse.co.uk; Mon–Fri noon–3pm, Mon–Sat 6–11.30pm, Sun noon–10.30pm; ££; tube: Farringdon; map p.152 B4

A renovated old Victorian café, serving traditional

wholesome food, in a nostalgic atmopsphere.

Smiths of Smithfield

66–67 Charterhouse Street, EC1; tel: 020-7251 7950; www.smithsofsmithfield.co.uk; Mon–Fri 7am–4.45pm, Mon–Sat 6–10.45pm; ££–£££; tube: Farringdon; map p.152 B3

Brunch on a Saturday or Sunday is great fun in this lively and buzzy post-industrial complex. Tuck into a cooked breakfast, grilled minute steak or corned beef hash. The more refined (and expensive) upstairs restaurant offers well-sourced meat and fish dishes.

St John

26 St John Street; tel: 020-7251 0848; www.stjohnrestaurant.co.uk; Mon–Fri noon–3pm, Mon–Sat 6–11pm; £££; tube: Farringdon; map p.152 C4

A stone's throw from Smithfield meat market, this restaurant is stark but elegant. In the main dining room, the meat and offal-heavy menu changes with the season Chef Fergus Henderson's signature roast bone marrow and parsley salad is always on the menu.

Sweetings

39 Queen Victoria Street; tel: 020-7248 3062; Mon–Fri 11.30am–3pm; ££; tube: Mansion House; map p.153 D2

A real institution: serves dishes such as smoked haddock and potted shrimps in friendly, if slightly shabby, surroundings.

South Bank and Bankside

The Anchor and Hope

36 The Cut; tel: 020-7928 9898; Mon 5–11pm, Tue–Sat 11am–11pm, Sun 12.30–5pm; ££; tube: Waterloo

All the produce is British, and the meat – featured strongly

Left (from top): flag carriers for traditional British dishes, Roast and St John's.

London's cultural diversity is reflected gastronomically but you often need to venture outside the centre to find authenticity: try the area around Southall and Wembley for Indian Punjabi and Gujarati cuisine (other decent subcontinental restaurants are also peppered all around the city), Edgware Road and Bayswater for Lebanese and Iranian food, Dalston and Hackney for authentic Turkish and Vietnamese fare, or New Malden for homely Korean spots.

on the menu – is butchered on the premises. Ratatouille makes a fine accompaniment to perfectly cooked roast neck of lamb. With keen prices, hefty portions and friendly staff, this gastropub is a definite winner.

Baltic

74 Blackfriars Road; tel: 020-7928 1111; www.balticrestaurant.co.uk; daily noon–3.30pm, 6–11.15pm; £££; tube: Southwark; map p.152 B1

The bar is glowing and glamourous, the restaurant space light and airy with excellent service. Food is a seasonally changing Eastern European and Baltic states menu, with excellent blinis and mains such as lamb with Georgian aubergine and garlic yoghurt.

Butlers Wharf Chop House

Butlers Wharf Building, 36e Shad Thames; tel: 020-7403 3403; www.danddlondon.com; daily noon–3pm, 6–11pm (Sun until 10pm); ££–£££; tube: London Bridge; map p.153 E1

The Chop House flies the flag for classic English food. Carnivores should head straight for the roast suckling pig with tangy apple sauce and lots of crackling. For dessert, the bread and butter pudding comes smothered in custard.

Champor-Champor
62–64 Weston Street; tel: 020-7403 4600; www.champor-champor.com; Mon–Sat 6.15–10.15pm; £££; tube: London Bridge; map p.153 D1
A tiny spicebox of a place. Champor-Champor means 'mix and match' in Malay, and this place specialises in creatively combined flavours and exotic meats. Asian cuisines are grafted onto Malay village roots, then cooked European style to produce fragrant and innovative dishes. Imagine king prawns with miso, curry leaf and mango.

Masters Superfish
191 Waterloo Road; tel: 020-7928 6924; Mon noon–3pm, Tue–Sat noon–3pm, 4.30–10pm (Fri until 11pm); £; tube: Waterloo; map p.149 E1
Huge portions of freshly prepared fish and chips in this old-fashioned eatery.

Mesón Don Felipe
53 The Cut; tel: 020-7928 3237; Mon–Sat noon–11pm; £££; tube: Waterloo
A busy little place with a great atmosphere and lots of tasty tapas. The drinks list is an education in Spanish wines. Bookings taken before 8pm, after that it's first come first served.

Roast
Floral Hall, Borough Market; tel: 0845-034 7300; www.roast-restaurant.com; Mon–Fri 7am–11pm, Sat 8am–11.30pm, Sun 11.30am–6pm; £££; tube: London Bridge; map p.153 D1
Spit roast meat, pan-fried fish, great sausages and fresh seasonal vegetables, this is full-bodied British cuisine. Interesting views over Borough Market are an added bonus.

RSJ
33 Coin Street; tel: 020-7928 4554; www.rsj.uk.com; Mon–Fri 12.30–2.30pm, Mon–Sat 5.30–11pm; ££; Waterloo, Southwark; map p.152 B1
This pretty restaurant offers smooth service and dishes like calves' liver with leeks. There's a great wine list.

Skylon
Royal Festival Hall, Belvedere Road; tel: 020-7654 7800; www.danddlondon.com; ££–£££; Grill: Mon–Sat noon–11pm, Sun noon–10.30pm, Restaurant: Mon–Sat noon–2.30pm, 5.30–10.30pm, Sun noon–4pm; tube/rail: Waterloo; map.149 D2
Modern European fare is the order of the day at the South-bank Centre's smartest restaurant, boasting great views out over the Thames and and a celebratory atmosphere. The grill is a more informal space with food to match; the restaurant menu includes a wide range of meat and fish dishes, such as rabbit with pancetta or pan-fried halibut with baby squid.

North London

Gem
265 Upper Street; tel: 020-7359 0405; www.gemrestaurant.org.uk; Mon–Thur noon–11pm, Fri–Sat noon–midnight, Sun noon–10.30pm; £; tube: Highbury and Islington
This homely Turkish/Kurdish spot serves up a range of excellent mezze and huge mains including kebabs, grills and vegetarian options. Service is friendly and the atmosphere alternately cosy and convivial.

Prices for an average three course meal per person, with half a bottle of house wine:
££££	over £50
£££	£30–50
££	£20–30
£	under £20

Below: Skylon offers smart modern European fare and a great view over the South Bank.

Lemonia

89 Regent's Park Road; tel: 020-7586 7454; Mon–Fri noon–3pm, 6–11.30pm, Sat 6–11.30pm, Sun noon–3.30pm; ££; tube: Chalk Farm

A Primrose Hill stalwart, Lemonia is said to be one of the top Greek restaurants in London. The set menus offer a good option for those unable to choose from the wide menu, the food is fresh and well-sourced, and the decor fittingly Greek-rustic.

Ottolenghi

287 Upper Street; tel: 020-7288 1454; www.ottolenghi.co.uk; Mon–Sat 8am–11pm, Sun 9am–7pm; ££; tube: Angel

Excellent, adventurous salads and marinated meats, eaten at shared tables in this popular restaurant.

East London

Canteen

2 Crispin Place, off Brushfield Street; tel: 0845-686 1122; www.canteen.co.uk; Mon–Fri 8am–11pm, Sat–Sun 9am–11pm; ££; tube: Liverpool Street; map p.153 E3

This spot has enjoyed a lot of attention, specialising in traditional, locally-sourced British food at good prices. The comfort-eating starts at breakfast with Welsh rarebit. Mains include roasts, fish and pies, as well as seasonal classics such as minted lamb with new potatoes. Also at the Southbank Centre (Royal Festival Hall, Belvedere Road; tel and opening times as before; tube: Waterloo; map p.149 D2).

The Narrow

44 Narrow Street; tel: 020-7592 7950; www.gordonramsey.com; Mon–Fro 11.30am–3pm, 6–11pm, Sat–Sun noon–4pm, 5–10.30pm (Sat until 11pm); ££; DLR: Limehouse

The first gastropub out of the Gordon Ramsey stable serves quite classic British

Prices for an average three course meal per person, with half a bottle of house wine:	
££££	over £50
£££	£30–50
££	£20–30
£	under £20

fare; highlights include the selection of starters on toast and the main of pig cheeks with mashed neeps. There are fantastic views out over the Limehouse basin.

Sông Quê

134 Kingsland Road; tel: 020-7613 3222; Mon–Sat noon–3pm, 5.30–11pm, Sun noon–11pm; £; tube: Old Street

Kingsland Road is the best place in London to track down authentic Vietnamese food at bargain prices, and this long-standing no-frills eatery is possibly the best of the bunch, with a legendary beef pho.

South London

Bamboula

12 Acre Lane; tel: 020-7737 6633; www.bamboulas.net; Mon–Fri 11am–11pm, Sat noon–11pm, Sun 12.30–9pm; £; tube: Brixton

This bright and cheerful Caribbean restaurant, attracts a mixed crowd, including many regulars. Curried chicken, lots of yams and pumpkins. There's a takeaway service, too.

Chapters All Day Dining

43–45 Montpelier Vale; tel: 020-8333 2666; www.chapter srestaurants.com; Mon–Sat 8am–11pm, Sun 9am–9pm; ££–£££; rail: Blackheath

Fresh, seasonal ingredients, an emphasis on fish and inventive puddings make this a winner. Offers a wide variety of meals all day, including breakfast and afternoon tea.

Chez Bruce

2 Bellevue Road; tel: 020-8672 0114; www.chezbruce.co.uk;

Mon–Fri noon–2pm, 6.30–10pm (Fri until 10.30pm), Sat noon–3pm, 6.30–10.30pm, Sun noon–3pm, 7–9.30pm; £££; rail: Wandsworth Common

Michelin-starred, enormously popular spot with large windows overlooking Wandsworth Common, a fixed-price menu of exquisite French food (three or four courses) with modern touches and a legendary cheese board. The knowledgable sommelier is invaluable for getting the most out of the fine wine list. Bookings advised.

Franklins

157 Lordship Lane; tel: 020-8299 9598; www.franklin srestaurant.com; Mon–Sat noon–11pm (Thur–Sat until midnight); ££; rail: East Dulwich

Crisp white tablecloths and fresh flowers give a good first impression, and the food and service live up to it. There are starters such as beetroot, lentil and goat cheese salad, main course dishes feature guinea fowl, butter beans and chorizo, and there are good old-fashioned puddings like rhubarb and creamy custard.

La Pampa Grill

4 Northcote Road; tel: 020-7924

Below: the River Café's idyllic garden setting.

Right: Taqueria is great for good-value Mexican food.

1167; Mon–Thur 6–11pm,
Fri–Sat 11.30am–midnight;
£–££; rail: Clapham Junction
Large, juicy steaks and good,
fresh vegetable side dishes in
this Argentinian parrilla.

West London

The Cow Dining Room
89 Westbourne Park Road;
tel: 020-7221 5400; www.the
cowlondon.co.uk; Sat–Sun
noon–3pm, daily 7–11pm;
££–£££; tube: Westbourne Park;
map p.157 D4
For discerning Guinness
drinkers the busy downstairs
pub pours the perfect pint, to
accompany the oysters and
shrimps served at the bar.
The upstairs dining room's
informal atmosphere belies
its status as a premier peo-
ple-watching spot. Food is
simple but expertly prepared.
Booking essential for the
restaurant.

Fishworks
13–19 The Square, Old Market;
tel: 020-8948 5965; www.fish
works.co.uk; Mon–Fri
noon–4pm, 6–11pm, Sat–Sun
11am–10.30pm; ££–£££;
tube/rail: Richmond
A big skylight and blue-and-
white decor give Fishworks a
bright, seaside feel. Lots of
shellfish, salads and a good
fish soup are on offer, along
with standards such as skate
with black butter. There are
other branches in Islington,
Westbourne Grove and
Marylebone High Street.

Hereford Road
3 Hereford Road; tel: 020-7727
1144; www.herefordroad.org;
daily noon–3pm, 6–10.30pm
(Sun until 10pm); £££; tube:
Bayswater; map p.157 E4
Hearty British cooking, bold
in its simplicity and innovative
use of classic native ingredients. Start with beetroot soup

or one of the offal dishes and
move on to a well-cooked
main of brill, lamb or pigeon,
before tackling a pudding like
gooseberry meringue.

Petersham Nurseries Café
Church Lane, off Petersham
Road; tel: 020-8605 3627;
www.petershamnurseries.com;
Wed–Sun noon–2.45pm; ££££;
tube/rail: Richmond, then bus: 65
Skye Gyngell's restaurant is
beloved of wealthy Richmond
locals, but retains a ram-
shackle, tucked-away charm.
The restaurant, inside one of
the nursery greenhouses, has
rustic garden tables and an
earth floor and serves a
changing lunch menu of
modern-European, seasonal
dishes using produce from the
nursery garden. Bookings
advisable, or for a lighter bite
such as sandwiches and
soup, try the adjoining Tea-
house: Tue–Sun 10am–4.30pm
(Sun from 11am).

The River Café
Thames Wharf, Rainville Road;
tel: 020-7386 4200; www.river
cafe.co.uk; Mon–Thur 12.30–
2.15pm, 7–11pm, Fri–Sat 12.30–
2.30pm, 7–11.20pm, Sun noon–
3pm; ££££; tube: Hammersmith
The River Café is a west London institution and its international reputation for fine
Italian food is well deserved
(as is its reputation for high
prices). Ingredients are

meticulously sourced by the
owners, Ruth Rogers and
Rose Gray. Dishes such as
char-grilled scallops with
deep-fried artichokes, beef
with tomatoes and spinach
are faultless. Booking some
time ahead is essential.

Taqueria
139–143 Westbourne Grove; tel:
020-7229 4734;
www.taqueria.co.uk; Mon–Thur
noon–11pm, Fri noon–11.30pm,
Sat 10am–11.30pm, Sun
noon–10.30pm; £–££; tube: Notting Hill Gate; map p.157 D4
Serving a mouth-watering
range of authentic Mexican
street foods, such as
tostadas, quesadillas and of
course, tacos. A good range
of beers and tequilas round
off this cheerful and good-
value experience.

In recent years, there has been
an explosion of traditional
boozers transforming
themselves into gastropubs
and with the smoking ban now
in force, further shifting the
focus of bars to food, this
seems set to continue. They
offer a more informal dining
experience than restaurants,
making them ideal venues for
families or groups of friends, as
it's acceptable if not everyone
eats. Food tends to be modern
British and European cuisine.

135

Shopping

Napoleon called England a nation of shop-keepers. London, with more than 30,000 shops, proves he had a point. The sheer variety of the goods for sale makes London a consumerist paradise, catering for all tastes in shopping. World-famous department stores and flagship chains can be found here amid smaller boutiques and offbeat markets, while the diversity of London's population means that different areas have very distinct shopping personalities. See also *Children, p.38, Fashion, p.52, Food and Drink, p.60, Literature, p.76, Music, p.98,* and *Pampering, p.110.*

The Shopping Map

Sundays and summer holidays are not sacred in London, unlike most other European capitals; in London, you can shop to your heart's content almost every day of the year. This remains appealing to millions of Londoners as well as the many visitors who pass through every year, taking advantage of the volume and quality of wares on offer.

Broadly speaking, the most famous shops and recognisable names are found in the jam-packed West End, with designer wares in wealthy **Mayfair**, and massive, often multiple branches of popular chains lining the jam-packed thoroughfare of **Oxford Street**. Meanwhile, **Tottenham Court Road** is a mecca of homewares and electrical goods. Even in this mainstream area, there are unusual enclaves lined with boutiques and galleries, such as **Shepherd Market** and **St Christopher's Place**.

Also in the centre, but more relaxed and alternative, is **Covent Garden**. There are many quirky shops amid the

> If you are shopping for souvenirs, a surprising resource are the museum and gallery gift shops. Far from just being good for a pen or a postcard, the shops in places like the Design Museum, V&A and Tate Modern produce interesting and varied collections, often inspired by their current exhibits.

better known names, especially as the area progresses west to the Seven Dials and then on into **Soho**, with streetwear, natural remedies and arty erotica all getting a look in. **Marylebone High Street** has an upmarket village atmosphere, with gourmet food shops, boutiques and several stylish homeware stores.

Knightsbridge is dominated by Harrods and Harvey Nichols, along with the international designer outlets lining **Sloane Street**. The 'Brompton Cross' is a particularly trendy spot, leading on to **Fulham**, which is spread out but features many good independent shops.

It's no longer as trendy as

in its heyday as home to 'swinging' Londoners and then punk culture, but the **King's Road** is a laid back alternative to the West End, with a good mix of fashion and home design stores, as is **Kensington High Street**.

In the west lies **Notting Hill**, home to a huge concentration of both edgy and posh boutiques and famed for **Portobello Market**. More antiques dealers can be found on **Kensington Church Road**. Further west still, in Shepherd's Bush, **Westfield London** Shopping Centre, the largest in Europe has branches of most shops in a smartly-designed, mall environment. Over to the east, at the fringes of the City, **Spitalfields** offers cutting-edge trends, reflecting the arty, inner-city aesthetic of the area.

Department Stores

Fenwick

63 New Bond Street, Mayfair; tel: 020-7629 9161; www.fenwick.co.uk; Mon–Sat 10am–6.30pm (Thur until 8pm), Sun noon–6pm; tube: Bond Street; map p.150 C1

Left: the iconic Harrods building dominates Knightsbridge.

plete without a visit to the flagship branch of the triumphantly revitalised British household institution. Supplier of the nation's underwear and 'posh' food, this largest branch of M&S also sells their different clothing lines and offers a bespoke tailoring service, as well as a useful bureau de change.

Peter Jones
Sloane Square, Chelsea; tel: 020-7730 3434; www.peter jones.co.uk; Mon–Sat 9.30am–7pm (Wed until 8pm), Sun 11am–5pm; tube: Sloane Square; map p.154 A2

All your home and interior needs can be catered for in this local institution. As part of the John Lewis group, there are several familiar ranges instore, known for their value and good quality. There's a Clarins beauty studio and foot clinic, in addition to fashion and homeware ranges and a good haberdashery.

Selfridges
400 Oxford Street, Marylebone; tel: 0800-123 400; www.self ridges.com; Mon–Sat 9.30am–9.30pm, Sun noon–6pm; tube: Bond Street; map p.150 B2

This iconic, pillar-fronted

Fenwick is well-stocked with chic, up-market fashion, and the style spreads to the home collections and beauty hall too. The accessories department is particularly good.

Harrods
87–135 Brompton Road, Knightsbridge; tel: 020-7730 1234; www.harrods.com; Mon–Sat 10am–8pm, Sun 11.30am–6pm; tube: Knightsbridge; map p.154 A3

Opened as a grocer's shop in 1849, today Harrods is a London landmark and one of the largest shops in the world, with an overwhelming range of goods, several restaurants and a deservedly legendary food hall. Even if you can't afford anything on sale, it's a fantastic place to browse and absorb the opulence.

Liberty
210–220 Regent Street, Soho; tel: 020-7734 1234; www.lib erty.co.uk; Mon–Sat 10am–9pm, Sun noon–6pm; tube: Oxford Circus; map p.148 A4

With its panelled interior and hanging chandeliers, Liberty

exudes elegance and style, something that is reflected in the quality and opulence of the goods on sale. While best known for its distinctive range of fabrics and patterned accessories, it also sells exquisite furniture, jewellery and high-end fashion.

Marks & Spencer
458 Oxford Street, Marylebone; tel: 020-7935 7954; www.mark sandspencer.com; Mon–Fri 9am–9pm, Sat 9am–8pm, Sun noon–6pm; tube: Marble Arch; map p.150 A2

No trip to London is com-

Right: stylish displays in the atmospheric Liberty.

S

department store successfully combines its 100-year heritage with contemporary style. The monumental one-stop shop has a vast range, covering virtually every luxury consumer need from fine bone china to cutting-edge fashion.

Design and Interiors
The Conran Shop
Michelin House, 81 Fulham Road, Chelsea; tel: 020-7589 7401; www.conranshop.co.uk; Mon–Fri 10am–6pm (Wed–Thur until 7pm), Sat 10am–6.30pm, Sun noon–6pm; tube: South Kensington; map p.156 B2
The flagship store of Sir Terence Conran's home interior empire is housed in the former headquarters of the Michelin Tyre Company, distinguished by its tiles and stained glass windows. The shop sells stylish contemporary furniture, beautiful kitchenware and many home accessories.
Divertimenti
33–34 Marylebone High Street, Marylebone; tel: 020-7935 0689; www.divertimenti.co.uk; Mon–Fri 9.30am–6.00pm (Thur until 7pm), Sat 10am–6pm, Sun 11am–5pm; tube: Baker Street; map p.150 B3
This wonderful kitchen shop, the largest in London, is crammed full of good-quality cooking equipment and everything else you would need to create and serve food. At the back of the store, there's a cosy café set around a communal wooden table.
Heal's
196 Tottenham Court Road, Fitzrovia; tel: 020-7636 1666; www.heals.co.uk; Mon–Wed 10am–6pm, Thur 10am–8pm, Fri 10am–6.30pm, Sat 9.30am–6.30pm, Sun noon–6pm; tube: Goodge Street; map p.151 D3

Sharing an entrance with another home furnishings behemoth, Habitat, the long-established Heal's is a reliable source of sophisticated furniture, lighting and stylish kitchenware. The store is vast, but there's a smart cafe on the first floor that makes a handy stopping point.

Gifts and Specialist
Cath Kidston
51 Marylebone High Street, Marylebone; tel: 020-7935 6555; www.cathkidston.co.uk; Mon–Sat 10am–7pm, Sun 11am–5pm; tube: Baker Street; map p.150 B3
Gifts, accessories and clothes all in Cath Kidston's unmistakable fabrics: exquisite floral designs, polka-dots, strawberries and stars are her trademark. You can buy her fabric by the roll too, in her charmingly colourful stores.
Oliver Bonas
23 Kensington Park Road, Notting Hill; tel: 020 7727 4932; www.oliverbonas.com; Mon–Fri 10am–6.30pm, Sat 10am–6.00pm, Sun noon–6.00pm; tube: Ladbroke Grove; map p.157 C4
Crammed with a range of home furnishings, fashion and beauty accessories, stationery and novelty pieces, this expanding franchise of shops is a great place to find gifts.

With the exception of food, books and children's clothes, goods are subject to a 17.5 percent tax, which is generally included in the quoted price of an item. Non-EU residents may be able to claim back this value added tax (VAT) on goods priced over a certain amount; you'll need to pick up a form in-store and have it stamped at Customs on leaving the country.

Smythson
40 New Bond Street, Mayfair; tel: 020-7629 8558; www.smythson.com; Mon–Fri 9.30am–6pm, Thur 10am–7pm, Sat 10am–6pm; tube: Bond Street; map p.150 C1
The vibrantly coloured and classic leather diaries, wallets and gifts are not cheap, but highly desirable, as are the luxurious paper and bespoke stationery at this sophisticated British stationers.

Antiques
Alfie's Antique Market
13–25 Church Street, Marylebone; tel: 020-7723 6066; www.alfiesantiques.com; Tue–Sat 10am–6pm; tube: Edgware Road
With over a hundred dealers based in a converted Edwardian department store, London's largest indoor antiques market has a lively atmos-

Right: cheerful fabrics at Cath Kidston.

Right: shopping for cut flowers at the Columbia Road market.

phere. Picks include The Girl Can't Help It, selling American pin-up and vintage clothing, and Da Silva Interiors, for 1950s to 1970s period furnishings, including wind-up telephones. Church Street is lined with further dealers.

Antiquarius
131–141 King's Road, Chelsea; tel: 020-7823 3900; www.antiquarius.co.uk; Mon–Sat 10am–6pm; tube: Sloane Square; map p.156 C1

The oldest and most famous of London's treasure troves, Antiquarius houses a wide variety of artefacts, including books, arts and ceramics, collectables and timepieces, in stylish surroundings.

Grays Antique Market
58 Davies Street, Mayfair; tel: 020-7629 7034; www.graysantiques.com; Mon–Fri 10am–6pm; tube: Bond Street; map p.150 B2

Tucked in between Oxford Street and Mayfair, this venerable antiques market is like another world from the one outside, from the greeting by a liveried doorman onwards. Jewellery traders line the front, but there is a diverse range on sale here, including Asian and Islamic artefacts.

Markets

Brixton Market
Electric Avenue, Brixton; Mon–Sat 10am–6pm; tube: Brixton

With over three hundred stalls, this is Europe's largest Caribbean food market and it's very atmospheric, with reggae sounds from the stalls and exotic foods and spices on offer, in addition to the usual local market goods, such as music and cut-price clothes.

Camden Market
Chalk Farm Road, Camden; Mon–Fri 10.30am–6pm (reduced stalls), Sat–Sun 10am–6pm; tube: Camden Town, Chalk Town

Comprising several busy indoor and outdoor markets, Camden Market is enormously popular on the weekends. You can spend hours wandering from Camden Lock into bazaars selling food, 'alternative' fashions, jewellery, arts and crafts, furnishings and antiques.

Columbia Road Market
Bethnal Green; Sun 8am–2pm; tube/rail: Liverpool Street, then bus: 26, 48

Columbia Road's cobbled street is taken over by a blaze of colour on Sundays, when the flower market takes place. All types of cut flower and houseplant are sold at wholesale prices, some even more cheaply after midday.

Petticoat Lane Market
Middlesex Street, Spitalfields ; Mon–Fri 10am–2.30pm (reduced stalls), Sun 9am–2pm; tube: Aldgate; map p.153 E3

London's oldest market, dating back to 1608, is so-named for the petticoats and lace once sold here by the French Huguenots. This traditional market, spread over 1,000 stalls, sells Asian fabrics, cheap clothes and leather goods, as well as electronic items.

Portobello Road Market
Notting Hill; Mon–Sat 8am–6.30pm (Thur until 1pm), Antiques Market: Fri–Sat 4am–4pm; tube: Ladbroke Grove, Notting Hill Gate; map p.157 C4

Renowned for its antiques, visit the iconic market early on Saturday morning to catch the best of what's on offer, or Friday is good if you want to avoid the crowds. Second-hand clothes, contemporary art and general bric-a-brac can also be found here.

Spitalfields Market
Commercial Street, Spitalfields; Thur–Fri, Sun 9.30am–5pm; tube: Liverpool Street; map p.153 E3

This redeveloped, historic covered market is a good place to spot up-and-coming talent, as young fashion and accessory designers often ply their trade here. Amidst the hand-dyed items, you can find vintage fashion, handmade soap, childrenswear and organic food.

139

Sports

London is a major sporting city, boasting some of the most spectacular venues and hosting some of the biggest events in the world. With the 2012 Olympics coming up, the focus on sport is set to get even greater. In the meantime, Londoners support their football, rugby and cricket teams passionately. Aside from the enthusiasm for watching sport, many Londoners take to the parks at the weekends to play games themselves, or go running, riding or rowing, while historical lidos and picturesque ice-skating rinks prove hugely popular in season. These listings suggest the pick of what to see and do.

Cricket

This quintessentially British game, both in Test Match and the shorter Twenty20 form, is played April–Sept. Both of these stadiums also host international matches in addition to county fixtures.

Brit Oval
Kennington; tel: 020-7582 6660; www.surreycricket.com; tube: Oval
The home of Surrey County Cricket Club and scene of England's dramatic Ashes victory in 2005.

Lord's
St John's Wood; tel: 020-7432 1000; www.lords.org; tube: St John's Wood
Tours of Middlesex County Cricket's home take in the famous Long Room, museum and architecturally-daring media centre.

Football

London's top sport, with 13 professional teams. Arsenal and Chelsea are the top London sides in the Premiership (which also features Fulham, Tottenham and West Ham) but tickets to see their games are tough to come by; how-

The upcoming 2012 Olympics is generating a flush of new interest and public funding in sports. The Olympic Park in Stratford will be the setting of world-class facilities. Currently, you can see future Athletics champions in action at **Crystal Palace National Sports Centre** (tel: 020-8778 0131; www.gll.org).

ever, tours can be taken of the stadiums.

Arsenal
Emirates Stadium, Ashburton Grove; tel: 020-7704 4040; www.arsenal.com; tube: Arsenal

Chelsea
Stamford Bridge, Fulham Road; tel: 0871-984 1905; www.chelseafc.com; tube: Fulham Broadway
For a grassroots football experience, plus tickets that are cheaper and easier to get, try to see a Championship side.

Crystal Palace
Selhurst Park, Whitehorse Lane, Selhurst; tel: 0871-200 0071; www.cpfc.co.uk; rail: Selhurst

Queen's Park Rangers
Loftus Road Stadium, South Africa Lane, Shepherd's Bush; tel: 0870-112 1967; www.qpr.co.uk

Greyhound Racing

For a fun, cheap night out, having a flutter at the tracks is hard to beat. Stakes start low.

Wimbledon
Plough Lane, Wimbledon; tel: 020-8946 8000; www.lovethe dogs.co.uk; meets: Tue, Fri, Sat 6.30pm; rail: Haydon's Road
Great options for dining and a good atmosphere.

Horse Riding

A fantastic way to discover London's leafier side.

Mudchute Equestrian
Mudchute Park and Farm, Pier Street, Isle of Dogs; tel: 020-7515 0749; www.mudchute.org; DLR: Mudchute, Island Gardens

Ridgeway Stables
93 Ridgeway, Wimbledon Common; tel: 020-8946 7400; www.ridgewaystables.co.uk; tube: Wimbledon

Ross Nye's Riding Stables
Bathurst Mews, Bayswater; tel: 020-7262 3791; www.rossnyesta bles.co.uk; tube: Lancaster Gate

Ice-skating

Enormously popular in winter, when several picturesque, temporary rinks are erected, including at Broadgate and

Left: Wembley Stadium is the UK's national sports venue.

Legendary pools in a dreamy setting, with single-sex, mixed and nude areas. There is also a lido on Parliament Hill.

Oasis Sports Centre
32 Endell Street, Covent Garden; tel: 020-7831 1804; www.gll.org; tube: Holborn; map p.149 C4
Indoor and outdoor pools, with a popular sun terrace.

Watersports

The famous **University Boat Race** takes place on the Thames between Putney and Mortlake every spring. Those wanting to row should contact the **Amateur Rowing Association** (tel: 020-8237 6700; www.ara-rowing.org).

Docklands Sailing and Watersports Centre
Westferry Road, Isle of Dogs; tel: 020-7537 2626; www. dswc.org; DLR: Crossharbour
Sailing, canoeing and rowing in Millwall Dock.

London's bigger parks offer gentle boating in row-boats or pedalos.

Hyde Park
Tel: 020-7298 2100; tube: Knightsbridge; map p.156 C4
Hire boats on the Serpentine.

Regent's Park
tel: 020-7724 4069; tube: Baker Street; map p.150 A4
Row around the boating lake.

Below: swimming in the Hampstead Heath Ponds.

Hampton Court Palace:
Somerset House
Strand, Holborn; tel: 020-7845 4600; www.somersethouse.org. uk/ice_rink; late Nov–late Jan; tube: Temple; map p.149 D3
Very popular seasonal venue.
Queens Ice Bowl
17 Queensway, Bayswater; tel: 020-7229 0172; www.queen siceandbowl.co.uk; tube: Queensway; map p.157 E3
Year-round ice-skating rink.

Rugby

The rugby union code is dominant in the south of England and the season runs from Sept–May.
Harlequins
Stoop Memorial Ground, Langhorn Drive, Twickenham; tel: 0871-527 1315; www.quins. co.uk; rail: Twickenham
The nearest ground to central

London is home to both a rugby union side and the city's premier rugby league club.
Twickenham Stadium
Rugby Road, Twickenham; tel: 020-8892 2000; www.rfu.com; rail: Twickenham
Home of English Rugby Union. Offers stadium tours.

Tennis

All eyes are on **Wimbledon** for two weeks each summer, as the most prestigious grand-slam tournament, takes place. You can play on public courts throughout London; contact the **Lawn Tennis Association** (tel: 020-8487 7000; www.lta.org.uk) for details.

Swimming

London offers idiosyncratic, outdoor swimming options:
Brockwell Lido
Brockwell Park, Dulwich Road, Herne Hill; tel: 020-7274 3088; www.brockwell-lido.com; rail: Herne Hill
Beloved, recently renovated, Art Deco lido in South London.
Hampstead Heath Ponds
Hampstead Heath; tel: 020-7332 3773; tube: Tufnell Park, rail: Hampstead Heath

Wembley Stadium (Wembley; tel: 0844-980 8001; www.wem bleystadium.com; tube: Wembley Park), is the national sports stadium and boasts world-beating architecture and the biggest football events. See also *Architecture, p.33.*

Theatre

London's theatre scene is world-famous. The West End ranks with Broadway as a venue for top-class productions, from drama to musicals, and continues to be a draw for some of the most respected names in theatre. The glitziest shows seek to appeal to a wide audience, but there is usually something playing to suit all tastes: the National Theatre stages new and classic plays in repertory; the Royal Court has a strong reputation for performing the work of new playwrights, as well as established names. In addition, there is a thriving and ever-growing fringe theatre sector, staging the new, bold and avante-garde.

The London Stage

London has long been known for the quality and variety of its theatre. A night out at the theatre has been a staple of Londoner's entertainment since the days of Shakespeare, when playhouses were considered bawdy and morally suspect, through the Regency comedies and Victorian drama to the politically-charged offerings from the 1950s on. The theatre scene in London remains vibrant and ranges from internationally high-profile productions to new works performed in intimate venues. The current enthusiasm of Hollywood actors for appearing on the London stage (to varying degrees of critical success, but generally strong commercial results) and Kevin Spacey's role as artistic director of the Old Vic has further amplified the media attention given to the London theatre.

There is a also a high number of long-running musicals in the West End, which continue to enjoy huge popularity. Andrew Lloyd Webber's forays into finding stars for the revivals of *The Sound of Music, Joseph and the Amazing Technicolour Dreamcoat* and *Oliver!* through Saturday night TV contests has given a great deal of publicity to the genre. And, of course, there is *The Mousetrap*, the Agatha Christie thriller that has been playing at St Martin's Theatre since 1952 – the longest running play in the world – and still attracts audiences.

Tickets

Ticket prices are fairly high, although not as high as on Broadway, and there is an additional booking fee if you reserve seats through one of the ticket agencies, and usually from the theatres themselves if you book online or by phone. However, seats booked in person do not incur this fee, and it is sometimes possible to get last-minute tickets at lower prices.

Left: the National Theatre.

Left: Shaftesbury Avenue is the heart of London's theatreland.

Evening Standard, and in the weekly *Time Out* magazine, as well as in free sheets available in the foyers of many theatres.

Barbican Centre
Silk Street, The City; tel: 0845-120 7550; www.barbican.org.uk; tube: Barbican, Moorgate; map p.153 C3
Esoteric, intelligent theatre regularly finds a home at the eclectic Barbican arts centre. They run an annual season called BITE – Barbican International Theatre Events – staging a mixture of drama and dance by international companies.

National Theatre
South Bank; tel: 020-7452 3400; www.nationaltheatre.org.uk; tube/rail: Waterloo; map p.149 E2
The prestigious National comprises three theatres, the Olivier, the Lyttelton and the Cottesloe, and stages an exciting mix of classic and contemporary plays. Artistic Director Nicholas Hytner continues to stage impressive, wide-reaching works and the Travelex season *(see opposite)* encourages new audiences.

Old Vic
The Cut, Waterloo; tel: 0870-060 6628; www.oldvictheatre.com; tube/rail: Waterloo; map p.149 E1
This atmospheric theatre is under the artistic directorship of Kevin Spacey, which has brought a considerable amount of attention to the plays being staged. After a few wobbles, the repertoire of classic and new plays such as *The Entertainer*, *Speed-the-Plow* and *Pygmalion*, Christmas celebrity-starring pantos and a smattering of strong Shakespeare productions is ensuring that theatre at the Old Vic is both popularist and well-received. In 2009,

If you are happy to stand, some theatres offer very low prices for standing only tickets, usually with a restricted view. These only go on sale in the hour or two before a performance.

All seats at the Royal Court are priced at £10 on Monday, and the National Theatre has for several years been running the Travelex season, during which two-thirds of all seats for certain plays are sold for £10.

tkts in Leicester Square sells reduced-priced tickets on the day of performance, but you need to queue and buy them in person (www.officiallondontheatre.co.uk/tkts). There are other outlets around the West End offering reduced price tickets for popular shows.

West End

The major commercial theatres are concentrated in and around **Shaftesbury Avenue** – roughly between Piccadilly Circus and Covent Garden – and in the **Strand** and **Drury Lane**. The bulk of 'West End' theatres are Edwardian in design and

If you find it more convenient to book through a ticket agency, despite the booking fees, try **Ticketmaster** (tel: 0844-277 4321; www.ticketmaster.co.uk).

consequently often surprisingly cramped and ill-facilitated for the prestige and price of the shows being staged there. However, what they lack in leg room they often make up in atmosphere and elegance. Shows staged in these theatres tend to be necessarily commercial, and feature musicals, classic plays by the best-known writers, or transfers of plays that were successful in smaller theatres.

However, the sophisticated venues listed below are also termed as being 'West End' venues, in spite of their geographical locations. These theatres stage some of the best and most innovative shows.

Performance listings can be found in weekend sections of national broadsheet newspapers, in the daily

Right: the striking Young Vic was rebuilt in 2007.

Sam Mendes's Bridge Project, an English-American collaboration with the Old Vic, staged two plays here in tandem: *The Cherry Orchard* and *The Winter's Tale*.

Royal Court
Sloane Square, Chelsea; tel: 020-7565 5000; www.royalcourttheatre.com; tube: Sloane Square; map p.154 A2

One of the most respected theatres in the world, the Royal Court has been staging high quality, often groundbreaking new writing for the past 50 years. Dedicated to producing new work by interesting writers, it has long been the site of risk-taking plays that defined British drama for their times, notably John Osbourne's *Look Back in Anger*, Carol Churchill's *Top Girls* and Timberlake Wertenbaker's *Our Country's Good*.

Shakespeare's Globe
21 New Globe Walk, Bankside; tel: 020-7401 9919; www.shakespeares-globe.org; tube: Southwark; map p.153 C1

Built in the image of the famed Globe of Shakespeare's time, this loving reconstruction, complete with standing pit for the hardy, stages classical and imaginative productions of the Bard's works, interspersed with plays by modern playwrights.

Fringe
There are a number of off-West End theatres with excellent directors, staging works old and new that sometimes end up transferring to the West End. Tickets are cheaper and the work often riskier, so while some can be hit or miss, there is a lot of potential for seeing something truly exciting on stage.

Almeida
Almeida Street, Islington; tel: 020-7359 4404; www.almeida.co.uk; tube: Angel

Under the artistic direction of Michael Attenborough, British and international plays in translation are performed at this respected Islington theatre. The space is intimate, and popular with the cream of London's theatre actors.

Arcola Theatre
27 Arcola Street, Dalston; tel: 020-7503 1646; www.arcolatheatre.com; rail: Dalston Kingsland

On the premises of a former textile factory in Dalston, the Arcola opened in 2000 and has built a strong reputation for quality work by new writers and directors, as well as its many community-inspired projects and workshops; Turkish theatre is also performed here.

In the summer, Regent's Park opens their **Open Air Theatre**, which stages Shakespeare's plays, among others. See www.openairtheatre.org for this year's details.

Bush
Shepherd's Bush Green, Shepherd's Bush; tel: 020-8743 5050; www.bushtheatre.co.uk; tube: Goldhawk Road

The small, quirky space produces up to eight new plays a year, as well as productions by visiting companies and artists. A vociferous champion of new voices and powerful contemporary stories, offbeat gems often turn up here.

Donmar Warehouse
41 Earlham Street, Covent Garden; tel: 0870-060 6624; www.donmarwarehouse.com; tube: Covent Garden; map p.148 C4

One of the most lauded and successful of the smaller theatres, the Donmar continues to boast high-profile actors, directors, writers and alumni, who create high-quality, high-profile dramas, such as the

productions *Frost/Nixon* and
A Doll's House.

Gate Theatre

11 Pembridge Road, Notting Hill;
tel: 020-7229 0706; www.gate
theatre.co.uk; tube: Notting Hill
Gate; map p.157 D3

A small 70-capacity space
above the Prince Albert pub,
the Gate is the only London
theatre dedicated to producing foreign drama. Bold works
are often specially translated
for productions here.

Menier Chocolate Factory

Southwark Street, Bankside;
tel: 020-7907 7060; www.menier
chocolatefactory.com; tube/rail:
London Bridge; map p.153 C1

Once the site of a chocolate
factory, this space with a
handy restaurant attached
serves up a range of plays
with popular appeal.

Soho Theatre

21 Dean Street, Soho; tel: 020-
7478 0100; www.soho
theatre.com; tube: Tottenham
Court Road; map p.148 B4

The Soho Theatre strives to
encourage and stage new
writing from a diverse range
of backgrounds, and markets
intelligent work at a broad
audience. Political work is
featured heavily recently, as
have comedy and cabaret.

Tricycle Theatre

269 Kilburn High Road, Kilburn;
tel: 020-7328 1000; www.tricy
cle.co.uk; tube: Kilburn

The Tricycle continues to
make political drama its
mainstay, with the Tribunal
Plays, documenting cases
from the Hutton Inquiry to
Guantanamo Bay, bringing
great acclaim to the theatre
and BBC televisations of several of these plays. The theatre also stages a variety of
other plays, and is known for
work that reflects the diversity
of the community in Kilburn.

Young Vic

66 The Cut, Waterloo; tel: 020-
7922 2922; www.youngvic.org;
tube/rail: Waterloo

The Young Vic is based in a
distinctively funky space on
the Cut, where it stages its
repertoire of classic revivals
and new writing. The emphasis is on encouraging young
people's work and interest in
the theatre, so there are many
incentives available for young
audiences, as well as seasons
of work by young directors.

Musicals

Musical theatre continues to
be enormously popular and
the quality is generally high.
Revivals of classic shows have
been successful in recent
years, but newer shows and
exports from Broadway have
also made their mark. There
are some shows that are
pretty permanently based at
their theatres; these are listed
below, along with some newer
popular shows.

Billy Elliot the Musical

Victoria Palace Theatre, Victoria
Street, Victoria; tel: 0870-895
5577; www.victoriapalace
theatre.co.uk; tube: Victoria;
map p.154 C2

Scored by Elton John, this
adaptation of the film has
been a smash critically and
commercially.

Chicago

Cambridge Theatre, Earlham
Street, Covent Garden; tel:
0870-890 1102; www.cam

bridgetheatre.co.uk; tube:
Covent Garden; map p.148 C4

Perenially popular, with a regular turnover of starlets in the
role of Roxie Hart.

Les Misérables

Queen's Theatre, Shaftesbury
Avenue, Soho; tel: 020-7494
5040; www.queens-
theatre.com; tube: Leicester
Square; map p. 151 D2

Les Mis, the longest-running in
the West End, is based on Victor Hugo's novel and is now a
very well-oiled machine.

The Lion King

Lyceum Theatre, Wellington
Street, Covent Garden; tel:
0844-844 0005; www.disney.
co.uk; tube: Covent Garden;
map p.149 D3

Wildly successful and imaginative take on the Disney
musical, beloved by children.

Mamma Mia!

Prince of Wales Theatre,
Coventry Street, Covent Garden;
tel: 0844-482 5115;
www.mamma-mia.com; tube:
Piccadilly Circus; map p.148 B3

Internationally successful
jukebox musical featuring the
hits of Abba.

Phantom of the Opera

Her Majesty's Theatre,
Haymarket, St James's; tel:
0870-534 4444; www.her
majestys.co.uk; tube: Piccadilly
Circus; map p.148 B3

Andrew Lloyd Webber's
gothic masterpiece is one of
London's longest-running
musicals currently staged,
performed here since 1986.

Right: the Royal Court in
Sloane Square.

145

Transport

L ondon is well-connected to the rest of the world through its five airports, as well as by the Eurostar link. Once in the city, the system isn't always as clean or efficient as in other metropolitan centres and the costs are higher, but the system is comprehensive and options numerous, from iconic red double-decker buses, to black taxis and the sprawling tube network. Meanwhile, the increasing use of the river, development of new train lines and option of cycling everywhere continues to open up the city to locals and visitors alike. For comprehensive London travel information, see www.tfl.gov.uk.

Getting There

By Air

Heathrow: London's major international airport, 15 miles (24km) to the west, with mainly scheduled flights. The fastest way to central London is by Heathrow Express train to Paddington station, which runs every 15 minutes from 5am–11.45pm, taking 15 minutes. Paddington connects with several tube lines (see map inside back cover). The fare is £16.50 one way (tel: 0845-600 1515). A cheaper option is the 25-minute Heathrow Connect service, which stops at several stations; a one-way ticket costs £7.40 (tel: 08457-484 950).

Alternatively, the Piccadilly tube line runs direct to central London in around 50 minutes, via Kensington to King's Cross, daily from 5am (6am on Sun) until 11.40pm.

National Express runs coaches from Heathrow to Victoria; journey time is 45–90 minutes, depending on time of day and traffic, and a one-way ticket costs from £4. (For information, tel: 0870-580 8080, www.nationalexpress.com)

Gatwick: London's second big international airport is 25 miles (40km) to the south and offers scheduled and budget flights. The Gatwick Express train leaves for Victoria every 15 minutes from 4.35am–1.35am. It takes 30 minutes and costs £16.90 one-way. You can also take non-express services to Victoria, costing £11 one-way and taking 35–40 minutes.

Luton: Offering mainly budget and charter flights, Luton is 32 miles (51km) to the northwest. Luton Airport Parkway rail is connected by Thameslink services to King's Cross (£11.50 one-way), averaging 40 minutes journey time and running every 15 minutes.

Stansted: Budget and charter flights dominate at Stansted, 35 miles (56km) northeast of central London. The Stansted Express rail link runs every 15 minutes to Liverpool Street; journey time is 45 minutes and a one-way ticket costs £18.

London City: Primarily a business airport connecting to other European cities, City is 6 miles (10km) from central London. The adjoining DLR station is six minutes from Canning Town tube, (Jubilee line), running every 8–15 minutes from 5.30am–1.15am.

By Rail

Eurostar services from Paris Gare du Nord take 2½ hours (tel: 00-33-892 35 35 39) or 2 hours from Brussels (tel: 00-32-252 828 28) to **London St Pancras**. (Bookings, tel: 0870-518 6186; www.eurostar.com)

No matter how much you will be travelling, it is worthwhile buying an **Oyster Card**, as it significantly reduces all travel costs (for example, a single Zone 1 journey with an Oyster card costs £1.60 instead of the cash fare of £4). You can choose the amount of credit you add, which can then be topped up if necessary; all of this can be done at tube stations, Oyster ticket stops in some newsagents or post offices, or online at **www.tfl.gov.uk**. Note that the Oyster pay-as-you-go system covers tubes, buses, trams, the DLR and London overground trains, but cannot as yet be used on rail services.

Left: a District Line tube train pulls into Sloane Square station.

By Boat

River cruises are a great way to experience London and various routes run between Hampton Court and the Thames Barrier. Thames Clippers (www.thamesclippers.com) run a frequent and reliable service for £5 one-way, or £12 for a 'River Roamer'.

By Bike

Confident cyclists can obtain route maps and information from the London Cycling Campaign (www.lcc.org.uk). London Bicycle at Gabriel's Wharf offer reasonably priced bike hire (tel: 020-7928 6838; www.londonbicycle.com).

By Taxi

Black cabs are licensed and display the charges on the meter. They can be hailed in the street or there are ranks at major train stations. Mini-cabs should only be hired by phone; they're not allowed to pick up passengers on the street (for details of reputable firms, see *Nightlife p.104*).

By Car

Central London is very expensive to drive in. The congestion charge is £8 a day *(see Environment, p.48, for details)*. Car owners are fined if payment is not made by 10pm the same day (tel: 0845-900 1234).

Getting Around

London's transport map is divided into six zones, spreading outwards from central London (zone 1). Tube and rail fares are priced according to which zones and what time of day you travel in (peak time is before 9.30am). Day travelcards enable unlimited tube, DLR, rail and bus travel in specified zones and start at £5.30 for Zones 1–2 (off-peak).
SEE ALSO CHILDREN P.41

By Underground (Tube)

The fastest way to get around London is by tube. Try to avoid rush hour (8–9.30am and 5–6.30pm) when trains are packed with commuters. Services run from 5.30am to just after midnight. Keep hold of your ticket after you have passed through the barrier; you will need it to exit.

There is a flat rate of £4 for a single tube journey across any zones. Oyster Cards *(see box)* are a wise buy if you plan to travel a lot by tube. Enquiries tel: 020-7222 1234; www.tfl.gov.uk.

By Bus

Buses are a good way of seeing London; the bus network is very comprehensive. The flat fare is £2 or £1 on Oyster pay-as-you-go (bus use on Oyster is also price-capped at £3.30 per day). You can also get a one-/seven-day pass for £3.80/£13.80. Many buses run a 24-hour service, in addition to special night buses. Full bus route maps are available at Travel Information Centres.

By Docklands Light Railway (DLR)

The DLR runs from Bank and Tower Gateway to east and southeast London destinations. Tickets are the same type and cost as for the tube.

By Rail

London's commuter rail network provides useful links to areas not on underground lines; travelcards are valid on rail services for journeys within the correct zones. Thameslink services run through the city centre while the London Overground connects Richmond with Stratford. Other services run out of London's major rail stations, including Waterloo, Victoria, Euston, Paddington, King's Cross, London Bridge and Liverpool Street. Enquiries tel: 0845-748 4950; www.national rail.co.uk.

Below: black cabs line up.

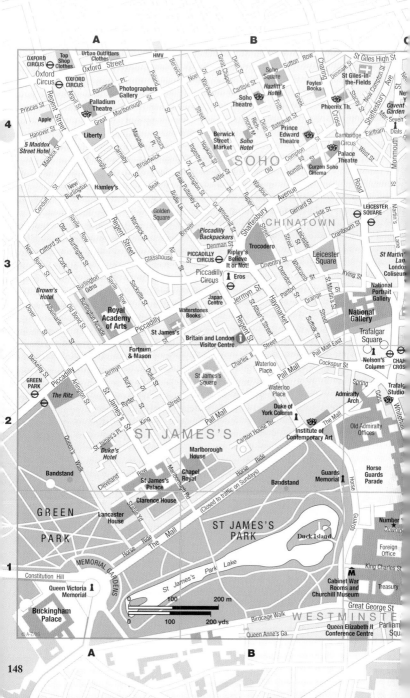

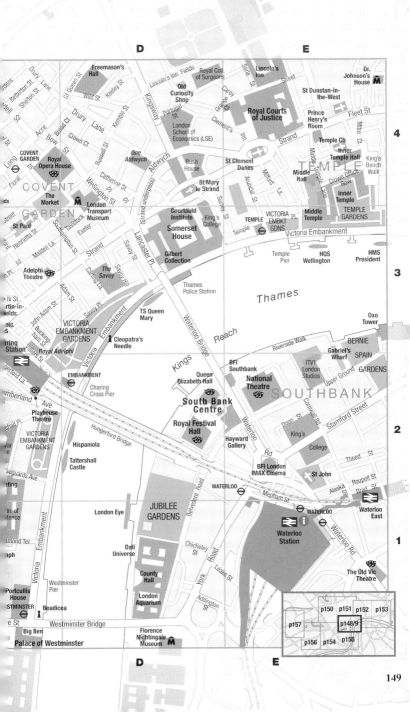

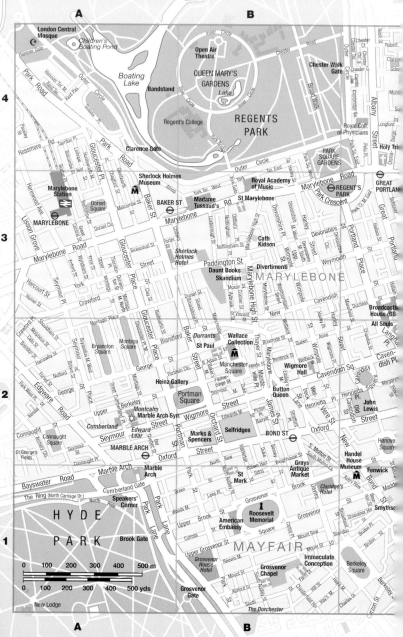

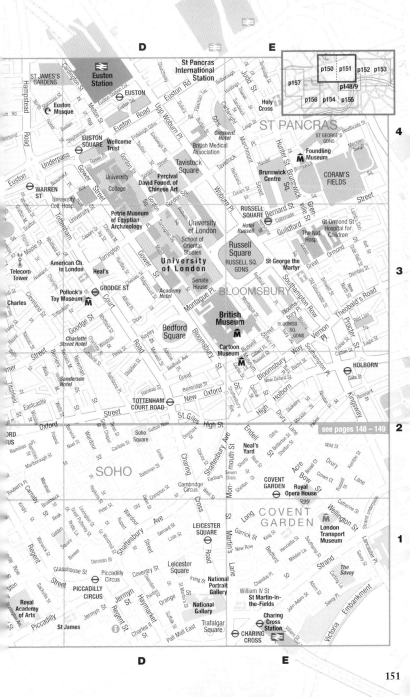

ST JAMES'S GARDENS

Hampstead

Euston Station

ST PANCRAS INTERNATIONAL STATION

EUSTON

Euston Mosque

EUSTON SQUARE

Underpass

Upp Woburn Pl

Euston Road

Crescent Hotel

British Medical Association

Holy Cross

ST PANCRAS

ST GEORGE'S GDNS

p150 | p151 p152 p153
p157
p148/9
p156 p154 p155

WARREN ST

University Coll. Hosp.

Wellcome Trust

University College

Gower Street

Tavistock Square

Gordon Square

Percival David Found. of Chinese Art

Brunswick Centre

Foundling Museum

CORAM'S FIELDS

Telecom Tower

American Ch. in London

Heal's

Petrie Museum of Egyptian Archaeology

University of London School of Oriental Studies

University of London

RUSSELL SQUARE

Hotel Russell

Guildford

Colonnade

Gt Ormond St Hospital for Children

The Nat. Hosp.

Charles

Pollock's Toy Museum

GOODGE ST

Senate House

Academy Hotel

Montague St

BLOOMSBURY

Russell Square

RUSSELL SQ. GDNS

St George the Martyr

Great Ormond

HOLBORN

Theobald's Road

Charlotte Street Hotel

Goodge St

Bedford Square

Bloomsbury

British Museum

BLOOMSB. SQ. GDNS

Vernon Pl

Southampton Row

Red Lion

Sanderson Hotel

Cartoon Museum

Eastcastle Street

Oxford Street

New Oxford Street

TOTTENHAM COURT ROAD

St Giles High St

Great Russell

High Holborn

Kingsway

HOLBORN

see pages 148 – 149

Soho Square

Neal's Yard

Seven Dials

Wild St

Drury Lane

SOHO

Shaftesbury Ave

Cambridge Circus

COVENT GARDEN

Royal Opera House

Acre Bow

Crown Ct

Charing Cross Rd

LEICESTER SQUARE

COVENT GARDEN

London Transport Museum

Wellington St

Shaftesbury Avenue

Leicester Square

Garrick St

New Row

Bedford St

Strand

The Savoy

PICCADILLY CIRCUS

Piccadilly Circus

Coventry St

Irving St

National Portrait Gallery

St Martin's Lane

Chandos Pl

William IV St

St Martin-in-the-Fields

Adam St

Victoria Embankment

Royal Academy of Arts

Jermyn Street

Haymarket

Regent Street

National Gallery

Charles II St

Trafalgar Square

Pall Mall East

Charing Cross Station

CHARING CROSS

Piccadilly

St James

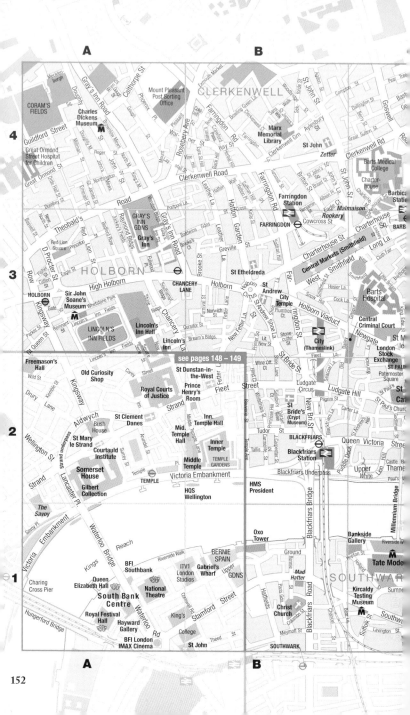

CLERKENWELL

4

Mecklenburgh Sq
Doughty St
Calthorpe St
Gray's Inn Road
Wren St
Phoenix Pl
Mount Pleasant Post Sorting Office
Exmouth Market
Bowling Green Ln
Rosoman St
Aylesbury St
St John St
Compton St
Pear Tree
Bast

CORAM'S FIELDS
Charles Dickens Museum
War…
Pine
Farringdon Road
Ray St
Clerkenwell Grn
St John
Marx Memorial Library
Great Sutton St
Zetter
Clerkenwell Rd
Barts Medical College
Charterhouse

Guildford Street
Great Ormond Street Hospital for Children
Great Ormond St
Roger St
John's M.
North Mews
King's Rd
Clerkenwell Road
Leather La
Hatton
Farringdon Rd
Briton St
St John's La
St John's Sq
St Broad St
Albion Pl
Charterhouse St
Clerkenwell Rd
Rookery
BARB
Barbican Statio

Road
Theobald's
Bedford Row
Raymond Bldgs
GRAY'S INN GDNS
Gray's Inn Road
Baldwins
Brooke's St
Greville
Portpool La.
Hatton Cross
Saffron Hill
Farringdon Station
Cowcross St
Central Markets (Smithfield)
Smithfield
Long La.
Charterhouse St
BARB

New North St
Boswell St
Dombey St
Red Lion Square
Princeton
Eagle St
D Procter St
Catton St
Theobald's
Red
Bedford Row
Jockey's Fields
Gray's Inn
FARRINGDON
West Smithfield
Hosier La.
Cloth Fair
Little Britain

3

HOLBORN
High Holborn
CHANCERY LANE
Holborn
Holborn Circus
St Etheldreda
St Andrew
City Temple
Far…ringdon St
West Smithfield
Cock La.
Barts Hospital

HOLBORN
Sir John Soane's Museum
Whetstone Park
Stone Bdgs
Cursitor St
Furnival St
Norwich St
Holborn Viaduct
Plumtree Ct.
Stone-cutter St
Central Criminal Court
Newgate
St M

Kingsway
Parker St
Gate
Remnant St
Lincoln's Inn Fields
LINCOLN'S INN FIELDS
Lincoln's Inn Hall
Lincoln's Inn
Bream's Bldgs.
New Fetter La.
New St
Fleet
City (Thameslink)
Old Bailey
London Stock Exchange
ST PAUL
Paternoster Square
St
Cat

Great Queen St
see pages 148 – 149
St Dunstan-in-the-West
Prince Henry's Room
Fetter
Street
Wine Off. Ct.
St Bride St
Fleet
Ludgate Circus
Salisbury Ct.
Pilgrim St
Ludgate Hill
Carter La.
St Paul's Churc

Freemason's Hall
Wild St
Old Curiosity Shop
Carey Street
Royal Courts of Justice
Strand
Inn. Temple Hall
St Bride's (Crypt Museum)
New Bri St
Creed La.

Drury Lane
Kingsway
Aldwych
Bush House
St Clement Danes
Mid. Temple Hall
Inner Temple
Carmelite
Whitefriars St
Tudor
Kingscote St
Tallis
BLACKFRIARS
Queen Victoria Stree
St Andrew's Hill

2

Wellington St
Strand underpass
St Mary le Strand
Courtauld Institute
Somerset House
Gilbert Collection
Surrey St
Arundel St
TEMPLE
Middle Temple
TEMPLE GARDENS
Temple
Victoria Embankment
HQS Wellington
Blackfriars Station
Blackfriars Underpass
Puddle Dock
Upper White
Castle
Thame
Paul's

The Savoy
Savoy Pl
Victoria Embankment
Lancaster Pl
Waterloo Bridge
HMS President
Blackfriars Bridge
Millennium Bridge

Charing Cross Pier
Hungerford Bridge
Kings Reach
Riverside Walk
Oxo Tower
BERNIE SPAIN GDNS
Ground Rennie
Mad Hatter
Bankside Gallery
Riverside W
Tate Mode

1

Queen Elizabeth Hall
BFI Southbank
ITV1 London Studios
Gabriel's Wharf
Upper
Paris Gdn
SOUTHWARK

South Bank Centre
National Theatre
Cornwall Rd
Stamford Street
Blackfriars Road
Hopton St
Kircaldy Testing Museum
Sumne
Southwa

Royal Festival Hall
Hayward Gallery
BFI London IMAX Cinema
Waterloo Rd
King's College
St John
Theed St
Hatfields
Colombo St
Christ Church
Meymott St
SOUTHWARK
Lavington
Blackf'rs La

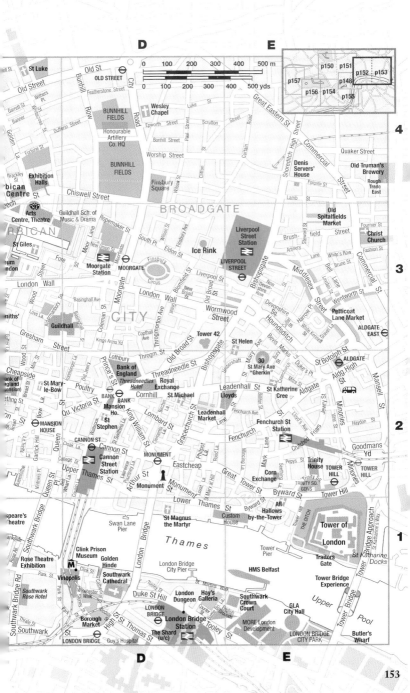

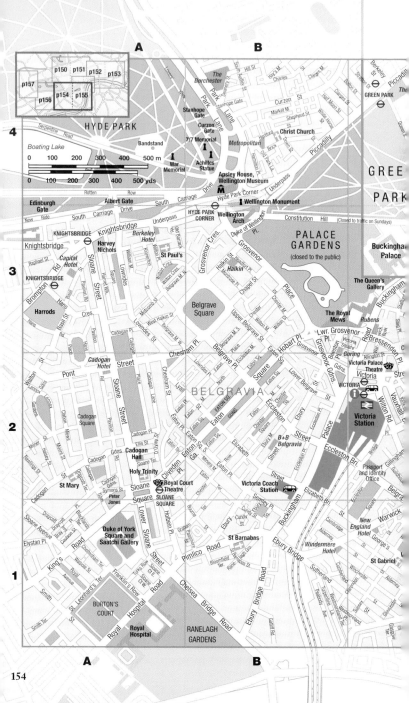

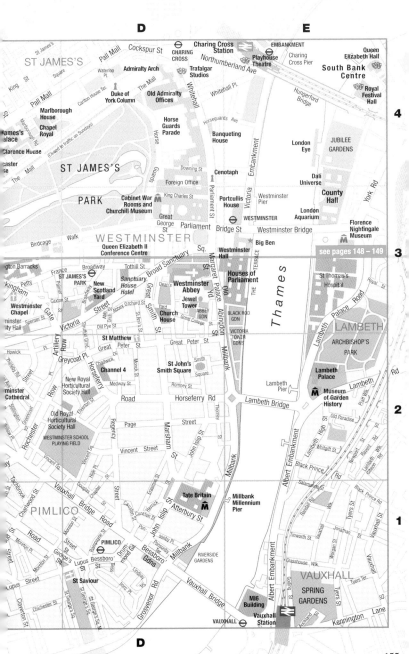

D **E**

St James's ST JAMES'S

Pall Mall
Cockspur St
King St
Square
Waterloo Pl.
Admiralty Arch
Carlton House Ter.

Charing Cross Station
CHARING CROSS
Trafalgar Studios
Northumberland Ave
Whitehall Pl.

EMBANKMENT
Playhouse Theatre
Charing Cross Pier

Queen Elizabeth Hall
South Bank Centre
Royal Festival Hall

Pall Mall
Marlborough House
Chapel Royal
James's Palace
Clarence House
caster se
The Mall

Duke of York Column
Old Admiralty Offices
Whitehall

Hungerford Bridge

4

Marlborough Rd
(Closed to traffic on Sundays)

Horse Guards Parade
Horseguards Ave
Banqueting House

Horse

London Eye
JUBILEE GARDENS

ST JAMES'S
Downing St
Foreign Office

Embankment

Dali Universe

PARK
Guards
Cabinet War Rooms and Churchill Museum
King Charles St
Cenotaph

County Hall

Birdcage Walk

Great George St
Parliament St

Portcullis House
Westminster Pier
WESTMINSTER
Westminster Bridge

London Aquarium
Florence Nightingale Museum

York Rd

WESTMINSTER
Queen Elizabeth II Conference Centre

Sq.
Westminster Hall
Big Ben

see pages 148 – 149

3

gton Barracks
France
Broadway
Tothill St
ST JAMES'S PARK
New Scotland Yard
Sanctuary House Hotel
Broad Sanctuary
Dean's Yard
Westminster Abbey
Margaret St
Houses of Parliament

St Thomas's Hospital
Royal St

kingham
Petty
Caxton St
Broadway
Victoria
Street
Great Smith St
St Ann's St
Church House
Jewel Tower
ABBEY GDN
Great College
Abingdon

T h a m e s
THE TERRACE
BLACK ROD GDN
VICTORIA TOWER GDNS

LAMBETH
ARCHBISHOP'S PARK

Palace

Westminster Chapel
minster ity Hall
Gate
Spenser St

Old Pye St

St Matthew
Great Peter St
Smith Square

Lambeth

Howick
Artillery ROW
Greycoat Pl.
Chadwick St
Monck St
St John's Smith Square
Romney St
Smith Square

Lambeth Pier
Lambeth Palace
Museum of Garden History

Pratt Wlk

2

minster Cathedral
New Royal Horticultural Society Hall
Channel 4
Medway St
Horseferry Rd
Lambeth Bridge

Rd

Rochester
Old Royal Horticultural Society Hall
WESTMINSTER SCHOOL PLAYING FIELD
Regency
Road
Page
Street
Marsham St
Thorney St

Old Paradise
Lambeth High St
Whitgift St

Lambeth Rd
Lambeth Rd

Vincent Street
Vincent Sq.

Albert Embankment
Black Prince Rd

Tachbrook St
Vauxhall Bridge Road

Tate Britain
Millbank Millennium Pier

Salamanca St

Black Prince Rd

1

PIMLICO
Moreton Pl.
George's Sq
Lupus St
PIMLICO
Drummond Gt
Bessborough Gdns
Millbank
RIVERSIDE GARDENS

Glasshouse Wlk.

VAUXHALL
SPRING GARDENS

Tyers St

St Saviour
St George's Sq

Vauxhall Bridge

MI6 Building
VAUXHALL Station
Vauxhall

Albert Embankment
Bondway
Auckland St
Kennington Lane

D

A   B

p150 p151 p152 p153
p157   p148/9
   p156 p154 p155

4

Peter Pan

The Long Water

0   100 200 300 400 5
0   100 200 300 400 500m

Physical
Energy

Temple
Lodge

Norwegian/
British Monument

Serpentine Bridge

Boat Houses

SUNKEN
GARDEN

Round
Pond

The Serpentine

Kensington
Palace

KENSINGTON   Bandstand

Serpentine Road

Diana
Memorial
Fountain

The Lido

HYDE

The Broad Walk

Serpentine
Gallery

GARDENS

Rotten   Row

PARK

The Flower Walk

Albert
Memorial

New   Ride

Prince of
Wales Gate

3

Palace
Gate

Queen's
Gate

Alexandra
Gate

Rutland
Gate

South Carriage Dr

Hyde Pa
Barrack

Kensington   Road

The Gore

Kensington   Gore

Kensington   Road

Cambridge Pl

De Vere Gdns

Albert Pl

Douro Pl

St Albans
Grove

Cottesmore
Gdns

Eldon Rd

Palace   Gate

Victoria Rd

Canning Pl

Victoria Grove

Canning Pl

Launceston Pl

Royal Coll
of Art

Royal
Albert Hall

Royal Geographical
Society

Prince's Gate

Russian
Orthodox
Cathedral

Montpelier

Prince Consort Road

Museum of
Instruments

Ennismore Gdns

Ennismore M.

Rutland

Montpelier
Sq

KNIGHTSBRIDGE

Ha
Rd

Kynance

Cornwall

Cornwall

Gloucester   Road

Hyde Park Gate

Queen's Gate

Kensington
Gate

Queen's Gate M.

Queen's Gate Ter.

Petersham Pl.

Elvaston Place

Ashburn Pl

Callender
Rd

Imperial College

Imperial   College   Rd

Ayrton Rd

Weals Way

Prince's Gdns

Prince's Gdns

Prince's
Gate
Mews

Holy
Trinity

Cottage Pl

Brompton

Ennismore

Ennis
Gdns

Chapel

Brompton   Rd

Egerton Ter

The Be
Beauch

Yeoman's Row

2

Emperor's Ga

McLeod's M.

Emperor's Ga.

St Stephen

Cromwell   Road

Elvaston Place

Elvaston
M.

Queen's Gate
Gdns

Southwell
Gdns

Queen's Gate

Queen's Gate

Queen's Gate M.

Atherstone
M.

Queen's Gate Pl. M.

Queen's Gate Pl.

Science
Museum

Natural History
Museum

WILDLIFE
GARDEN

Cromwell Road

Exhibition Road

Exhibition   Rd

SOUTH
KENSINGTON

Victoria & Albert
Museum

Cromwell Gdns

Cromwell
Rd

Thurloe
Pl.

Thurloe
Square

Brompton
Oratory

Brompton
Road

Alexander Pl.

Thurloe Sq.

Egerton Gdns

Egerton Cres

Walton

First St

Ovington St

Hasker St

Draycott Pl

Moore St

BROMPTO

GLOUCESTER
ROAD

Ashburn Pl

Stanhope Gdns

Stanhope M. E.

Queensberry Pl.

Queen's Gate

Cromwell
M.

Harrington Rd

Thurloe St

SOUTH
KENSINGTON

Pelham Street

St Jude's

Courtfield   Road

Cunningham Pl

Harrington Gardens

Wetherby Pl.

Clareville
St.

Gloucester   Road

Rosary Gdns

Harcourt Tce

Rosary Sq.

Clareville
Gardens

Onslow St

Onslow
Square

Onslow Sq.

Sydney
Place

Pelham Cres.

Lucan

Pelham Pl

Sloane

Avenue

The Conran Shop

Elysta

SOUTH
KENSINGTON

Old   Brompton   Road

Bolton Gdns

The Little Boltons

The Boltons

Tregunter Rd

St Mary

Drayton
Gardens

Cresswell Place

Thistle
Grove

Roland Wy

Evelyn
Gdns

Charles Mews

Gardens

Selwood Terrace

Old   Brompton   Road

Fulham   Road

Onslow
Gdns

Selwood
Place

Sumner Pl.

Sumner
Place

Cale

Bury Walk

Pond Pl

Sydney   Street

Fulham   Rd

Royal
Marsden
Hospital

Royal
Brompton
Hospital

Old   Church   Street

Elm Park Gdns

Manresa Rd

Chelsea Gardener
Nursery & Farmers
Market

St Luke's

St Luke

St Luke's St

Britten St

Jubilee Pl

Chelsea Manor St

Dovehouse St

Godfrey St

Burnsall St

Markham St

Whitehea

Anderson St

CHELS

Welsh Unit
Reformed Ch

Heal's

King's

Antiquar

Old Chelsea
Town Hall

King's   Road

1

A   B

156

Index

Insight Smart Guide: London
Compiled by: Sarah Sweeney, Tom Stainer, James Macdonald, Maria Lord

Edited by: Sarah Sweeney
Proofread by: Sue Pearson
Indexed by: Erica Brown

Photography by: All pictures © Apa/Ming Tang Evans except: Apa 45T; Cannizaro House 75; Austin Clark 121; Comedy Store 104, 105; Elemis 110C; English heritage 106/107, 107B, 109; Fabric 102/3T; Jay Fechtman/Apa 4T; Firmdale Hotels 73, 74; Getty 46/47, 142; Glyn Genin/Apa 2B, 3B,4B , 7B, 12, 13T, 14, 15C, 20, 21B, 24, 32, 38/9T, 41B, 43B, 45B, 51B, 80/1T, 86, 87B, 119, 147; Groom 110/11T; Halkin Hotel 72; Britta Jaschinski/Apa 8, 13B, 36, 37, 55B, 56B, 57TR, 60B, 62, 63T&B, 71B, 79B, 117B, 121, 123b, 124BL&BR, 125, 126TL,C&BL,127, 128, 130, 131, 132BL, 138; Britta Jaschinski 64/5T, 65B, 67BL/BR; Kensington Roof Gardens 102; London Transport Museum 95; Alisdair Macdonald 15T, 31B, 48/9T, 50/1T, 78/9T, 78C, 115, 146/7T; James Macdonald 19, 69b, 77,

98/99, 100/101; National Portrait gallery 5B, 80B, 81; Andrea Pistolesi 42/3T; Sarah Sweeney/Apa 60/1T, 132CL; Philip Vile 144; Andreas Von Einsiedel 70/1T

London Master Atlas reproduced by permission of Geographers' A-Z Map Co. Ltd. Licence No. B4676. © Crown Copyright 2009. All rights reserved. BLicence number 100017302.

Picture Manager: Steven Lawrence
Maps: James Macdonald
Series Editor: Jason Mitchell

Second Edition 2010
First Edition 2008
© 2010 Apa Publications GmbH & Co. Verlag KG Singapore Branch, Singapore.
Printed in Canada

Worldwide distribution enquiries:
Apa Publications GmbH & Co. Verlag KG (Singapore Branch) 38 Joo Koon Road, Singapore 628990; tel: (65) 6865 1600; e-mail: apasin@signet.com.sg

Distributed in the UK and Ireland by:
GeoCenter International Ltd
Meridian House, Churchill Way West,

Basingstoke, Hampshire RG21 6YR; tel: (44 1256) 817 987; e-mail: sales@geocenter.co.uk

Distributed in the United States by:
Langenscheidt Publishers, Inc.
36–36 33rd Street 4th Floor, Long Island City, New York 11106; tel: (1 718) 784 0055; e-mail: orders@langenscheidt.com

Contacting the Editors
We would appreciate it if readers would alert us to outdated information by writing to:
Apa Publications, PO Box 7910, London SE1 1WE, UK; fax: (44 20) 7403 0290; e-mail: insight@apaguide.co.uk

No part of this book may be reproduced, stored in a retrieval system or transmitted in any form or by any means (electronic, mechanical, photocopying, recording or otherwise), without prior written permission of Apa Publications. Brief text quotations with use of photographs are exempted for book review purposes only. Information has been obtained from sources believed to be reliable, but its accuracy and completeness, and the opinions based thereon, are not guaranteed.

MAYOR OF LONDON